D1213871

The University of Kentucky Press

The Frontier Mind
Arthur K. Moore

McGraw-Hill Book Company, Inc.

New York   Toronto   London

First McGraw-Hill Paperback Edition, 1963

*Publication of the original hardcover
edition of this book
was possible partly because of a grant
from the Margaret Voorhies Haggin Trust Fund
established in memory of her husband
James Ben Ali Haggin*

To
Lalla, Claire, Rebecca, Adalene

Preface

MY ORIGINAL TITLE was—as titles should be—clear, crisp, and modest, but it could not by any amount of stretching be made to cover the book which finally evolved. At the beginning, I had no reason to believe that the Kentucky backwoods could lead to anything requiring so solemn a label as *The Frontier Mind*, which possibly recalls the ponderous treatises of the last century and may appear to deny humor and levity. The buckskin Kentuckian, never one to underestimate his importance, changed my plans by demanding something larger than a regional stage on which to display his quality. So acceding, I widened the perspective considerably and implicated him in the cultural development of the West. The record of his strenuous daily living and his ferocious amusements I did not diminish, and the reader is likely to discover most of the materials that a book on the frontier ordinarily presents, though not the familiar interpretations. Yet, it is only fair to acknowledge that the Kentuckian, as I have dealt with him, is a great deal more complex than the simple-minded Indian fighter imaged in frontier chronicles.

This book began as one of those fleeting intuitions which a student working with source materials frequently experiences and more often than not discounts. While searching the ante bellum newspapers of New Orleans for a variety of information in 1949, I noticed—with barely enough interest to record them —a few sketches and anecdotes relating to the Kentucky frontiersman. During the next two years I was occupied with working up for publication the immediately usable material gathered from the newspapers and with studying and writing in the field which I mainly profess. Meanwhile, the Kentuckian had developed some attraction for me, though I had no confidence that my training fitted me to survey his habitat. It was a hunch rather than a legitimate insight which drew me on, and many months passed before the plan of the whole study was even vaguely perceptible. The search for solutions to fundamental problems carried me into alien fields far beyond my anticipation and left me with a sense of having over-extended myself. I mention these circumstances to make plain the naïveté with which I began to deal with the early Kentuckian and the difficulties I encountered before finishing him off. What I have accomplished may very well strike the professional historian as overly ingenuous, but it has the advantage of being a fresh look at a subject of continuing importance for American civilization.

It should be perfectly evident that my conclusions were in no way preconceived. In all truth, I was unprepared to accept them, so uncongenial were they to the comfortable traditions which I early acquired and previously saw no reason to question. By way of routine analysis I came to realize how far the western expansion committed itself to ideas which were originally put forward very tentatively in Europe and which were in important instances open to serious objection both on practical and theoretical grounds. It gradually occurred to me that some of the more troublesome, not to say harmful, attitudes of the present were traceable to presumptions about man and society which noisily declared themselves on the frontier. The difference between the American West as represented by historians whose references were largely national and the American West considered as a cultural extension of the Old World became annoyingly evident, and I saw a real need to reassert how far the past lives on in the minds of men and positively or negatively affects their decisions. I could discover no valid excuse for the widespread pretense that America somehow produced her own intellectual capital and accordingly developed with little debt to Europe. It seemed to me that from ignorance, tact, or plain chauvinism certain pleasant but none too healthful illusions had been fostered and theories even devised to support them. I could not allow that a nation which upholds the ideal of scientific objectivity is morally justified in glossing over the fundamental miscalculations in its past and evaluating its accomplishment by local rather than universal standards.

While this book may be fairly described as a fresh approach, it is ·yet very extensively indebted, and anything less than special acknowledgment of the fact would be ungenerous. The notes at the back give too little indication of the extent to which I have been guided to indispensable source materials and helped to crucial insights. Lacking merely the scholarship produced in the history of ideas since World War II, I should have been able to formulate only very simple explanations of frontier cultural phenomena and nothing approaching a workable model for the western expansion. My understanding of both the immediate and the remote background of the American experience benefited immeasurably from the work of Gilbert Chinard, Ernst Cassirer, Shirley J. Case, Arthur O. Lovejoy, George Boas, and Lois Whitney. For the frontier scene I placed uncommonly heavy reliance upon the basic writings of Thomas P. Abernethy, Ralph H. Gabriel, Merle Curti, William W. Sweet, R. E. Banta, Niels H. Sonne, and Thomas D. Clark, of whom the last favored my work with his personal attention. I was enabled to proceed much more rapidly than otherwise would have been the case by J. Winston Coleman, Jr.'s *A Bibliography of Kentucky History* (1949) and Lawrence S. and Algernon D. Thompson's *The Kentucky Novel* (1953), the latter of which I was privileged to examine in manuscript.

I wish to express my appreciation to the Research Fund Committee of the University of Kentucky for two modest grants, which enabled me to employ clerical aid and to search the newspaper holdings of the Alabama and Mississippi Departments of Archives and History, the Arkansas History Commission, the Missouri Historical Society, and the Historical and Philosophical Society of Ohio. In these and other repositories of early records which I visited the very kindest service was extended to me.

I am grateful to my wife for undertaking to examine a large quantity of frontier travel literature and to Roy W. Battenhouse, who criticized my work out of his very full knowledge of Renaissance thought and of theological systems in general.

To Roy Harvey Pearce I doubtless owe most. His extensive writings on American civilization were originally of great assistance, and his meticulous and critical reading of an early draft of this book proved invaluable.

For errors of fact and judgment I alone am responsible; on occasion I have preferred, perhaps regrettably, my own intuitions over authoritative opinions.

February, 1957   **A. K. M.**

Contents

1 A Long View of the Frontier

"Thus the advance of the frontier has meant a steady movement away from the influence of Europe."—THE FRONTIER IN AMERICAN HISTORY

THE PIONEERS, it is widely agreed, abandoned the Old World on or around the Kentucky frontier and stepped the more lightly toward the far-distant Pacific. Writers concerned with the West have very often created the impression that the break with the burdensome European past was a wise and deliberate choice, on the whole beneficial to the emigrants and to the republic. This view tends to confer high purposefulness and keen foresight upon the pioneers as a group; by the same token the expansion becomes in its main lines an orderly movement directed toward rational ends. In this favorable regard, Transappalachia appears as a culture peculiarly American and in most things peculiarly successful, a monument to the statecraft of men who were poorly educated but nonetheless enlightened and surprisingly competent to solve the problems which had long confounded the nations. The legitimate objection to this construction is not that it is absolutely false but that it leaves certain conspicuous facts out of account; numerous other selective interpretations, though less congenial to national sympathies, claim equal consideration. The settlement and growth of the West may be attributed with as much justice to a mad lust for wealth and advantage as to a rational desire for a liberal political system, and in fact the economic case has often been argued. Recent historians, aware of the weaknesses of the various limited approaches, have tended to emphasize the multiplicity of factors involved in the westward movement; none, however, has devised an inclusive model, and perhaps most confess to some partiality for the frontier theory of Frederick Jackson Turner, which is nothing if not exclusive.

Whether a comprehensive theory can be devised to organize the changing complexity of the American West during the formative period is highly problematical. It is apparent, however, that the oversimplified models of the expansion bravely set forth in textbooks of history can be deepened and refined. The special and local studies produced by historical scholarship in this century call in question all of the popular views of the frontier experience, and there is accordingly pressing need for a general reexamination of basic assumptions and conclusions, whatever the effect on the soft focus in which the West has been conventionally held. A mature understanding of American civilization requires severer and more objective ways of conceiving the emigration and its aftermath, for in the beliefs, customs, standards, and biases crystallized in this great cultural spasm the modern American predicament was largely forecast, if not foreordained.

Kentucky, the first settlement of importance beyond the mountains and a principal channel of the westward movement, is a superior, if somewhat neglected, vantage point for studying the origins of western culture. Tennessee is another such point, though perhaps less revealing. The claim might justly be made that without such insights as Kentucky permits, the great emigration cannot be well understood. As an extension culturally speaking of eighteenth-century Virginia, it was in some sense a boundary between Europe and the wilderness. It was the ground, moreover, upon which the frontier mind, ultimately the western mind, acquired definite form and challenged the Old World in fundamental concerns. The forces which shaped the West converged there and fell into a perceptible pattern. Admittedly, not all things western are implied in the Kentucky settlement, but the beginning can be shown to have prefigured the end in those things most significant for cultural history.

Rumor transformed Kentucky into something rich and strange a century before the first settlements. What Daniel Boone saw from Pilot Knob in June, 1769, was not only a magnificent forest enveloped in a blue haze but also a fabled garden interpenetrated with myth. From extravagant reports of Indians and white wanderers, the tramontane region embraced by the Ohio and Cumberland rivers came early to be involved, although tenuously, with the tradition of the Earthly Paradise, the existence of which Europe had affirmed more or less seriously the thousand years past. For the hopeful emigrants entering from the east by way of the Ohio and through Cumberland Gap along the ancient Warrior's Path, Kentucky connoted abundance in all desirable things and boundless liberty for all, thus a new life immeasurably superior to that before and equal to the idyllic modes of existence after which the human race has always yearned. In the romantic view the settlers achieved something resembling the life they sought, and from their ranks sprang the buckskin hero of the Kentucky frontier, symbolizing various ideal states of being. Thus, the real frontiersman, obsessed with the garden myth and behaving accordingly, became entangled in several versions of the same myth projected into the wilderness by the romantic imagination. Existing both as abstractions derived from European ideas about nature and man and as objective realities embodying the practical consequences of those ideas, Kentucky and the Kentuckian may be said to have mediated between Western civilization and the civilization which evolved in the American West.

Kentucky during the eighteenth century claimed the attention of the East and indeed of Europe more than any other Transappalachian area. Owing to wonderful reports of it as a region temperate and fertile, abounding in wildlife of many sorts, Kentucky was widely regarded as promised land. What was known recalled the Earthly Paradise, which, though traditionally located in the Orient, was thought after the voyages of Columbus to be accessible from the west. Despite plausible reports of Indian barbarities and appalling hardships, the oppressed and the idealistic of Europe for more than three hundred years had contemplated America through a prism streaked with myth, and out of the refracted colors formed images of Eden. Although explorers in the end dissipated the mystery of America as of all the other terrae incognitae with which early cartographers filled up remote spaces of the globe, Kentucky remained for a considerable period a principal focus of the myth and acquired an enduring paradisiacal character. California and Polynesia inspired Edenic imagery at one time or another in the eighteenth and nineteenth centuries, but Kentucky was substantially the last rumored paradise to fill large numbers of people with serious expectation. In the period of the expansion Kentucky was then a particular geographical location but also an ideal condition founded in long-standing myth.

Even after the frontier had been pushed far beyond the Mississippi, Kentucky was a compelling symbol; and when the West as a whole came to be regarded as a garden by prospering settlers, the conviction remained that Old Kaintuck was *the* Garden of the West. Although the splendid herds of big game were gone before 1800 and with them much of the forest, the fertile land remained a conspicuous reminder of the departed glory. Many travelers probably expected to find the inhabitants in the state of nature, lolling beneath the shade of the forest primeval. Instead of wild nature, unmistakable signs of wealth everywhere met their gaze. The reaction of Count Francesco Arese, who toured the new nation during 1837-1838, is significant: "The most sincere and least bombastic Americans tell you that the country around Lexington is the garden of the United States: the others tell you it is the garden of the *world!* In reality it is very beautiful, but in a positive, numerical way, a money-beauty, in short an American beauty."[1] Unfortunately for the hopes of hungering emigrants, the Blue-

grass was never a poor man's land. Yet even for the disappointed multitudes who moved on west in search of untenanted
gardens, Kentucky remained a bright pastoral thought.

Their removal to Kentucky worked two kinds of change in
the backwoodsmen of the Virginia frontier. The expectation of
a life in all things pleasurable, the escape from constituted
authority, and the hardships of the actual settlement intensified
in them qualities which suit a heroic age decidedly better than
a settled state of society. While living on the eastern slopes of
the Appalachians, the backwoodsmen were in the urbane view
unshirted barbarians. Certainly not less barbarous following
the emigration and from all indications rather more, they
acquired after a time an admirable character in the civilized
imagination. The real Kentuckian, as far as circumstances
permitted, arranged his life and used the garden according to
the paradisiacal archetype—that is, with the utmost profligacy—
but the legendary one leaped into the several myths in which
the expansion was framed. Willing enough to accept the manifold benefits conferred upon him by optimistic philosophers,
the natural man of the wilderness was least of all concerned
with substantiating their social theories. As a matter of fact,
he emphatically repudiated his idealized portraits and by his
excesses gave thoughtful observers cause to ponder the nature
of man. Kentucky was then something of a laboratory in which
the noble savage of the primitivists had every opportunity to
fulfill himself and thus disclose his actual quality—and fulfill
himself he did, though not as the Enlightenment had anticipated. Almost from the outset, moreover, he set himself in
opposition to the cultural program of the class of society which
had come to romanticize him as the indomitable Indian fighter.

The eighteenth-century stage of Western civilization known
as the Enlightenment demonstrably passed into Kentucky with
the Virginia gentry, but powerful countercurrents prevented its
success there and its extension westward. Upper-class settlers
intended besides profiting themselves in the wilderness to
plant a culture expressive of the best part of their Old World

6 The Frontier Mind

legacy, and for a time they appeared to labor effectually, as the early achievement of Lexington suggests. Their ambitions were finally frustrated somewhat by their own misconceptions but rather more by irrational forces embodied in the ignorant generality of emigrants, who had the sense of moving out of a circumscribed life dominated by magistrate and priest into a largely unrestrained condition. Although it is incorrect to assert that license and ignorance triumphed altogether, the emigrants seldom listened to wise and educated counsel in vital matters. The decisive turn came in Kentucky, and the cultural development of the West beyond was essentially the same story rewritten at each stage with a change of local details.

Frontier historians have commonly described the revolt from Europe in such a way as to conceal its grave implications and to exalt the pioneers for their temerity. Thus, Turner's widely applauded interpretation, though true as far as it goes, is selective, uncritical, and lacking in rear vision: "The men of the 'Western World' turned their backs upon the Atlantic Ocean, and with a grim energy and self-reliance began to build up a society free from the dominance of ancient forms."[2] This statement invites ironical contemplation, because it ignores the fact that the emigration, while in some measure a rational protest against the social, religious, and political forms of Europe and the East, was yet enacted in the context of the ancient paradisiacal myth, which is a structure of irrational expectations. Strongly influenced by romantic patterns imposed upon the West in the nineteenth century and by personal sympathies, Turner assumed that men in a state of nature could somehow create an adequate culture virtually from nothing. He tended to slight the continuing influence on the emigrants of some of the noblest concepts of the Enlightenment, and he took small account of the recrudescence of ancient and generally primitive modes of behavior in the West in consequence of the loss of a rational frame of reference. The "movement away from the influence of Europe" unquestionably benefited the pioneers in some things, but it was nevertheless a retreat of sorts and as such entailed large and probably permanent cultural losses.

Perhaps fortunately, frontier Kentucky is not remembered as the place where the westward movement went wrong but as the beginning of the short-lived heroic age in America. The settlement was in all ways a remarkable experience for the actual participants and one which five or six generations of adolescents have eagerly re-created. It was doubtless written in the myths which hovered over the Middle Ages that when arrived in Eden the men of the Western world would go "hog wild." The frenzied pilgrims who invaded the Kentucky Eden unquestionably went "whole hog" and by their exploits and excesses produced an incomparably rich legendry. The old Garden of the West and its picturesque tenant speak of many things—of big-game hunting and Indian fighting, of high living and ferocious brawling, and something too of cultural aspiration and cultural failure. Kentucky is the most colorful chapter in early American history and studied against the European background possibly the most instructive.

I *The Garden of the West*

2 Eden Recovered

*"O my dear honeys, heaven is a Kentucky
of a place."*—THE CHRISTIAN TRAVELLER

THE EARTHLY PARADISE is by tradition a far-distant
region of extraordinary fertility, blessed with noble trees, foun-
tains, and rivers, and screened by a perilous barrier—mountain
or sea—over which only the valiant may pass. Men have variously located it—the Venerable Bede in Ireland, Michael
Drayton in Virginia—though usually to the westward of the
limit of precise geographical knowledge. Kentucky, according
to report, substantially fitted the archetypal pattern and not
unaccountably became in the eighteenth century the focus of
the paradisiacal myth in the New World, although only the
Blue Limestone triangle—with the base on the Ohio River
between present Mason and Trimble counties and the practical
apex in Lincoln county—was uncommonly rich. It was this
section which was always best known, because first settled and
consequently easier of access to travelers, whether they came
up from Cumberland Gap by way of the Hazel Patch or over
the trace from Limestone (Maysville) on the river. The soil
was generally a fine loam, containing available lime and phos-
phoric acid and abundant organic matter, as an unidentified
but perceptive observer clearly recognized in 1792:

After you are got fairly into Kentucky, the soil assumes a black appearance, rich and light in substance; and should you visit the country in the spring, you will be surprised at finding no leaves under the trees. The reason is, the ground is so rich and damp, that they always rot and disappear with the winter, except where the soil is evidently poor, for that country. It then bears the appearance of the better sort of land in Pennsylvania and Jersey, though differing widely in substance, there being no sand to be met with in the soil of Kentucky.

There is a species of flat, or split limestone that pervades all the country, lying at unequal depths. In the rich and black-looking soil, it lies near the surface, and in general, the nearer the stone lies to the surface, the richer the land is found to be. At the same time, the stone does not, as I expected, impede the growth of the trees, as they grow every where to an amazing height, except near the salt licks, where the influence of the saline particles seems to check their growth.[1]

Some early prospectors studied the trees for indications of the quality of the soil. F. A. Michaux, who visited Kentucky in 1802, thought that the best land lay beneath cherry, white walnut, buckeye, ash, hackberry, slippery elm, blackjack oak, coffee tree, honey locust, and papaw—the last three denoting the highest fertility.[2] Harry Toulmin, a young Unitarian minister from Lancashire, took in addition black walnut, black locust, hickory, sugar maple, poplar, and sycamore, among others, as proof of superior land.[3] Michaux consigned chestnut, red oak, black oak, sassafras, persimmon, and sweet gum to the second class of land. Whether reliable indexes or not, all these and many other varieties of deciduous trees flourished in the Bluegrass. Conspicuously absent were the acid-loving conifers, like hemlock and pine, and the broadleaf evergreen shrubs. The only evergreen in the limestone country was the ubiquitous *Virginia juniper*, misnamed red cedar, which usually points to thin land. Where the soil was especially rich, oak and locust often grew five feet in diameter, beach four to five, and poplar between five and six, the last two species reaching as much as one hundred twenty feet in height.[4] No doubt there were exceptional individuals much exceeding these

measurements. Travelers frequently noticed gigantic syca-
mores along the Ohio and tributary streams, and some excellent
specimens of these yet survive—because commercially value-
less.

The fertility of the soil considered, the forests were surprisingly open, and extensive meadows, not altogether treeless
but with trees wide apart, appear to have spotted the inner
Bluegrass. Generally, the uplands were carpeted with white
clover, rye grass, fern, wild ginger, Shawnee cabbage and
lettuce, and a sort of bluegrass, or "greensward,"[5] or, according
to Gilbert Imlay, with rye, clover, pea-vine, and "buffalo,
orchard, spear, blue, and crab grasses."[6] The woodland pastures
furnished excellent grazing, and occasionally were left undis-
turbed until the trees had been leveled by wind, lightning, or
disease. Even more abundant grazing was provided on low
ground by large tracts of giant cane, an evergreen plant growing three or four inches in diameter and seven or eight feet
tall in central Kentucky.[7] It is no great wonder that "Kaintuck"
was thought to mean "Canetuck" by some of the early settlers
whose cattle battened on the green shoots before grain became
plentiful.[8] After clearing, the best land for a time yielded corn
bountifully without exceptional care—from forty bushels the
first year to more than a hundred the third.[9] Clear streams, fed
by countless springs issuing from the Silurian limestone,
watered park land and canebrake before emptying into the
Licking and Kentucky rivers, which in turn swelled the Ohio.

Observation then confirmed rumor wonderfully. The land
beyond the mountains was as rich as any Eden need be, and
nature flourished accordingly. For those individuals caught
up in the wild enthusiasm for the new land, ancient descriptions of the Earthly Paradise merely prefigured Kentucky. The
historian and Federalist legislator Humphrey Marshall, who
moved to Kentucky from Virginia in 1780 and therefore knew
something of the original appearance of the region, described
the Bluegrass in the context of the myth which had enveloped
it from the first, representing Daniel Boone as a "second Adam"

entered into a "second paradise": "By this time, he had advanced some distance into the extended wood; and progressing, gained an eminence; whence looking around with astonishment —on the one hand he beheld the ample plain, and beauteous fields; on the other, the river Ohio, which rolled in silent dignity, marking the north-western boundary of Kentucky, with equal precision, and grandeur. The chirping of the birds, solaced his ears with music; the numerous deer, and buffaloe, which passed him in review, gave dumb assurance that he was in the midst of plenty—and cheerfulness once more possessed his mind."[10]

Wild animals figured importantly in the American conception of Eden; the backwoodsman's terrestrial paradise was, like the Indian's Elysium, a happy hunting ground. The reports of an incredible abundance of game in Kentucky no less than the reports of fertile land stirred the interest of the colonies and even of England and France. Hunting was certainly in the blood of a majority of those who wandered across the mountains before 1775, and the fondest recollections of old settlers generally concerned the enormous concentrations of wildlife in the wilderness. Boone's friend, John Finley, entered western Kentucky in 1752 while a member of a hunting party in the employ of the astute Indian trader George Croghan, and French hunters before 1767 harried the buffalo along the Ohio.[11] Yet game was little diminished when the Long Hunters —forty venturesome frontiersmen from the New River and Holston valleys—hunted in 1770-1771 through northern Tennessee and the Kentucky Barrens as far as Green River.[12]

Every account of this expedition supports the impression that the land teemed with game of all sorts but especially with deer. By February, 1771, the party had prepared approximately fifteen hundred peltries when a band of Cherokee seized the whole lot. Some of these hunters elected to continue and reportedly secured a quantity nearly as great on the Cumberland and Green rivers. But the noblest of the ruminants was the wapiti, the American elk, which seems to have disappeared more rapidly than any other large animal, although found in impressive herds during the period of exploration. Because of number, size, and habit, the buffalo deeply stirred the first hunters, who, much to the hurt of these majestic creatures, acquired a keen taste for the tender flesh of their humps. The buffalo was chiefly responsible for beating the broad roads along the ridges of central Kentucky and for digging great channels in the saline earth about the licks. One old hunter, according to John Filson, saw a thousand of the animals milling around Blue Licks at one time, and Simon Kenton observed fifteen hundred at the same place.[13] Despite constant harassment, the buffalo survived in Spencer County until 1793[14] and in the western part of the state perhaps longer.

Among the other really formidable animals, the bear plays a large and often humorous role in the annals of Kentucky. Not much interest attaches to the panther, a fundamentally cowardly animal given to the fatal habit of treeing. The wolf, despised by all, prowled through the region, preying originally on the deer and later on the livestock of the settlers. But the bear, hunted incessantly and eventually driven to the mountains, gained wide respect as a hard antagonist and as a source of warm fur, nutritious though gamy flesh, and strong oil. Wonderfully adaptable, the bear acquired a taste for the staples of human diet—eating corn green off the stalk, pork raw off the settler's pig, and honey out of hollow trees. It is no great wonder that tall tales by the score collected around this animal, including those of Davy Crockett, the greatest enemy (according to legend) the bear ever had.

Birds of many kinds frequented Kentucky, as the Audubon accounts disclose, but it was chiefly the wild turkey which interested the settlers. These birds—remarkably plentiful, tame, and fat—posed agreeably for the hunter's aim and sometimes burst open on striking the ground.[15] Settlers without meal thought the breast a tolerable substitute for bread[16]—doubtless because dry. Filson's colorful account of birdlife in the Ohio Valley supported the myth impressively and yet departed only slightly from the truth: "The land fowls are turkeys, which are very frequent, pheasants, partridges, and ravens: The perraquet, a bird every way resembling a parrot, but much smaller; the ivory-bill wood-cock, of a whitish colour with a white plume, flies screaming exceeding sharp. It is asserted, that the bill of this bird is pure ivory, a circumstance very singular in the plumy tribe." His description of the fish, though oddly omitting the bass, is very nearly correct: "The fish common to the waters of the Ohio are the buffalo-fish, of a large size, and the cat-fish sometimes exceeding one hundred weight. Salmons have been taken in Kentucke weighing thirty weight. The mullet, rock, perch, gar-fish, and eel, are here in plenty. It is said that there are no trouts in the western waters. Suckers, sun-fish, and other hook-fish, are abundant; but no shad, or herrings."[17]

Scarcely less interesting to Europe than the abundant wildlife were the remains of Pleistocene mammals imbedded in the mud of Big Bone Lick (Boone County). At least until the end of the sixteenth century, monsters of a sort familiar to medieval legend were widely thought to inhabit Cathay and other remote lands, and the discovery of the huge bones in America, which for long had been confused with the Orient, perhaps freshened the tradition. Kentucky was plainly no place for a defenseless man when occupied by such creatures as those identified from the remains—ground sloths the size of elephants, beavers as large as bears, elephants of several kinds, and mastodons. Among the less fearsome animals were horses, deer, elk, caribou, and bison.[18] Thomas Ashe was deeply impressed by the Big Bones and, to judge from his reconstruction, particularly by those of the great sloth—"With the agility and ferocity of the tiger; with a body of unequalled magnitude and strength; this monster must have been the terror of the forest, and of man!" He was not quite certain that the *Megalonyx*, as Thomas Jefferson named the animal, was extinct, though thinking it probable.[19] The presence of the bones at the lick was a matter of common knowledge to the Indians of the Ohio Valley and by the middle of the eighteenth century even to white men beyond the mountains. Baron de Longueuil noticed the remains in 1739, Christopher Gist in 1751, and Nicholas Cresswell in 1775. Following the Revolution curio seekers thoughtlessly despoiled Big Bone Lick of its ancient treasure.

Before many years large game went the way of the Pleistocene monsters. The causes are familiar—unrestrained hunting and agriculture, although the hard winter of 1779-1780, during which man and beast suffered frightfully, accelerated the process.[20] During much of the period enveloped in the paradisiacal haze, however, Kentucky was as rich in game as in other things, and the abundant wildlife no less than the land supported Timothy Flint's bold claim that the region was "the home of all that is good, fertile, happy, and great."[21] A boatman on the Ohio, quoted by Charles Fenno Hoffman, testified in even more sweeping terms to the power of the garden myth: "No, stranger, there's no place on the universal 'arth like old Kaintuck: she whips all 'Out-west' in prettiness; and you might bile down cr'ation and not get such another State out of it."[22] The boatman's declaration was novel in nothing except imagery, for Kentucky had long been described in terms familiar to the tradition of the lost paradise.

Perhaps the first account available to Europe appeared in 1663 in one of the series of reports from America known as the *Jesuit Relations*.[23] The author was apparently the Jesuit Hierosme Lalemant, who sent this relation, covering the years 1661-1662, to his superior in France. He had no personal knowledge of Kentucky, but relied on vague reports originating with Iroquois braves who ventured there and took prisoners from among the Shawnee. Such facts as the Indians provided, this Jesuit father assimilated to the medieval pattern of the Earthly Paradise. Though perhaps not a direct influence on travelers of a later date, his account wonderfully anticipates the descrip-

tions of Kentucky preserved in publications widely read during
the next two centuries and substantially forges the connection
of the Kentucky paradisiacal tradition with the ancient myth:

Proceeding rather Westerly than Southerly, another band of
Iroquois is going four hundred leagues from here in pursuit of a
Nation whose only offense consists in its not being Iroquois. It is
called Ontôagannha, signifying "the place where people cannot
speak"—because of the corrupt Algonquin in use there. Furthermore, if we believe our Iroquois who have returned thence, and
the Slaves whom they have brought thence, it is a country which
has none of the severity of our winters, but enjoys a climate that
is always temperate—a continual Spring and Autumn, as it were.
The soil there is so fertile that one could almost say of it, within
bounds, what the Israelite discoverers said of the Promised land; for,
to mention the Indian corn only, it puts forth a stalk of such extraordinary thickness and height that one would take it for a tree,
while it bears ears two feet long with grains that resemble in size
our large Muscatel grapes. No Moose or Beavers are seen there,
as they live only in cold countries; but, to make up for this, Deer,
Buffalo, wild Hogs, and another species of large animal wholly
unknown to us, inhabit those beautiful forests, which are like so
many Orchards, consisting almost wholly of fruit-trees. In their
branches live very peacefully birds of all colors and of every note,
especially little Paroquets, which are so numerous that we have
seen some of our Iroquois return from those countries with scarfs
and belts which they had made from these birds by a process of
interweaving. One finds there also a kind of Serpent of prodigious
size and two brasses in length; but these are harmless Snakes, their
venom not being hurtful or their sting injurious. The people are
not so inoffensive as the snakes, for they make use of a poison
with which they understand perfectly the art of infecting springs,
and even whole rivers; and they do it with such skill that the water
loses nothing of its fair appearance, although it be tainted throughout. Their villages are situated along a beautiful river which serves
to carry the people down to the great Lake (for so they call the
Sea), where they trade with Europeans who pray as we do, and
use Rosaries, as well as Bells for calling to Prayers.[24]

It can hardly be doubted that Father Lalemant thought of
Kentucky in connection with the Earthly Paradise, visions of
which had filled the European mind since the Middle Ages.

Perhaps the most widely known of a dozen or so medieval
accounts was the voyage of St. Brendon, which Jacobus de
Voragine included in the *Golden Legend,* a popular collection
of saints' lives. St. Brendon, an Irish monk of the sixth century,
reportedly sailed far into the east and found an island which,
from its altogether pleasant accommodations, he recognized as
the Earthly Paradise. Much the same luxurious situation,
implying abundance and felicity supreme, was sketched by
the author of the Anglo-Saxon *Phoenix* and by the twelfth-
century Platonist of Chartres, Bernard Silvestris *(De mundi
universitate);* and these strangely resemble the descriptions of
the Bluegrass of Kentucky written by Gilbert Imlay and other
"enthusiasts." Idyllic abodes were perhaps not regarded very
seriously in the Middle Ages so long as their location was
vaguely "eastward in Eden," but those regions described as
paradises and located with apparent geographical exactitude
unquestionably excited a great deal of interest even among the
sophisticated. The description of the Earthly Paradise in the
Travels of Sir John Mandeville, a fourteenth-century work of
uncertain authorship, produced a measure of conviction because attached to what purported to be a guidebook to the
Holy Land. The author merely expanded a standard description like that contained in the *De imagine mundi* of Honorius
of Autun by adding topographical and other particulars, which
probably had the effect of authenticating the account and, it
might be added, of discouraging those who longed to undertake the journey. The prospect of perilous waters, mountains,
and deserts, however, little deterred the numerous adventurers
who two centuries later were minded to cross over the sea to
the Earthly Paradise by the supposed western shortcut to
Cathay.

More than a hundred and fifty years after Father Lalemant
an unidentified French writer betrayed in himself similar preconceptions about Kentucky, which he described as a region
favored by a Côte d'Azur climate, where snow rarely fell and
then remained only a short time. His description of the Elk-

horn Valley of the Bluegrass hardly suggests firsthand knowledge, but it tends to show that the garden myth remained
attached to Kentucky even after agriculture had replaced the
forests: "Let us speak of Elkhorn Creek: the lands that it
waters are so fertile and so beautiful, the air there is so pure, so
serene almost all the year, that this country is veritably a
second terrestrial paradise. The farms are already so close
together that one would take it for an immense village. The
soil is consistently five to six feet deep. One knows of no
kinds of grains, fruits, or vegetables, which succeed not mar-
velously there: they gather also a quantity of excellent cotton,
and the hemp is of a beauty equal to that of the kingdom of
Naples."[25] The author's enthusiasm over this prospect owed
much to French political philosophy, which worked alterations
in the conception of the Earthly Paradise during the eighteenth
century. Admittedly, in many native-born Americans the
thought of an orderly and relatively crowded garden could
only evoke the profoundest melancholy; there were no fields
of cotton or hemp in the hunter's paradise imagined by
Humphrey Marshall. While obviously unlike, these two con-
figurations are equally valid in the context of the myth, which
chiefly promises abundance and freedom in a vaguely pastoral
state. The Earthly Paradise may be organized as legitimately
by the principles of Jeffersonian agrarianism as by those of
Rousseauistic naturalism; both concepts trace ultimately to
the same myth of the lost garden.[26]

The Arcadian character of the Kentucky wilderness first
became widely rumored with the publication of *A Topographical Description of the Western Territory of North America*
(1792), which reached a numerous audience in America and
Europe and inspired some confidence. Gilbert Imlay, the
author, in 1784 owned and occupied a tract of land in Fayette
County but returned to Europe before the end of 1786. His
description of central Kentucky agrees in essentials with that
contained in the *Jesuit Relations*, but in raising the expectation that "all the useful minerals will be found in abundance"[27]

he touched a theme which, though explicit in St. Brendon's voyage and in most explorations of the New World,[28] was hardly congenial to the Society of Jesus. The prototype of the garden which he sketched is unmistakably medieval:

Every thing here assumes a dignity and splendour I have never seen in any other part of the world. You ascend a considerable distance from the shore of the Ohio, and when you would suppose you had arrived at the summit of a mountain, you find yourself upon an extensive level. Here an eternal verdure reigns, and the brilliant sun of lat. 39°, piercing through the azure heavens, produces, in this prolific soil, an early maturity which is truly astonishing. Flowers full and perfect, as if they had been cultivated by the hand of a florist, with all their captivating odours, and with all the variegated charms that colour and nature can produce, here, in the lap of elegance and beauty, decorate the smiling groves. Soft zephyrs gently breathe on sweets, and the inhaled air gives a voluptuous glow of health and vigour, that seems to ravish the intoxicated senses. The sweet songsters of the forests appear to feel the influence of this genial clime, and, in more soft and modulated tones, warble their tender notes in unison with love and nature. Every thing here gives delight; and, in that mild effulgence which beams around us, we feel a glow of gratitude for that elevation our all-bountiful Creator has bestowed upon us. (pp. 42-43).

This absurd flight, because written toward the sentimental close of the eighteenth century, escapes suspicion of parody. A "man of feeling" rather than a satirist, Imlay seems to have been perfectly serious and has been so regarded. The paradisiacal character of Kentucky was unquestionably known to him beforehand, and, expectation rewarded, he gave the myth powerful support.

In all likelihood influenced by both Imlay and Filson, the romancers James Hall and Emerson Bennett continued the paradisiacal tradition well into the nineteenth century. The latter freely affirmed in the *Renegade* (1848) that "Kentucky, when first beheld by the white hunter, presented all the attractions he would have envied in Paradise itself." Although little originality can be claimed for their re-creations of the primeval landscape, both emphasized rather more than Imlay the possibilities of good hunting in the "paradise of brute creation," as Hall described Kentucky in *Legends of the West* (rev. ed., 1853). For at least two decades Hall and Bennett entertained a substantial public with their romances of the frontier, and credit is accordingly due them for perpetuating and even strengthening the Kentucky myth. Although not as exuberant as Imlay, Judge Hall sketched in *Legends of the West* much the same idyllic situation: "The beautiful forests of Kentucky, when first visited by the adventurous footsteps of the pioneers, presented a scene of native luxuriance, such as has seldom been witnessed by the human eye. So vast a body of fertile soil had never before been known to exist on this continent. The magnificent forest trees attained a gigantic height, and were adorned with a foliage of unrivalled splendour. The deep rich green of the leaves, and the brilliant tints of the flowers, nourished into full maturity of size and beauty by the extraordinary fertility of the soil, not only attracted the admiration of the hunter, but warmed the fancy of the poet, and forcibly arrested the attention of the naturalist" (p. 237). In the *Phantom of the Forest* (rev. ed., 1868), Bennett exhibited a certain Byronic interest in the wilder aspects of Kentucky scenery but otherwise adhered to the familiar pattern.

Novelists in this century, while generally disinclined to employ high-flown diction, have yet put in the mouths of rustic characters much the same description of Kentucky which the early romancers and chroniclers standardized. In the *Crossing* (1904) Winston Churchill assigned to a precocious lad, David Trimble, a Virgilian appreciation of the wilderness which clearly recalls the ante bellum romances. A florid image ascribed by James B. Finley to Boone is echoed by Simon Kenton in Hal G. Evarts' *Tomahawk Rights* (1929): "Kentucky is the cream of the world, with wild honey throwed in for good measure" (ch. 11).[29] Elizabeth Madox Roberts, whose *Great Meadow* (1930) is perhaps the best novel concerned with the frontier scene, exploited the Edenic tradition extensively. Her rustic, an old hunter returned from Kentucky, avers, "Like paradise it is, so beautiful and good." The Middle Ages would have immediately recognized the land—the "promise land"— which he describes: "Yea, it is a good land, the most extraordinary that ever I knew. Meadow and woodland as far as eye can behold. Beauteous tracts in a great scope, miles. A fine river makes a bound to it in the north, and another fine river flows far to the west, another boundary. To the east is a boundary of rugged mountains. And set above the mountains is a great cliff wall that stands across the way. Yea, you would know you had come to the country of Caintuck when you saw that place. A cliff wall makes a steep barrier across your path beyond any man's strength to climb. But high up in the mountains, cut in the cliff, is a gate" (ch. 1).

Poets as well as romancers have had a considerable hand in perpetuating the Kentucky myth. Much nineteenth-century verse concerned with the frontier period reflects the paradisiacal tradition in a general way through expressions of strong affection for Kentucky and sentimental recollections of the olden times. Though perhaps only the Miltonic epic *The Mountain Muse* (1813) by Daniel Bryan is as extravagantly rhetorical as the romances, a great deal of Kentucky poetry uses the commonplace but significant garden image. The context is plainly Edenic in the *Banks of Ohio*, a popular "come-ye-all" from the period 1812-1818,[30] and in *Boone's First View of Kentucky*, attributed to Timothy Flint:

> Such was Kentucky then,
>   With wild luxuriance blest;
> Where no invading hand had been,
>   The garden of the West. (st. 4)

The sheer bulk of paradisiacal similitude lavished upon Kentucky suggests that the most pretentious one of all was not uttered entirely with humorous intent. The anecdote containing this figure has been repeated often enough by nineteenth-century writers and recent historians of the Ohio Valley frontier. Perhaps the most circumstantial version is Isaac Reed's, recorded in a letter dated February 10, 1818: "The preacher [a Baptist] was descanting upon heaven, and the heavenly state. He wished his hearers to get a just idea of that place, and he attempted to give it by comparison: it was in the meeting-house [near Paint Lick], not half a mile from where I now write, where the preacher said to his hearers, 'O my dear honeys, heaven is a Kentucky of a place.' "[31]

The Edenic metaphor became conventional in accounts of frontier Kentucky after the publication of Imlay's *A Topographical Description* and admittedly sprang from affectation as often as from conviction. Even so, the original conception of this land of majestic forests, rich soil, and limpid streams seems not to have deteriorated significantly. Repetition of the image from whatever cause can only have attracted greater attention to Kentucky as the focus of a myth which represented the end of all man's desiring no less in the nineteenth century than in antiquity. Although Robert Montgomery Bird in *Nick of the Woods* (1837) doubtless exaggerated the appeal of Kentucky, his estimate agrees substantially with sober reports from the pioneer period: "The Dorado of the Spaniards, with its cities built of gold, its highways paved with diamonds and rubies, was not more captivating to the brains of Sir Walter Raleigh and his fellow freebooters of the 16th century, than was the Kentucky of the red men, with its fertile fields and ever-blooming forests, to the imaginations of their descendants, two hundred years after. It was not unnatural, indeed, that men should regard [it] as an Eden" (ch. 1). The illusion was repeatedly denied by objective reality, for, however idyllic at times, Kentucky was a land visited periodically by extreme heat and cold, drought and flood. That the illusion should have prevailed and even yet sustains the high price of Bluegrass acreage can best be explained by the rich content of the myth of the Earthly Paradise, which has always had power to move men beyond reason.

3 The Garden Archetype

"Ask these Pilgrims what they expect when they git to Kentuckey the Answer is Land."—MOSES AUSTIN

THE ECONOMIC motive has been most often advanced in late years to explain the willingness—indeed, eagerness—of the hardy race on the Virginia frontier to risk life and limb in the danger-filled wilderness beyond the topmost Appalachian ridge. C. W. Alvord declared with rigorous dogmatism that a "vision of sudden wealth in the exploitation of free land" acted like a magnet to attract settlers,[1] and in this view American historians have tended to concur. It is significant of a deepening understanding of the emigration, however, that R. H. Gabriel, while agreeing that the most powerful factors in the western expansion were "earth hunger" and the "desire for profit," frankly admits religious, utopian, escapist, and primitivistic motivations.[2] Perhaps few historians would now grant unqualified approval to the exclusive economic interpretation, which, though comprehending the speculator's transparent purpose, tends to confuse the means with the end and leaves unconscious impulsions wholly out of account.

There is no question that emigrants on all frontiers were obsessed with land, but it may be doubted that the generality conceived the new land as wealth in the ordinary sense. The myth which first overspread Kentucky and invested it with a rich symbolic content touched elsewhere in the West and produced comparable illusions. What chiefly motivated the western movement was assuredly a vision but hardly one of quick riches to be gained from the exploitation of land. The almost mystical concern with Kentucky which Moses Austin perceived in the stream of suffering humanity flowing over the Wilderness Road in 1796 appears to have owed far less to the desire for assessable real estate than to an irrational expectation of a paradisiacal situation with negligible economic problems:

Ask these Pilgrims what they expect when they git to Kentuckey the Answer is Land. have you any. No, but I expect I can git it. have you any thing to pay for land, No. did you Ever see the Country. No but Every Body says its good land. can any thing be more Absurd than the Conduct of man, here is hundreds Travelling hundreds of Miles, they Know not for what Nor Whither, except its to Kentucky, passing land almost as good and easy obtain.d, the Proprietors of which would gladly give on any terms, but it will not do its not Kentuckey its not the Promis.d land its not the goodly inheratence the Land of Milk and Honey. and when arriv.d at this Heaven in Idea what do they find? a goodly land I will allow but to them forbiden Land. exausted and worn down with distress and disappointment they are at last Oblig.d to become hewers of wood and Drawers of water.[3]

A more revealing commentary than Austin's on the psychology of the emigration can hardly be discovered in documents of the eighteenth century and not often in those of the nineteenth. Among formal historians perhaps only Humphrey Marshall fully acknowledged the paradisiacal connotations of Kentucky; Mann Butler and Lewis Collins were utterly sober annalists who concerned themselves with the hard facts of the political and military record rather than with the mind of the settlers. Audubon recognized that more was involved than the desire for land and suspected that the sheer beauty and richness of the Ohio Valley attracted the Virginians quite as much as the opportunity for gain.[4] Certainly the great ornithologist bothered himself little about property while any considerable part of that splendid wilderness remained undefiled by ax and plow. But none so well as Timothy Flint understood what moved the settlers. This perceptive Yankee preacher, journalist, and novelist, who spent much of his life in the Mississippi Valley, studied the same pathetic spectacle which so amazed Austin, and his insights into the emigrant unconscious reveal what was for the period unusual awareness of the garden myth and its dynamics:

There is more of the material of poetry than we imagine, diffused through all the classes of the community. And upon this part of the character it is, that the disposition to emigration operates, and brings in aid the influence of its imperceptible but magic power. Very few, except the Germans, emigrate simply to find better and cheaper lands. The notion of new and more beautiful woods and streams, of a milder climate, deer, fish, fowl, game, and all those delightful images of enjoyment, that so readily associate with the idea of the wild and boundless license of new regions; all that restless hope of finding in a new country, and in new views and combinations of things, something that we crave but have not,— I am ready to believe, from my own experience, and from what I have seen in the case of others, that this influence of imagination has no inconsiderable agency in producing emigration. Indeed, the saturnine and illiterate emigrant may not be conscious that such motives had any agency in fixing him in his purpose. But I need not observe, that those who examine most earnestly what passes in their own minds, are not always aware of all the elements of motive that determine their actions.[5]

The author was not concerned with the speculators but with the firmly resolved emigrants, for whom land, taken literally, signified no more wealth than labor could extract. Without a fairer prospect than swinging a mattock in new ground, the latter group would have stayed at home. As Flint recognized, it was the myth attached to Kentucky and other western territories, rather than cold economic considerations, which especially excited these people. This is not of course to deny either the presence or importance of economic factors in the actual development of the West. While all the early settlers naturally desired whatever of good things the earth might yield, few can have expected land or gold as capital to provide ease and abundance in the immediate future. Gold, of which there was none in the Ohio Valley, is meaningful somewhat as insigne but chiefly as a lien on the food and labor supply; and the advantage of property ownership depends directly on the availability of labor. Where land is abundant and every man privileged to be his own employer, neither money nor real estate will procure a luxurious mode of existence. Although man acts economically—building, gathering, exchanging—wherever he goes in company, his primary motivation is not by that fact economic. In truth, he often emigrates to escape the eternal struggle with economic reality, though usually finding the promised land to be more exacting in this respect than the old. Common sense dictates a coming to terms with present circumstances, for change dissipates whatever goods labor has produced; but the imagination tricks people into emigration through creating a distant life in which the laws of wild and human nature are miraculously suspended. More or less consciously, they seek the lost garden, where, as Horace represented the Fortunate Islands, "yearly the earth un-ploughed brings forth grain, and the unpruned vine flowers continuously, and buds the branch of the never-failing olive." Ironically, emigrants very often flourish because the new situation is in fact no Eden and, far from affording ease and abundance, compels extraordinarily energetic responses.

For the emigrants observed by Moses Austin, Kentucky assuredly symbolized wealth, but wealth viewed as an ideal life rather than as treasure to be displayed or borne away or as land to be turned and harrowed. True, they thought of bread but had no thought of living by bread alone. Without comprehensive freedom—freedom from social, religious, polit-ical, and even moral repressions—bread has no savor and life is a burden. To agree with Alvord that a vision of wealth peopled the tramontane region is to oversimplify and debase a movement enacted in the context of a splendid myth. When man sets out for the Earthly Paradise, he anticipates felicity unlimited but not economic problems; that he discovers the latter and becomes accordingly avaricious merely underscores the difference between vision and reality. Perhaps few of the early settlers of Kentucky realized that once subdued the garden would be turned by greed (a synonym for economic anxiety) into a legal battleground, as it was unthinkable that occasions for strife could arise where there was milk and honey aplenty and boundless freedom for all. But then peoples have generally minimized the trials and tribulations of Canaan.

To assert the strong influence of myth on the emigration to Kentucky and other western lands is not to maintain that all settlers were moved in identical ways or that the simple desire for profits was limited to speculators. Some sought material wealth and privilege as means to the ideal life, for the lack of these had rendered mature societies distasteful to them. Yet others proposed to found utopian communities without distinctions based on property or class.[6] Perhaps many of those drawn westward had no well-defined program but only a vague expectation of betterment. Some wanderers were doubtless moved by no other conscious motive than curiosity, like the bear which "went over the mountain to see what he could see." A considerable number were of that nomadic sort described by F. A. Michaux as "a kind of men who cannot settle upon the soil that they have cleared, and who under pretence of finding a better land, a more wholesome country, a greater abundance of game, push forward, incline perpetually towards the most distant points of the American population, and go and settle in the neighbourhood of the savage nations, whom they brave even in their own country."[7] Even more contemptuous of the attractions of property and the amenities of civilization than the ordinary frontiersmen were those eccentric individuals who relinquished the fruits of a millennium of progress in order to enjoy a free, communal life with the Indians.[8] But whatever the means sought, the new mode signified release from onerous obligations, satisfaction of unexpended desire, and a general suspension of all those inexorable processes of nature and society which use men up and cast them back unfulfilled into the common clay. To forgo the

advantages of civilization out of dissatisfaction with the restraints is to act regressively and of course impractically, but
the image of the Earthly Paradise emotionally apprehended
makes backward movement seem forward.

The "flowery and enchanting fables" of enthusiasts and
knaves, according to Thomas Ashe, produced the frenzied
emigration to Kentucky.[9] Oversimple to be sure, this explanation has a significant core of truth; for Imlay, among other
knaves and enthusiasts, intensified the mythic connotations of
the tramontane garden land. In other words, the primordial
longing for the Earthly Paradise actualized as emigration to
Kentucky to some extent as a consequence of *A Topographical
Description* and similar accounts, which described the region
in terms familiar to the tradition. It goes without saying that
speculators exploited the myth. Many individuals in Europe
and the East were seduced by the vision of paradise in Kentucky and hastened there without much concern for the realities of settlement. The solicitations of the speculators would
have fallen on deaf ears, however, had people not been emotionally prepared at the end of the eighteenth century for the
discovery of an Eden. Since antiquity, the Aryan imagination
had been obsessed with the idea of a far-western paradise, and
Europeans had come to view America as its likely location.
For the present study, this long-continuing tradition has uncommon importance, as it closely supports Timothy Flint's
intuitions about the expansion and provides needful perspective for the cultural development of Kentucky and the West.

The fiction of the Earthly Paradise is a perennial flower of
the imagination, springing from ascertainable causes and
assuming forms which owe something to racial memory and
something also to pious and secular literature. The existence
of an archetypal pattern can scarcely be doubted in view of
the fact that much the same images appear in ancient and
modern descriptions of paradisiacal states. When the problems of the present become unsolvable and the miseries insup-
portable, the mind postulates an existence without problems,

without miseries, that is, a paradise, which may be the re-
creation of an ancestral mode or even a spiritual state wrought
out of suggestions in Holy Writ. Man can find necessary relief
from the compulsions of his culture by imagining himself
either gathered with the saints in the City of God at the
millennium or reborn at the golden dawn of the world. Neither
as primitive being nor as one of the chosen of God is he
susceptible to the miseries which rend the flesh and torment
the spirit. Significantly, in religious thinking these two conditions tend to become confused, and in the mind of those
entertaining what E. L. Tuveson calls the "millennial expectation," the New Jerusalem and the Earthly Paradise are in
content not substantially different.[10] Paradise may be conceived as a Rousseauistic state of nature, a millennial situation,
or a utopian community, and be located in the Fortunate
Islands, Kentucky, or Polynesia, but psychologically considered
it is simply a projected haven from the harsh demands of the
social order and nature and an existence which without toil
or trouble satisfies desires of every fundamental kind.

By the time Columbus discovered America, several discrete
paradisiacal traditions, for having natural affinities, had become confused, if not interwoven. The myth of the Earthly
Paradise had assimilated features from the Golden Age of
classical antiquity and in some measure had coalesced with
the biblical Eden and the Fortunate Islands of the Romans.
Further, some Christians throughout the Middle Ages placed
a literal construction on the millennial forecast of St. John the
Divine and thus anticipated a future state rather like the idyllic
situations of pagan conception. While the impact of this con-
texture of myth on European thought is difficult to estimate,
it is abundantly clear that Europe had paradise on the mind
when the penetration of the Western Hemisphere began. To
ignore this complex of traditions is accordingly to misunder-
stand in some part the meaning of America for the Old World
and thus the preposterous expectations of the emigrants.

The myth of the Golden Age descended to the medieval

period directly from Ovid and Boethius, who had drawn the tradition out of the Hellenic stream. More than seven centuries before the Christian era, the Greek poet Hesiod in *Works and Days* outlined the history of mankind within the context of the familiar theory of cultural degeneration. First in this scheme—certainly not original with Hesiod—was a golden race dwelling in a terrestrial Elysium, after which came in succession the silver and the bronze races, the demigods or heroes, and finally the present inhabitants of the earth, each progressively worse. In the *Metamorphoses* Ovid called special attention to the evils unknown to the Golden Age and thereby intimated the sources of discontent in his own era, for which, in the opinion of Juvenal, nature possessed no metal commensurately debased. At the beginning, according to Ovid and sentimental primitivists during the next eighteen hundred years, man behaved virtuously without law. Where all men were righteous, there was no need for judges or law courts. And since men had not yet learned to build ships and sail with hostile intent against foreign lands, defenses were useless. Thus, the human race lived in peace and plenty without labor or constraint. Doubtless influenced by Seneca, Boethius in his exceedingly popular *Consolation of Philosophy* gave a decidedly ascetic tone to the Golden Age existence, limiting men to a diet of acorns and water and emphasizing contemplation rather than frivolity. This view, because essentially moral and primitive, held an understandable appeal for Christians, who accepted an ethics of renunciation and made a virtue of poverty. It cannot be maintained, however, that Christian paradisiacal thinking during the Middle Ages and after was free of libertinism.

First the Greeks and afterward the Romans were intrigued by the thought of finding wonderful islands beyond the Pillars of Hercules. The former even located the Islands of the Blest, though conceived as heavenly, in the unknown Atlantic waste. In his sixteenth epode Horace urged strife-torn Rome to seek in the western seas the Fortunate Islands, which by repute preserved Golden Age conditions. For Horace, the Fortunate Islands were identical with the Islands of the Blest, which had been understood by Hesiod and Pindar as abodes of the dead, not as earthly states. How real the Fortunate Islands of the Roman poets had become in the European imagination by the time America was discovered may be judged from a report issued June 19, 1493, by Bernardino de Carvajal, Spanish ambassador to the papal court: "Christ has set under their sway (Ferdinand and Isabella's) the Fortunate Islands, whose fertility is wonderful."[11] Columbus merely confirmed long-standing legend, which had been credited all along. People had known in good reason that paradisiacal states lay over the western ocean, including the Earthly Paradise, which, if located in the vicinity of Cathay, might be reached across the Atlantic.

The Earthly Paradise, widely sketched in the literature of the Middle Ages and associated particularly with St. Brendon, tended to be identified with the Garden of Eden, which, never reported destroyed by God or man, was thought to continue in existence. Whether represented in religious or secular literature, the Earthly Paradise ordinarily resembles the Golden Age scene sketched by Hesiod rather than that of Boethius, and is accordingly something of a bower of bliss, though perhaps not very different from the popular conception of Eden. Virgil had contributed somewhat to the confusion in the Christian mind by forecasting in his fourth—the so-called Messianic—eclogue a return to the Golden Age, with a little child leading the way. This alleged prefiguration of Christ gained the Mantuan considerable credit among the Christians of the Middle Ages, some of whom were disposed to believe that Eden might one day be recovered. Significantly, Matilda suggests to Dante in the *Purgatorio* that the Golden Age hymned by the classical poets represents a distorted tradition of the Age of Innocence.

The promise of a joyous millennium was a major attraction in Christianity from the outset, and early missionaries used it to win souls from paganism. Toward the end of the ancient world there must have been general dissatisfaction with the state of civilization (witness the persistent paradisiacal myth) and a corresponding desire for a better hope for the future, which millenarianism abundantly satisfied. The medieval church, supported by the well-considered opinions of Origen and Augustine, condemned the doctrine and generally disabused the faithful of the millennial illusion; but its recrudescence was likely whenever peoples endured hard afflictions. In the twelfth century Joachim of Floris, an Italian monk, gave millenarianism a new impetus and a new twist, predicting that the end of the world and thus the beginning of Christ's rule on earth would come when the church had been regenerated through the return of the Holy Spirit and apostolic conditions had been restored. This reputed heresy persisted despite opposition, and four centuries after Joachim's time it found a ready reception among Protestant sectaries of the Reformation, who on the authority of the Book of Revelation, taken literally, believed the Great Day to be imminent. Though perhaps never actually confused with the pagan paradises, the millennial state seems to be in content their Christian equivalent, and it unquestionably alleviates the same discontents.

Modern man would surely have created some form of paradise for his heart's ease even though lacking a traditional pattern, as the ultimate source of such conceptions is the universal longing for a state in which problems are simple or nonexistent. But as in most vital affairs, the medieval imagination wrought splendidly in weaving the primitivistic urge for a condition without painful issues into a tapestry filled with sense images of an altogether seductive kind. The conjoined paradisiacal myths were by the end of the Middle Ages imbedded in Christian thought and formed a part of that foundation upon which Renaissance speculative thinkers reasoned and wrote. During the Enlightenment ingenious philosophers elaborated the central ideas into systematic social structures, which even yet have adherents enough. The energy expended during the last five hundred years as a consequence of the myth of the Earthly

Paradise .is frightful to consider, although a world without it might be an even more frightful prospect. It is now a matter of common knowledge that the New World from the period of discovery until the nineteenth century was searched both for paradisiacal locations and for evidence to substantiate social theories founded in the paradisiacal myth. As one of those locations, Kentucky received much of the weight of the tradition and an enduring impression from it.

Reminiscences of the Earthly Paradise colored accounts of both real and imaginary voyages in the sixteenth century, with the consequence that the character of faraway and little-known lands—America in particular—became increasingly mythical. Moreover, the aborigines, never really understood, came to be regarded as noble savages living in a Golden Age environment free from the evils of corrupt societies, their obligations, according to Montaigne *(Des cannibales)*, consisting only of "bravery against their enemies and tenderness for their women." The sanguine and oversimple reports of voyagers fluttered the expectations of Europe and provoked elaborate social theories. With the experiences of Columbus and Amerigo Vespucci fresh in memory, Thomas More wrote *Utopia* (1515), a somewhat ironical account of a more or less Platonic commonwealth on an island in the western world. Following More over a century later, Francis Bacon commenced but did not finish a comparable book, the *New Atlantis*. Rabelais sent Pantagruel and his whimsical companions to visit idyllic islands in the west, and, while intending satire, disclosed how much information about medieval island paradises descended to the Renaissance.

The real voyages of Cabot, Balboa, Magellan, Cartier, and numerous others, often fancifully related, were set in a mythic context by Europeans yearning for Eden—an Eden by the end of the sixteenth century, it is well to add, abundantly furnished like St. Brendon's paradise with gems and precious metals, which More's Utopians despised. To Raleigh and the Spanish adventurers who searched South America for Eldorado it was only reasonable that the Golden Age should have gold, and the motive of material gain entered increasingly into the paradisiacal illusion, though not to the exclusion of social and religious programs. In this connection, it is well to remark that the English, slower than the Spanish or French to perceive the opportunities in the Western Hemisphere, behaved rather singularly when embarked on conquest. While seeking to mine the treasure of America, they meant besides to possess the land physically forever, with or without the leave of the aborigines. For all Europe, America was an Eldorado to be looted; but for the English more than others, it was also an Eden to be occupied. No other peoples displayed such enthusiasm for expending their strength in the conquest of a wilderness with so little prospect of immediate gain.

Admittedly, not all emigrants to America were blinded by myth to the hard realities of settlement, though it seems likely that few were wholly free of some sort of paradisiacal expectation. Chinard maintained that the accounts of voyages, novels of adventure, and the utopias of the philosophers had so powerfully conditioned the popular mind that by the beginning of the seventeenth century the desirability of returning to the state of nature was seriously considered.[12] His proposition accounts in some measure for the extravagance of Michael Drayton's *Ode to the Virginian Voyage* (1606), a poem based on the romanticized chronicles of Richard Hakluyt. No adventurer himself, Drayton described for the "brave heroic minds" about to set sail not Virginia, which he calls "Earth's only paradise," but the archetypal garden, "To whose the golden age / Still nature's laws doth give." He encouraged the colonists to expect "pearl and gold," venison, the juice of the "ambitious vine," and bountiful crops, as well as a mild climate —in short, the conspicuous delights of both the Golden and the present age without the inconveniences of either. This poem particularizes the content of the Edenic scene in a somewhat gross manner, though it scarcely exceeds the bounds of wish-fulfillment fantasies. The settlers quickly discovered that

Virginia was something less than idyllic, but the original conception was not immediately dissipated. More than a century later, Samuel Jenner described Virginia in Edenic terms in the *Neu-gefundenes Eden* (1737), an early example of an American report meant to attract settlers from Europe. But even as Jenner wrote, the focus of the paradisiacal myth was shifting westward to a more or less permanent location in Kentucky.

How man ought to occupy himself in paradise, neither ancient nor modern writers state quite clearly, although it is evident that a second Adam, spared the necessity of labor, would have time on his hands. Whether conceived as physical or spiritual, the state of blessedness implies some activity; the alternative is inertia, a condition achieved by Tennyson's wan lotus-eaters and the feeble shades of Persephone's garden, without, however, any sign of true felicity. The desire for rich spiritual experience unquestionably enters into the conception of paradise, and yet the conventional imagery suggests that paradise is a state of the flesh rather more than of the spirit. So much was perceived by the witty Syrian rhetorician Lucian in the second century of the Christian era, and in the *Verae narrationes* he represented the Islands of the Blest as ridiculously luxurious, with the greatest heroes there engaged much as on earth, disporting themselves with women and feasting sumptuously. The *Land of Cokaygne*, a thirteenth-century English poem adapted from a French source, is a comparable treatment of the Earthly Paradise. In Cokaygne, conventionally located in the western ocean, certain worldly monks and nuns live in exceeding felicity—eating, drinking, and making merry—with no thought for the spirit. A modern American instance, *The Big Rock Candy Mountains,* is for all its rich good humor a no less shrewd commentary on the sensuous quality of human wishes. The underlying argument of these satires is that paradise is chiefly a condition gratifying to the senses, and in truth there is no substantial evidence to the contrary. Quite understandably, the matter is not closely examined in serious accounts of paradisiacal states, but these

nonetheless imply unlimited food, leisure, love, and freedom
from restraint.

Kentucky at a distance was probably like other promised
lands a bright and shining pastoral image—bountiful, peaceful,
and fulfilling; yet from the first settlement it was disturbed not
only by Indian hostilities but also by a "wild and boundless
license." Paradise promises total satisfaction, and such "pilgrims" to the Kentucky Eden as Moses Austin observed meant
to indulge themselves at whatever frightful cost to the forest,
the creatures, and society. It is a matter of common knowledge
that they exploited nature with appalling profligacy, and it is
a reasonable conclusion from contemporary reports that in the
absence of social, religious, and civil constraints they frequently and spectacularly disturbed the peace of the garden.
The arm of the law reached no farther than the edge of the
forest surrounding the few settlements and had far less bone
and muscle than needful to restrain the willful immigrants.
However pervasive the effects of the Great Awakening, the
grip of the church relaxed considerably during the pioneer
period. Indeed, the influence of religion seems to have been
limited in Kentucky from the first settlements in 1775 until
the second quarter of the nineteenth century, camp meetings
notwithstanding.[13] In the opinion of R. L. Rusk, the evangelists may not be said to have corralled the lusty sinners of the
Garden of the West much before 1840,[14] by which time the
hardiest of the buckskin breed had topped the Continental
Divide.

While seldom absolutely candid, the literature of the Kentucky frontier taken as a whole leaves an impression of wanton
and reckless behavior. The presence of sober, conservative
settlers cannot be denied, or their concern with establishing
law and order; yet there are good reasons for thinking that
a large fraction of the approximately one quarter of a million
residents credited to Kentucky by the census of 1800 would
have had some difficulty staying within legal and social bounds
in the East. Nor should the presence of a large number of

unruly persons in the population occasion surprise, for the rebellious and the adventurous rather than the well-adjusted citizens tend to emigrate. The movement to Kentucky was in part a protest against the restrictions, arbitrary and otherwise, of the original colonies; since connoting liberty unlimited, Transappalachia attracted not only the congenitally restless backwoodsmen of the Valley of Virginia but also assorted incorrigibles, for whom the older settlements held out the prospect of a life behind bars.

Crediting the lamentations of frontier preachers rather than the effusions of the primitivists or the rank sentimentalism of Walt Whitman and Theodore O'Hara, W. W. Sweet declares the pioneers far less virtuous than generally supposed and attributes their depravity to the very influences—the wilderness and the savages—which by the calculations of the romantics should have ennobled them.[15] The experiences of the formidable Methodist circuit rider Peter Cartwright suggest that cooling the ardor of the backwoods was often a necessary prelude to conversion, and he sometimes used force to prepare ruffians to receive the word of God. Revivals were social no less than religious events; while the meek and the pious listened to the preaching, the more spirited habitually engaged in decidedly secular activity, including gambling, drinking, shooting, and brawling. Sunday meetings were convenient occasions for settling disputes, and fights were accordingly commonplace. While the womenfolk behaved less spectacularly than the men, they were cut from much the same cloth and at church often used their time for fair dalliance rather than worship, as the unbelievably candid autobiography of Daniel Isgrig (1775-1854) suggests.[16] In large part the confessions of a masterful libertine, this work has a special value for revealing the easy sexual relationships of frontier Kentucky. The moral laxity of the backwoods, though by no means unsuspected by historians, cannot be closely documented from printed sources.[17] Whereas Elias Pym Fordham merely acknowledged himself unable to "speak in high terms of the manners or of the virtue" of frontier women,[18] Isgrig described in lurid detail the kind of irregularities which apparently revolted cultured travelers. Brought by his family from Maryland to Bourbon County in 1789, Isgrig spent his youth and early manhood in the Bluegrass, moving to Ohio in 1806 only after having lost his land through the by then familiar judicial process. Whether from a congenital distrust of the church or from a preference for a libertine existence, Kentuckians seem to have been unusually refractory heathen well into the nineteenth century despite the frenzied exhortations of the evangelists. There is a large question, moreover, whether many of the genuine alligator-horses ever achieved a state of grace, for they appear to have kept one jump ahead of the preacher, as well as the sheriff, all the way to the Pacific.

The worldliness of the pioneers was not a subject the later nineteenth century dwelt much on, although doubtless disturbed by the thought that spiritual matters were not a chief concern in the old Garden of the West. E. G. Cattermole's conclusion to a sketch of Simon Kenton illustrates the way Victorian chroniclers preferred to think of the early settlers: "For many years before his death, he lived not only a patriotic but a well-ordered Christian life, being a zealous member of the Methodist Episcopal Church, and laying up treasures in the other world, as well as leaving a fragrant memory to posterity."[19] Whatever the truth about doughty Simon in old age, most of the frontiersmen died unchurched and in the orthodox view unregenerate. Moreover, they established a tradition of barbarism which gained strength with the years. It has lately been reaffirmed by the eminent British historian Arnold J. Toynbee, who seems, however, to confuse the original Indian fighters with subsequent waves of Scotch-Irish who lodged in the high Appalachians.[20] Early travelers into Kentucky admired the land but not the inhabitants, whom they considered something less than civilized. Yet what the early Kentuckians were—licentious, exuberant, violent—they were to some extent in consequence of the paradisiacal illusion, which holds out the promise of complete fulfillment in all desirable things.

The Kentucky paradise—if ever a paradise—was doomed by a sad commonplace: population increases in new ground. And the multiplication of the population directly threatens the ease and abundance fundamental to the idea of idyllic abodes. The eternal dream of a lost paradise might prove less compelling if man considered why he was once deprived of his bliss and would again be deprived of it. Eden is Eden only so long as fertile and uncrowded, but the human race has small power and less desire to practice the restraint necessary to the preservation of any primeval garden. Man pretends that he desires the garden for his children, when in fact he disinherits them through the pursuit of pleasure. Jonathan Swift recognized that excessive procreation posed a threat to all societies, however soundly ordered, and on that account instituted birth control among the rational Houyhnhnms, in whose utopia Gulliver lived for a time. The absolute continence practiced from religious principles by the Shakers of Kentucky made little impression on their neighbors, to judge from a notice printed in the *Arkansas Gazette,* April 22, 1820: "David Wilson, of Portwilliam, Gallatin county, Ky. is 81 years of age. He had four wives, and by them forty-two children. His second wife had five children at two births, in eleven months. Mr. W. has but two ribs in his body, there being a solid smooth bone on each side. He is a man of small stature, and very active."

While it is likely that the increase of the original pioneers would have taxed the abundance of Kentucky in time, the operation of the Malthusian principle was much accelerated by wave after wave of immigrants drawn by the magnetic force of the myth into the Garden of the West. Neither the Proclamation of 1763, forbidding settlement beyond the sources of the rivers flowing into the Atlantic, nor the threat of Indian massacre proved effective against the overwhelming desire to possess some part of the promised land, there to wax and multiply with little toil and less restraint from constituted authority. The frontiersmen may have been a comparatively homogeneous group, native Americans from the eastern slopes of the Appalachians; but those who came after were of every conceivable character—gentlemen from the Tidewater and Piedmont of Virginia who proposed to found a squirearchy in the garden, tidy French bourgeoisie with poor qualifications for pioneering, Jacobin philosophers intent on establishing utopian communities, thrifty Swiss and German farmers, fundamentalist preachers from the uplands of North Carolina and Virginia, expectant millennialists like the Shakers and Millerites, and, in addition, the inevitable rout of gamblers and lawyers, speculators and highwaymen, agents of foreign powers and common politicians, whores and thieves, mechanics and drunken Irish laborers. In 1790, according to the census, there were 73,677 people in Kentucky; in 1800, 220,955; in 1810, 406,511; and by 1820, 564,317.

A quarter of a century after the founding of Boonesboro and Harrodsburg, the buffalo and the elk had vanished from the land and the bear and deer had retreated to remote areas; the forests were irreparably damaged and the best lands had come into the possession of individuals who had suffered few of the hardships of settlement. Never had there been a comparable assault on nature and never such a rapid alteration. Moreover, Kentucky had become the scene of violent struggles for choice sites, with speculators and lawyers usually winning titles in fee simple. This was not an unexpected consequence of crowding, for man has never shown a marked disposition to share his real estate. The comment on the condition of Kentucky elicited from a planter by William Faux is somewhat amusing but rather tragic too, for it proclaims the vanity of paradisiacal myths: "Kentucky is morally and physically ruined. We have been brought up to live without labour: all are demoralized. No man's word or judgment is to be taken for the guidance and government of another. Deception is a trade, and all are rogues. The west has the scum of all the earth. Long ago it was said, when a man left other States, he is gone to hell, or

Kentucky. The people are none the better for a free, good government. The oldest first settlers are all gone or ruined."[21]

For a time, however, the Garden of the West sustained the illusion, and that interval was sufficient to permit faith and emotion to congeal, with the result that the Kentucky myth entered the cultural stream as a hardy organism, proof against fact and reason. The American imagination seized upon the short period when the forest was indeed majestic and the tenant heroic, and wove the golden threads into a superlative tapestry which, like good whisky, improves with age. Timothy Flint perceived an almost mystical fervor in the oldest settlers as they recalled the surpassing beauty of Kentucky in their youth, when they set about destroying the scene which was ever to be their fondest recollection.[22] As if in atonement for their wanton acts, the pioneers preserved for posterity not the real but the mythic configuration, and their well-wrought image of Eden has now become a part of the national heritage.

II *The Heroic Age*

4 The Tenant of the Garden

"You are of the class, mammalia; order, primates; genus, homo; species, Kentucky."—THE PRAIRIE

WHILE THE topography of primeval Kentucky shows fairly distinctly beneath the Edenic imagery of the early chronicles, the portrait of the frontiersman who discovered and for a time possessed the garden behaves like a kaleidoscope. Historians have insisted that a definable type arose in the wilderness, but none has yet removed the accretions of legend from the real character. The impressions of the Kentuckian recorded by early observers commonly betray a bias, either contempt for the backwoods in general or a disposition to idealize men living in a state of nature. There is of course strong antecedent probability of a Kentucky frontier type, but the very conception depends upon tradition and tradition upon colored accounts. His elusiveness notwithstanding, the real man demands attention, as he evolved into an important social and political force in the nineteenth century and gave rise besides to the legendary Kentuckian, whose significance for cultural history will appear hereafter. What he may actually have been can be known somewhat through contemporary portraits but rather better through his background, the circumstances of the settlement, and the unvarnished history of his exploits in the wilderness.

Those who conquered Transappalachia were demonstrably filled with bright visions of racial destiny and with a strong

spirit of aggression. Mere desire for the promised land, fortunately for the peace of the world, actualizes as concerted
movement only when the energy level is high throughout a
people; not even a Joshua can lead an apathetic race to the
land of Canaan. There was in the backwoods during the
middle eighteenth century considerable curiosity about western lands, and there must have been besides a degree of
unconscious hostility toward the Allegheny-Cumberland barrier. Obstacles pose a challenge and evoke in warlike men a
blind passion to conquer, or, as Spengler says, "the mere *fact*
of the frontier—the limit of one's own power—arouses the old
instincts to hate, to attack, to annihilate."[1] Moreover, the backwoodsmen were denied the wonderful garden land by the royal
Proclamation of 1763 and by the opposition of the Indians,
both of which deterrents probably had the psychological effect
of provoking them. Of course, nothing hindered the powerful
impulse toward the tramontane region, but the dangers and
hardships precipitated a heroic age without parallel since
medieval times. The response of the backwoods folk to the
challenges lying on their frontier was more violent than the
Indians could have anticipated, for prior to the avalanche
which came in the period of the Revolution, there had been
for a quarter of a century only innocent probings—weakly supported hunting and surveying expeditions—which gave cause
for mild apprehension at most. Nonetheless, it was as certain as
death that the fabled Garden of the West would not be neglected forever, as the reports of explorers served to intensify
the paradisiacal vision.

Who first of the white race saw Kentucky may never be
known, though that honor has been bestowed upon Boone by
legend. Certainly Boone was far from the first. The French
knew of the existence of Kentucky in the third quarter of the
seventeenth century, though their information was unquestionably sketchy. La Salle conceivably spent the winter of
1669-1670 on the Ohio, and in 1673 Louis Jolliet and Père
Marquette on their voyage down the Mississippi observed the

mouth of the Ohio and, out of necessity, some part of the
western extremity of Kentucky. Gabriel Arthur, a Virginia lad,
while in the company of a band of Cherokee in 1674, was cap-
tured by Shawnee braves and taken to their town on the Scioto
River. Released later in the year, Arthur returned over the
Warrior's Path to Virginia. A Dutch trader from Albany,
Arnout Viele, with a party of white men and Indians, entered
Kentucky in 1692 and remained in the Ohio Valley until 1694.
Sometime between 1690 and 1693 Jean Couture, a French-
Canadian explorer, perhaps viewed the Bluegrass; in 1700, at
any rate, he guided a party of South Carolina traders down the
Tennessee River to the Ohio. Thus, thirty-four years before
the birth of Boone, Kentucky was reasonably well known to
the French and by no means unknown to the English.

During the next fifty years the Kentucky shore was probably
scanned by many an unreported voyager on the Ohio and the
interior searched for game by nomadic hunters. In 1742 a
Swiss emigrant, John Peter Salley, and three others joined John
Howard, a daring Scotch-Irishman, in an expedition down the
Ohio and the Mississippi, which terminated abruptly with the
capture of the party by French and Indians. To what extent
the overland route through Cumberland Gap was used meanwhile by hunters is not known. In 1750 two surveyors acting
independently penetrated the wilderness and recorded something of what they discovered. As a representative of the Loyal
Land Company, holding a grant of 800,000 acres in Kentucky,
Dr. Thomas Walker led a party through the gap. Christopher
Gist, employed by the Ohio Company, traveled along the
northern bank of the Ohio, in 1751 crossing over into Kentucky
and returning to Virginia by way of Pound Gap. Boone's friend
John Finley visited Kentucky for the first time in 1752, Henry
Scaggs hunted on the Cumberland River in 1764, James Smith
with four others passed through Cumberland Gap in 1766, and
five hunters from South Carolina under Isaac Lindsey entered
Kentucky in the same year. James Harrod and Michael Stoner
just possibly visited the southeastern part of the state in 1767.

In 1769 Boone first reached the Bluegrass region and six years
later led a company of settlers to Boonesboro. In the same year
Harrod established Harrodsburg on a permanent basis. By
1775 the period of exploration was largely past and the settlement commenced by a people inured to hardships and violent
struggles. When Kentucky entered the Union in 1792, the
wilderness had been thoroughly subdued, the Indians largely
excluded from the central region, and a culture with aristocratic tendencies erected in the Bluegrass.

The "brave heroic minds" who landed at Jamestown were
scarcely equal to the task of accommodating themselves to the
relatively soft environment of the Atlantic seaboard, and their
descendants, in no apparent haste to exploit the hinterland,
required a century and a quarter to move the frontier to the
Valley of Virginia. In the valley, however, a new race came
into being, compounded largely of Scotch-Irish and English
stocks, which not only breached the Appalachian barrier but
drove all the way to the Pacific in a hundred and twenty-five
years.[2] The Indian understood when the "tall men came /
Whose words were bullets" that he had to reckon with a people
quite different from the pleasure-loving *coureurs de bois,* the
peaceful Quakers, and the English traders. These grim backwoodsmen were not concerned, as the Jesuit fathers, with his
salvation, or, as the traders, with his beaver, but came to kill
his deer and occupy his land permanently. Under the circumstances, it is not surprising that the Indian fought the settler
in buckskin. As E. D. Branch observed, the Scotch-Irish (the
dominant stock on the Virginia frontier) and the Indians
understood each other from the beginning and acted accordingly.[3]

The English were most numerous of the many nationalities
intermingled in the colonies during the eighteenth century, but
on the outer frontier the transplanted Ulstermen apparently
had a majority.[4] Called Scotch-Irish, they were not Irish and
only slightly Scottish, insofar as Celtic blood is implied. Their
original home was the Lowlands of Scotland, a region from

which the Gaels had been largely expelled sometime after the arrival of the Angles, Saxons, and Jutes in the fifth century. A predominantly Germanic people, the Lowlanders, like the Northumbrians, mixed freely with the Norse, who in the ninth and tenth centuries planted numerous settlements in northern England and southern Scotland, and by the end of the Viking period they were even less Celtic than before.

Whatever the significance of their Teutonic character, the Lowlanders survived under conditions extraordinarily trying. From the reign of Edward I (1272-1307) until sometime after the accession of James I in 1603, the region extending from the Grampian to the Cheviot Hills constituted a buffer between two hostile peoples and accordingly knew little peace. If the Scots never became as adept with the longbow or as skillful in open battle as the English, they much excelled them in executing ambushes and raids. For three hundred years the Lowlanders stood off the English and the Gaels, intrigued fiercely among themselves, and fought innumerable bloody feuds, in the end producing the incomparable moss troopers on the order of Kinmont Willie Armstrong, whom Sir Walter Scott immortalized. When James came to the throne, he called upon his old friend Scott of Buccleuch to pacify the border, and this ruthless veteran of raids on England and skirmishes over the Debatable Land succeeded well enough.[5] However, James' decision to grant the lands of the native chiefs of Ulster to English and Scottish nobles on the condition that they settle the region with tenants from Britain probably had some effect in bringing peace to the border and to the Lowlands in general, for the large shipments of colonists to Ireland, beginning in 1610, included a good many of the more belligerent Scots, who were bred to fight, not to farm. The Lowlanders, who had no love for Celts of any sort, treated the Irish of Ulster with no more consideration than their descendants treated the Indians, but drove the hapless remnants to the hills and kept them at a distance thereafter.

The emigration to America did not begin until the early

eighteenth century, when English rule had become intolerable. Prevented from developing their woolen industry, compelled to pay tithes to the English Establishment, and charged exorbitant rents for their lands, the Ulstermen learned the meaning of abject poverty. Perhaps 200,000—one third the Protestant population of Ulster—emigrated to America between 1717 and 1775, carrying with them their determined Calvinism and democratic inclinations as well as a fierce hatred of England, aristocracy, and Catholicism. J. R. Commons placed a high estimate on their contribution to the new nation: "Trained as they were in the representative democracy of the Scottish kirk, thrown on their own resources in the wilderness, mingling with the pioneers of many other races, they took the lead in developing that Western type which in politics and industry became ultimately the American type; yet they retained their original character, and the American to-day is more at home in Glasgow than in London."[6]

The Scotch-Irish entered in the main through the ports of Pennsylvania and without long delay moved in the direction of the back country, where land was cheap or free and restraint negligible. They originally had little in common with the inhabitants of the coast and never much esteemed the social and political modes familiar to English settlements. Though for the most part peasants, the Ulstermen were not disposed to truckle to aristocracy or to accept permanently the second-class lot of indentured servants. Generally neither Puritan nor Anglican, they were objectionable on religious grounds in New England and Tidewater Virginia, and, on account of their aggressiveness and clannishness, almost everywhere else. Indifferent to prior claims on the frontier land which sustained them, to the rights of the Indians, and to the laws of colonial legislatures, they went about the business of mastering the wilderness and developing farms without much regard for any authority. Other stocks—notably the German—proved equal to the rigors of frontier life, but no other flourished like the Scotch-Irish. The hunger and disease, the cold and heat, which daunted many of the English and prostrated the French of the artisan class, seem merely to have conditioned the Presbyterian Irish for the herculean task of seizing an empire from the Indians. Fanning out through Pennsylvania in the second and third quarters of the eighteenth century, they filled the valleys east of the Alleghenies and poured down the Valley of Virginia in mounting waves. Advanced groups of these settlers reached the headwaters of the Yadkin by 1740 and, augmented by backwoodsmen from the Virginia and North Carolina Piedmont, crossed the mountains in force less than thirty years after. Meanwhile, they had acquired a knack for land speculation and Indian fighting, politics and public affairs, which, together with their vigor and determination, made them a formidable force in American society throughout the next century.

Forwardly placed on the frontier, the Scotch-Irish deserve major credit for executing the pincer movement on Kentucky by way of Cumberland Gap and the Ohio River, although the role of the numerous English, German, Welsh, and French settlers in the emigrant stream should not be minimized on that account. Indeed, C. W. Alvord and Lee Bidgood maintained that the American frontiersman as a distinct type developed prior to 1700 (some years ahead of the Scotch-Irish immigration) in the course of the movement westward through Virginia to the falls lines of the rivers emptying into the Atlantic.[7] When the movement across the mountains commenced, these groups had unquestionably intermarried to a degree, there being no insurmountable racial or religious impediments. The backwoodsmen were then in most instances not foreign-born but native Americans and as often as not a mixture of the stocks represented on the frontier, though with the Scotch-Irish predominating.

The movement of these peoples from Maryland, Pennsylvania, and Virginia down the trough between the Blue Ridge and the Alleghenies was accompanied, under the impact of hardships, by a measure of regression to a more primitive condition. Although in some cases devoutly religious, the frontiersmen became increasingly prone to wild, lawless action, a tendency which, while invaluable for Indian fighting, earned them no enviable reputation in the East until the whole westward movement had been enveloped in a romantic haze. Yet, as a class, they can scarcely have been so barbarous as alleged by an urbane English traveler at the beginning of the nineteenth century:

It may not be improper to mention, that the backwoodsmen, as the first emigrants from the eastward of the Allegheny mountains are called, are very similar in their habits and manners to the aborigines, only perhaps more prodigal and more careless of life. They depend more on hunting than on agriculture, and of course are exposed to all the varieties of climate in the open air. Their cabins are not better than Indian wigwams. They have frequent meetings for the purposes of gambling, fighting and drinking. They make bets to the amount of all they possess. They fight for the most trifling provocations, or even sometimes without any, but merely to try each others prowess, which they are fond of vaunting of. Their hands, teeth, knees, head and feet are their weapons, not only boxing with their fists, . . . but also tearing, kicking, scratching, biting, gouging each others eyes out by a dexterous use of a thumb and finger, and doing their utmost to kill each other, even when rolling over one another on the ground.[8]

This traveler, like many others, reported rather more than he observed. By the end of the eighteenth century, the frontiersman had acquired an unequaled reputation for savagery, and visitors from the East and from Europe seldom resisted the temptation to support this widespread impression. Adept enough with claw and fang the pioneer may have been, but what is more significant, he became uncommonly skillful with rifle and ax, without which instruments of destruction the progress to the West would have been painfully slow.

Awkward by modern standards, the Kentucky rifle was nevertheless an economical and accurate weapon well suited to the needs of the settlers. It was, moreover, decidedly superior to any previously used extensively in the Mississippi Valley, whether by the French or the British. The arm which

came to be known after about 1770 as the Kentucky rifle owed
its form to Swiss and German gunsmiths located in eastern
Pennsylvania, particularly around Lancaster. Following the
development of clean-burning powder and the technique of
rifling, European artisans were able to manufacture increasingly efficient weapons, and the Pennsylvania immigrants, heirs
to Old World crafts, in time created a graceful and practical
rifle for the frontiersman and on that account deserve credit
for hastening the conquest of the West. This rifle had a barrel
forty-two inches long or longer, usually octagonal, with a stock
of curly maple, cherry, apple, or walnut, extending to the muzzle, a patch box, trigger guard, side plate, rod pipes, front
sight, and brass butt plate. The ball, approximately 3/100 of
an inch smaller in diameter than the barrel, was inserted in the
muzzle wrapped in a greased patch of buckskin and then
rammed home with a hickory ramrod. Although .70-caliber
rifles were preferred in Europe, the American hunter needed
a smaller bore, as powder and lead were difficult to procure
and to transport. From one pound of lead forty-eight bullets
were normally molded for the .45-caliber Kentucky flintlock,
while the same quantity of lead produced only a third as many
balls for the heavier European type. The consumption of
powder by the Kentucky rifle was correspondingly economical.
In this weapon the frontiersmen had an efficient complement
to their physical strength and animal cunning.

In novels, travelbooks, and folktales the range and accuracy
of the old flintlock are grossly exaggerated. Since the velocity
was hardly in excess of sixteen hundred feet—not quite two-
thirds that of the modern Springfield—shooting was unquestionably affected to a marked degree by the wind. Under good
conditions, however, the rifle was extraordinarily accurate up
to a hundred yards and effective at even twice that distance.
Penetration was necessarily low, but shocking power was high.
The ball, without jacket of any sort, tended to disintegrate on
impact. At the same time, close shooting was requisite, as
neither deer nor buffalo could be brought down with indis-

criminate hits. Out of the necessity for killing game and Indians and out of sheer love of weapons, the frontiersman developed his marksmanship to a degree of excellence that commands the respect even of modern experts who are accustomed to precision-built arms of high velocity and low trajectory, standardized ammunition, and telescopic sights.[9]

The ax with which the backwoodsman assaulted the forest was bit, helve, and balance as fine an instrument of destruction as his rifle and in the conquest of nature rather more decisive. Without the gauges and formulas of modern metallurgy, American craftsmen, both in the factories of the East and in the smithies of the frontier, forged out of good bar iron and cast steel a head notable for sharpness, durability, and lightness.[10] Handiness with the ax was one criterion of fitness in the wilderness, and men accordingly acquired extraordinary skill in the management of the tool. Their precision is evidenced by the notched logs of cabins surviving from the period of settlement and their speed by the records of rail splitting—as many as two hundred a day. Walnut and other straight-grained timber split like melons beneath axes, iron wedges, and dogwood gluts, manipulated by men who had acquired the strength, the rhythm, and the eye for the work. Whole forests of oak, beech, poplar, maple, and walnut, standing since Columbus, collapsed in a matter of years from girdling and deadening with fire. There was in the heart of the new race no more consideration for the trees than for the game until the best of both were gone; steel conquered the West but chilled the soul of the conqueror. This assault on nature, than which few more frightful spectacles could be imagined, owed much to sheer need, but something also to a compelling desire to destroy conspicuous specimens of the fauna and flora of the wilderness. The origin of this mad destructiveness may be in doubt, but there is no question about its effect. The Ohio Valley today has neither trees nor animals to recall adequately the splendor of the garden of the Indian which the white man found and used so profligately.

Without the rifle and the ax the rapid conquest of the wilderness would have been impossible; even with those superlative instruments settlement was difficult enough. Inexorable nature and provoked savages opposed the pioneers, whose only course was to meet the challenges with fortitude. Father Lalemant to the contrary, the climate of the Ohio Valley was far from Mediterranean; indeed, it was matched for severity by few places in the British Isles. Any lingering suspicion that Kentucky was subtropical vanished in the winter of 1779-1780, when the cane was killed and game perished in sickening numbers. Snow fell early and stayed late that winter, and the temperature may have been below zero nearly as often as above. But such losses as came with the winter's cold and the summer's heat were stoically accepted by the settlers, who had learned something of the mutability of fortune during the long journey from the Yadkin Valley along Boone's Trace over the Smokies and finally through the Cumberland Mountains into Kentucky.

The founding of homes in the wilderness demanded of the pioneers not only great endurance but also crucial judgments. Their line of communications was fairly long and unusually hazardous. From the Block House, five miles northeast of the South Fork of the Holston, to Harrodsburg or Boonesboro was approximately two hundred twenty-five miles, mainly through mountains.[11] On every mile of the way, disaster threatened from treacherous footing, sliding rock, high water, or Indian attack. These dangers avoided, meat had still to be obtained at frequent intervals to sustain the grueling march, and game was not always abundant on the laurel and pine slopes of the high mountains. No less acuteness was required for the selection of a homesite on the plateau of central Kentucky than for passing the mountains, as life depended on the availability of tillable land and water and on the defensibility of the chosen location in event of attack.

Land was taken up on the western side of the Appalachians during the eighteenth century much as on the eastern. A settler might obtain in Kentucky a homestead of four hundred acres by raising a crop of corn, tomahawking his initials in trees bounding his claim, and paying a nominal fee. He was privileged, in addition, to preempt as much as one thousand acres adjoining his homestead at the rate of forty dollars per hundred.[12] However this procedure worked in Virginia, in Kentucky it laid the foundation for an appalling legal circus which continued well into the nineteenth century and produced untold hardship and bitterness.[13] In the end the illiterate backwoodsmen, ignorant of law and careless of records, probably suffered most, though many of them were in fact squatters with no more than physical possession to support their claims. Some of the dispossessed passed in flotillas down the Ohio in the wake of the Boone family, while others trod the game trails into the Old Northwest, there to reenact the drama of settlement in the face of Indian opposition. While the Indians haunted the forests of Kentucky, however, there were few Virginia planters and lawyers to call in question the right of the settler to erect his cabin where he pleased.

Shelters ranged from lean-tos to substantial cabins, depending upon the industry and skill of the settler. Houses no larger than twenty by sixteen feet, more often than not unfloored, seem to have been commonplace at first. Since little time could be spared from hunting and cropping, the furnishings were usually as primitive as the cabins. Improvements came eventually, and in the early nineteenth century fairly comfortable houses were in evidence in the back country. John Woods, an English traveler, attempted to describe a typical specimen on the Illinois frontier in the period 1820-1821, which may be regarded as representative of cabins in the sparsely settled parts of Kentucky at the same date. Though the one-floor plan (a rectangle) remained standard, the outer dimensions were much increased—to thirty by twenty feet and sometimes larger. Notched logs, round or square, were built up from the ground nine or ten high, with the top logs cut three or four feet longer than the others to form eaves. The roof, built of logs of graduated length, was finally covered with clapboards cut four feet by six inches. Doors and windows were then chopped out and the windows in the more pretentious houses fitted with glass. As earlier, mud was used to fill the chinks. Floors consisted of notched puncheons laid on sleepers. Ceilings were sometimes constructed of saplings extended from wall to wall and overlaid with boards. Hearths in the better cabins were stone.[14] Daniel Drake, the prominent Cincinnati physician, recalled in later years the fireplace used by his family in Kentucky during the 1780's: "I know of no scene in civilized life more primitive than such a cabin hearth as that of my mother. In the morning, a buckeye backlog & hickory forestick resting on stone andirons, with a Jonny cake on a clean ash board, set before it to bake, a frying pan with its long handle resting on a split bottomed turner's chair, sending out its peculiar music, and the tea kettle swung from a wooden 'lug pole' with myself setting the table, or turning the meat, or watching the Jonny cake, while she sat nursing the baby in the corner, and telling the little ones to 'hold still' and let their sister Lizy dress them!"[15]

The diet of the pioneers consisted at first, according to Timothy Flint, of "Venison and wild turkeys, sweet potatoes and pies smoked on the table; and persimon and maple beer quaffed as well, at least for health, as Madeira or nectar";[16] and in truth there was usually an abundance of game, whatever else may have been lacking. As game dwindled, however, Kentuckians depended increasingly on less lordly fare, notably "hog and hominy." Thomas Ashe's circumstantial account of a dinner suggests that in eating as in other things they displayed little restraint:

The dinner consisted of a large piece of salt bacon, a dish of homslie, and a turreen of squirrel broth. I dined entirely on the last dish, which I found incomparably good, and the meat equal to the most delicate chicken. The Kentuckyan ate nothing but bacon, which indeed is the favourite diet of all the inhabitants of the State, and drank nothing but whiskey, which soon made him more than two thirds drunk. In this last practice he is also supported by the public habit. In a country then, where bacon and spirits form the favourite summer repast, it cannot be just to attribute entirely the causes of infirmity to the climate. No people on earth live with less regard to regimen. They eat salt meat three times a day, seldom or never have any vegetable, and drink ardent spirits from morning till night! They have not only an aversion to fresh meat, but a vulgar prejudice that it is unwholesome. The truth is, their stomachs are depraved by burning liquors, and they have no appetite for any thing but what is high flavoured and strongly impregnated with salt.[17]

Prices fluctuated, of course, but tended to be low during the interval between the settlement of Kentucky and admission to the Union. Gilbert Imlay reported beef, mutton, and pork as low as two pence per pound, chickens four to six pence each, ducks eight pence, and geese and turkeys one shilling three pence, butter for three and flour for twelve and six per hundredweight.[18] These prices are not particularly meaningful, for few besides those clustered in the forts and villages had occasion to buy much food. Hard money was invariably scarce, and meat, vegetables, and sweetening (honey and maple sugar) in any event were to be had from the land. Salt alone was regularly high.

The pioneers dressed plainly and practically. When their original clothing wore out, they turned to nettle thread and buffalo hair for the materials from which to weave garments. Once flax and wool became available, the familiar linsey-woolsey appeared. Cotton, though known, figured negligibly in the frontier economy. Housewives made dyes of varying quality from butternut (yellow), black walnut hulls (rusty black), oak bark mixed with copperas (black), indigo (blue), and madder (dirty red), and therewith invested their fabrics with a measure of distinction.[19] Men wore hunting shirts of linsey-woolsey or of buckskin, which extended halfway down the thigh, and they sometimes made breechclouts serve in place of breeches.[20] Of course, leggings were required as protection against briars and brambles. The feet of the settler were extremely vulnerable, for the moccasins which he wore for the lack of shoes availed little against cold and moisture; in consequence, rheumatism was endemic. Elias Pym Fordham, who traveled in the Ohio Valley during 1817-1818, left a vivid description of the simple hunter's garb: "Clothed in *dressed* not *tanned* buckskins:—a home-made, homespun hunting shirt outside;—belted to his waist with a broad belt, to which is appended a knife with a blade a foot long: or tomohawk, or powder horn, in the belt of which is sometimes a smaller knife to cut the patch of the bullet; a bullet-pouch; mocassins on his feet; a blanket on his saddle; and a loaf of Indian Corn."[21]

Unlike nature which exacted heavy tribute in privation and labor but returned a golden harvest, the Indian objected to every stroke of an ax, every shot at a deer, and offered nothing as compensation to the settler. Just though his cause was, the Indian drew down upon himself the wrath of a ferocious and implacable race, and after fifty years of intermittent and bloody skirmishing had no place to lay his head in the Ohio Valley. The valley tribes were a commendable lot—brave, intelligent, relatively energetic, and often humane. Algonquian for the most part, they maintained hostilities with many of their neighbors and with the dreaded Iroquois but were not on that account more warlike than the white invaders of their forests. By the Boonesboro period, they were of course thoroughly alarmed by white encroachments and acted with appalling savagery to drive the settlers back over the mountains. Although egged on by British agents, the Indians did not need to be told the ominous meaning of the spreading clearings. Whatever the intent of the Proclamation of 1763, humanitarian or political, it proved ineffectual; five years afterward the Iroquois at Fort Stanwix and the Cherokee at Hard Labor were called upon to relinquish their claims on Ohio Valley lands in exchange for commodities of dubious value. In 1775, Colonel Richard Henderson negotiated the purchase of perhaps twenty million acres of Kentucky and Tennessee territory and dispatched Boone up the Warrior's Path with a contingent of trailblazers. Whether the Indians merely behaved stupidly in selling, or, as more likely, recognized the inevitable and ac-

cepted all that was offered, only an act of God could have
halted the immigration or preserved the native mode of life.
At the same time, the Indians had no decent alternative to
resistance.

When the settlement commenced, the area bounded roughly
by the Ohio and Cumberland rivers and the Cumberland
Plateau had no permanent aboriginal residents. For reasons
not now clear, though long-standing taboos may have been
involved, Indians were reluctant to establish towns in Kentucky, but instead used the fertile land for protracted and
unquestionably profitable hunting expeditions. Since the herds
of big game figured critically in their economy, the wasteful
hunting practices of the frontiersmen filled them with concern.
Kentucky was apparently known to and visited by many
tribes, though hunting privileges seem to have belonged in
particular to the Cherokee and Chickasaw on the south and
the Delaware, Shawnee, Miami, and Illinois on the north,
numbering all told between five and six thousand warriors.[22]
During the Indian wars, however, tribes of the Six Nations,
Choctaw, Wyandot, and various non-Iroquoian Lake Indians
appeared occasionally in Kentucky.

Mississippi Valley Indians with few exceptions fought capably, but the northern proved generally the more formidable.
Though surprisingly receptive to civilized ways, the tribes of
the numerous Muskhogean family (Chickasaw, Choctaw,
Creek, Seminole) have received far less attention from historians than the more troublesome northern savages, who took
a fearful toll of the emigrant stream before retiring beyond the
Mississippi. When first known, the Cherokee, an Iroquoian
tribe, seem to have been vigorous enough but by 1776 were
generally decadent, with the exception of their rebellious off-
shoot, the Chickamauga under Dragging Canoe.[23] Even after
the high praise of James Adair has been properly discounted,[24]
the Chickasaw still tower above other southern tribes; but,
since located in northern Mississippi, they had less occasion
than the Ohio group to display their martial spirit before the

Kentucky settlements. The fact that the Tennesseans seldom lost an engagement to the Cherokee and the Kentuckians only occasionally won one from the Shawnee suggests how much greater the Indian menace was on the Ohio than on the Cumberland.

According to the dime novels, the Kentucky frontiersmen kicked the Indians out of the thickets like rabbits and shot them down on the run. The truth is quite otherwise. Perhaps no more than a handful of the canniest settlers learned to deal effectively with the Shawnee, Delaware, and Wyandot on their own ground, and the majority had small resource against scalping parties. Warriors of these tribes possessed not only serviceable weapons supplied by the British but also a wealth of experience from warfare with the whites on the Pennsylvania and Virginia frontiers. While possibly more effective in offensive than in defensive actions, the Ohio Valley Indians displayed great skill in checking and diverting expeditions into their own country. The repeated raids against their towns proved little more than that capable settlers, well mounted and flanked by alert scouts, could accomplish moderate destruction of dwellings and crops and return home without disastrous losses. Mann Butler declared from a wealth of information: "the truth is, the mounted expeditions of the early times, were more chivalric than effective, more brilliant than useful; they were inroads not conquests. In no one instance did they, or could they compel the enemy to a full trial of their strength, much less defeat them, as in the battles of the Maumee and of Tippecanoe."[25] Though accustomed to fight in small parties deployed through heavy cover, the Indians fought commendably in large actions, numbering among their notable victories, usually with British support, Blue Licks (1782), Harmar's campaign on the Scioto (1790), St. Clair's campaign (1791), and the River Raisin (1813). As often as not outnumbered, the red men over a period of nearly four decades engaged in innumerable skirmishes with Kentuckians and usually wrought more injury than they sustained. Prior to 1813, only General Anthony

Wayne at Fallen Timbers (1794) and General William Henry Harrison at Tippecanoe (1811) had won important battles against considerable forces of Indians, and it was not until the Battle of the Thames—thirty-eight years after the founding of Boonesboro—that Kentuckians acting with the regular army ended once and for all the terrible menace of a few thousand able warriors in the Old Northwest.

Generally inferior to the northern tribesmen in forest warfare, though possessing superior weapons and possibly abler leadership, the settlers yet had means to blunt the Indian threat and at the same time to diminish the enemy's military potential. The depletion of the herds of big game by the backwoodsmen, who were not conservationists in any sense, strained the economy of the Indians and forced them to go farther and farther afield in search of meat. Losses in battle, which were quickly repaired on the white side by immigration, left the tribes commensurately weaker. Even so, a concerted attack would have broken up the settlements at any time between 1775 and perhaps 1783, had the Indians possessed effective measures for breaching the walls surrounding the forts.[26] Their failure to capture Boonesboro (1778) and Bryan's Station (1782) indicates a fundamental weakness in the face of fortified positions, although the sagacity and fortitude of the Kentuckians in raising those sieges ought not to be discounted. In the matter of fortifications, the settlers usually wrought well, choosing commanding sites with available water and then erecting truly formidable barriers. To judge from the defenses surrounding the cabins at Bryan's Station, an enemy without artillery was unlikely to succeed:

The form was a perfect parallelogram, including from a half to a full acre. A trench was then dug, four or five feet deep, and contiguous pickets planted in it, so as to form a compact wall ten or twelve feet above the ground. The pickets were of hard and durable timber, nearly a foot in diameter; and formed a rampart beyond the power of man either to leap, or overthrow, by the exercise of individual and unaided physical power. At the angles were small

projecting squares, of still stronger material and planting, techni-
cally called flankers, with oblique port holes; so that the sentinel
within could rake the external front of the station without being
exposed to a shot without. Two folding gates, in the front and rear,
swinging on prodigious wooden hinges, gave ingress and egress to
the men and teams in time of security. At other times, a trusty
sentinel on the roof of an interior building, was stationed so as to
be able to descry at a distance every suspicious object.[27]

The settlers could not of course remain indefinitely in the
forts, as crops and stock required attention. Upon outlying
cabins, occupied by single families, the Indians fell at will,
shooting and scalping, though sometimes carrying their victims
into captivity. In a letter dated July 7, 1790, Judge Harry
Innes wrote Secretary of War Henry Knox that he had "been
intimately acquainted with this district from November 1783,
to the time of writing; and that fifteen hundred souls have been
killed and taken in the district and migrating to it."[28] Even
as late as 1800, according to a letter from Thomas T. Davis to
the Secretary of State, John Marshall, many Kentuckians were
still held captive by the Northwest tribes despite agreements
for the release of prisoners.[29]

Provocations considered, the deadly regard of the settlers
for the Indians was inevitable. Not even a tolerant and understanding people could have remained insensible of the atrocities committed periodically by the savages, and the frontiersmen were neither mild nor forgiving. Mere vengeance,
however, was incidental to the main issue, whether an agrarian
or a hunting economy should prevail. Every tree cut, every
deer slain by the advancing settlers directly affected the liveli-
hood of the Indian. He acted in the only way he knew to halt
the ever-deepening wedges in his hunting grounds, and the
backwoodsman in the end retaliated most effectively not by
repaying savagery with savagery but by transforming the
woods into farms. When resistance was no longer feasible, the
Shawnee and Delaware and Wyandot moved west to partake
of the fatal bounty of the government, but not before working

permanent alterations in the character of the people whom they besieged in the garden below the Ohio River.

A state of siege such as the Kentuckians endured for nearly twenty years evokes the very qualities which stable societies suppress, and when the threat of sudden death passes, the survivors are unlikely to adopt civilized modes at once. Even without human enemies, man in the wilderness undergoes significant changes, as St. John de Crèvecoeur perceived in Pennsylvania: "That new mode of life brings along with it a new set of manners, which I cannot easily describe. These new manners being grafted on the old stock, produce a strange sort of lawless profligacy, the impressions of which are indelible. The manners of the Indian natives are respectable, compared with this European medley."[30] The raw backwoodsmen filled the tidy Frenchman with alarm, but his conclusion is not less plausible on that account. When hostile savages vie with nature in assaulting a courageous folk, extraordinarily violent responses are to be expected, and the Kentuckians, from report, satisfied every expectation. Some part of their striking character ought properly to be attributed to the Scotch-Irish strain, for the Lowlanders were traditionally a warlike people and their continental ancestors before them. Even in Ulster they were yet surrounded by enemies and continued therefore in a state of watchfulness. Such martial qualities as they originally possessed, the rigorous life in Kentucky sharply accentuated. But backwoodsmen of whatever stock who met the challenge of the wilderness underwent notable changes and became through the toughening influence of an obdurate nature wonderfully fit for heroic actions, although rather unsuited to peaceful pursuits. James Kirke Paulding estimated the effect of the frontier on the Kentuckians in *Westward Ho!* (1832): "The result of their peculiar situation, habits, and modes of thinking has been a race of men uniting a fearlessness of danger, a hardy spirit of enterprise, a power of supporting fatigues and privations, an independence of thought, which perhaps were never associated with the pursuits and acquirements of civilized life in any other country than the United States" (vol. I, ch. 1). These "peculiarly American tendencies," in the opinion of Frederick Jackson Turner, were much intensified in the Kentuckian by isolation.[31] According to R. C. Buley, the Kentuckians who opened that part of the Old Northwest on the Ohio River were distinguished by a restless energy, freedom of thought, and a sense of destiny, all attributable to their military heritage.[32]

Yet neither race nor environment entirely explains the behavior of the tenant of the garden. Reckless, exuberant, lawless, violent, brave, the frontiersman of Kentucky acted the part of the utterly free agent and by word or gesture expressed a lively contempt for artificial ethical prescriptions. Admittedly, the cords which bind the individual to a given cultural frame may be snapped by prolonged danger and isolation, but such a consequence is by no means inevitable, at least not to an extreme degree, as witness the Puritan experience in New England. What the pioneer became in Kentucky was to an appreciable extent a result of his expectation of a paradisiacal situation, that is, an unrestrained existence. Whenever this illusion touches a people, a keen sense of social responsibility is not to be expected or indeed a deep concern with ideals of any noble kind. The signification of Kentucky was never preeminently religious or economic, though both sorts of motives drew people to the region; above all else, the rich new land stood for personal freedom and physical satisfaction—hence, the indifference to convention and the incidence of spectacular actions. Most of those who trudged over the Wilderness Road, while not officially rebellious against society, probably intended to achieve in the Garden of Kentucky a way of life conspicuously free of the impediments familiar to the East. Such an expectation of unalloyed freedom, intensified by and involved in myth, inevitably precipitated irresponsible acts ranging from gross to foolish and eventuated in an unusual state of mind— the frontier mind.

Although the objective reality of a distinct Kentucky type

cannot be positively asserted, it is clear that circumstances between the founding of Boonesboro and the end of the century favored the development of a definable type and that the image of an indomitable Kentucky frontiersman lodged in the popular imagination. Assuredly the legendary Kentuckian presupposes a substantial model. Precisely at what date Europe and the East came to regard the Kentuckian as a species separate and apart cannot be determined, although the fact that an exceptionally hardy backwoods breed was encamped in the very heart of the Indian country must have been widely known a few years after the struggle commenced. Moreover, a full-length portrait of Boone was available as early as 1784 in John Filson's *Discovery, Settlement and Present State of Kentucke*. It is noteworthy that in Cooper's *Prairie* (1827) the asinine naturalist Dr. Battius recognizes the Kentucky backwoodsman Paul Hover as a member of a distinct group: "You are of the *class,* mammalia; *order,* primates; *genus,* homo; *species,* Kentucky" (ch. 9). James Hall professed to recall the type from about 1800, though it is apparent that in the meantime legend had enveloped the personage whom he saw:

I shall never forget the intense interest which I felt, while a boy, in gazing at the brawny limbs and sun-burnt features of a Kentuckian, as he passed through the streets of Philadelphia. The rough, hardy air of the stranger, the jaded paces of his nag, the blanket, bear-skin, and saddle-bags—nay, the very oil-cloth on his hat, and the dirk that peeped from among his vestments, are still in my eye; they bespoke him to be of distant regions, to have been reared among dangers, and to be familiar with fatigues. He strode among us with the step of an Achilles, glancing with a good-natured superciliousness at the fragile butterflies of fashion that glittered in the sun-beams around him. I thought I could see in that man, one of the progenitors of an unconquerable race; his face presented the traces of a spirit quick to resent—he had the will to dare, and the power to execute; there was a something in his look which bespoke a disdain of controul [*sic*], and an absence of constraint in all his movements, indicating an habitual independence of thought and action.[33]

Hall's is the romantic view commonplace in frontier novels of the nineteenth century, though it is perhaps not for that entirely false. Charles Fenno Hoffman, while not insensible, of the faults of the Kentuckians, discovered in them several of the qualities praised by Hall—"an off-handedness . . . a fearless ardour, a frankness and self-possession."[34]

There was, however, another way of regarding an order of men who carried independence to the verge of anarchism, who were so forthright as to be rude, and so fearless and mischievous as to constitute a permanent menace to society. Flint protested what seems to have been a widespread opinion without much considering the evidence: "We suspect that the general impressions of the readers of this day is, that the first hunters and settlers of Kentucky and Tennessee were a sort of demisavages. Imagination depicts them with long beard, and a costume of skins, rude, fierce, and repulsive."[35] Elsewhere he charged the East with conceiving the backwoodsman as "a kind of humanized Ourang Outang, like my lord Monboddo's man, recently divested of the unsightly appendage of a tail."[36] Morris Birkbeck, who held no special brief for the frontiersmen, acknowledged that "the Kentuckians in general are supposed by their fellow citizens of the east to be semi-barbarians."[37] Charles Sealsfield pronounced the descendants of the pioneers a "proud, fierce, and overbearing set of people" upon whom the Indians took their revenge by infecting them with a "cruel and implacable spirit."[38] For choleric Thomas Ashe the Kentuckians were barbarous, in fact the most objectionable people in the whole of the United States.[39] A note of hope, however, was sounded by Estwick Evans after a tour of Kentucky in 1818. Having witnessed no spectacular displays of violence, he concluded, "The society of this part of the world is becoming less savage, and more refined."[40] It is not difficult to guess what Evans, a Down-Easter, had been led to expect on the frontier. The apologists like Flint excluded, both the friendly and the hostile observers found the Kentuckian on close examination to be not altogether civilized, although through the alchemy of romance he became like the Scottish borderer a heroic figure, his faults smoothed over and his virtues magnified.

Generalizations about peoples are necessarily oversimple and therefore misleading. Many early writers patently mistook the sensational exception for a type and accordingly reached some extravagant conclusions about the Kentuckian. Yet the intelligent Englishmen who toured the back country felt an unusual temper in the Kentucky people, and their intuitions must be given some credit. For the multiplicity of causes previously considered, the inhabitants in all likelihood possessed a distinctive character, perhaps compounded of equal parts of aggressive self-assurance bordering on arrogance, belligerent independence, and inordinate pride of person, family, possessions, and homeland. While all Americans of the period of expansion doubtless possessed these qualities to a degree, it is safe to assume from the testimony that they were greatly exaggerated in the Kentuckians. This is not to say, however, that all Kentuckians were equally imbued with the Kentucky temper, or that the Kentucky temper was expressed in identical ways by all Kentuckians; some were unquestionably offensive, others disarmingly hospitable and congenial.

The symbolic meaning of Kentucky considered, it is not surprising that the immigrants should have desired to reorder the old way of the world and to remove long-standing social, political, and religious irritations. There was in them a sense of achievement born of their conquest of the wilderness and a sense of having left behind a hard and vexatious way of life. Socially inferior but proud, poverty-stricken but resourceful, the frontiersmen sought to alter the humble role assigned them by their betters in the East and asserted in the Ohio Valley their natural prerogatives to level out class distinctions, tinker with political machinery, worship orgiastically, and set aside the Mosaic Decalogue at pleasure. The Kentuckians of the lower class, nature's uninhibited children, fortified themselves with buffalo loin and raw Monongahela and proceeded to assert with muscular rhetoric their own superior quality and the ineffable charm of the Garden of the West. To the hierarchy of values accepted by the genteel folk of the original colonies —intelligence, refinement, and Christian morality—these wild libertarians opposed strength, naturalness, and license. Both in fact and in fiction, the backwoodsmen realized the naturalistic doctrines of European reformers; William Godwin could not have wished a more anarchic mode than theirs, or Jean Jacques Rousseau a more primitive. In the lower South, aristocrats in broadcloth imposed a variety of Greek democracy (that is, a wise and benevolent oligarchy) on the lower classes as Jeffersonianism declined; in the Ohio Valley the transplanted Virginia squirearchy required all the artifices of Quintilian's *Institutes of Oratory* and a prodigious quantity of corn liquor to preserve the dignity of political office in the face of an electorate which knew its "inalienable rights" rather better than its responsibilities.

The class antagonisms which existed in Virginia were perpetuated in Kentucky, where many of the early arrivals sprang from Shenandoah stock and accordingly distrusted and disliked lace cuffs and powdered wigs on principle. Although large landowners dominated political affairs in the Valley of Virginia, the sympathies there tended to be democratic, by contrast with the Tidewater and Piedmont,[41] and transplanted to Kentucky concretized as a definable political attitude. Nevertheless, the backwoods element of Virginia and North Carolina had finally to contend with a superior class in Kentucky—eastern planters removed to the rich new land, sons of planters denied estates by entail and primogeniture, and yeomen risen through wealth to a genteel condition.

Scarcely less than the common folk the gentry of the Piedmont and even of the Tidewater responded to the paradisiacal vision, and many acted promptly and shrewdly to obtain Kentucky land. With few exceptions, aristocratic Virginians took a relatively minor part in the more difficult phases of settlement but acted through surrogates to procure desirable acreages, preferably by grant or preemption, otherwise by outright purchase from the occupants. Agents of Lord Dunmore under the direction of Thomas Bullitt and William Preston, the surveyor of Fincastle County, marked off some of the richest land in central Kentucky for political favorites during 1773 and 1774,[42] and in 1775 Colonel Richard Henderson and fellow speculators promoted the settlement of Boonesboro with the fond expectation of possessing for themselves much of Tennessee and Kentucky on the strength of a flimsy treaty with the Cherokee. The program of the Transylvania Company, while not implemented, has some interest as yet another instance of scheming for empire in the West. Less ambitious and astute and accordingly less dangerous than Aaron Burr and James Wilkinson, archconspirators of later date, Henderson had grandiose plans nonetheless and apparently meant to erect a feudal domain of unprecedented size. Whatever his inspiration—the English proprietors or the Dutch patroons of New York—the program was ill conceived and died a-borning at the hands of the Virginia legislature in 1776—not that it could have been instituted in the face of backwoods hostility to quitrents and arbitrary authority. In refusing to recognize the claims of the ambitious Transylvania proprietors, the Virginians acted a not altogether disinterested role, as some of them were speculating in Kentucky lands.

The true heroes of the Kentucky settlement, according to Alvord, were the speculators, who perceived the opportunities for quick profits in the fabulously rich land, and not the frontiersmen, who usually crossed the mountains for the first time as surveyors and explorers in the pay of men of substance.[43] A measure of exaggeration allowed for, this bald assertion from one point of view agrees with the circumstances. The keen interest in Kentucky, apparently widespread through the uplands of Pennsylvania, Virginia, and North Carolina, would have materialized sooner or later in settlement; but the problems of supply and defense involved in the large-scale occupation of the wilderness were beyond the solution of backwoods families of scant means. Although a steady infiltration of the Ohio Valley would certainly have occurred in the last quarter of the eighteenth century, no such rapid settlement as history records could have taken place without substantial financial support. Understandably, the prosperous Virginians by whose foresight and treasure the development of Kentucky was accelerated intended to protect their investment in the familiar political ways and, once the settlements were stabilized, proceeded to occupy their holdings and to act a part befitting their station. What happened thereafter might have been foreseen, as the very qualities which enable men to survive in a primitive state handicap them when the social mechanism reorders human relationships according to artificial though nonetheless compulsive values. The real pioneers like the Harrods, McAfees, Calloways, Boones, Bryans, Logans, and Floyds, who endured the privations of the raw frontier and the onslaughts of the Indians, figured progressively less in the affairs of the region, gradually giving way before men of wealth and education, such as the Browns, Todds, Bullitts, Breckinridges, McDowells, Harts, George Nicholas, Harry Innes, Caleb Wallace, Thomas Marshall, and James Wilkinson, many of whom had been leaders previously in southwestern Virginia.

Even worse, many of the earliest settlers had to surrender their land on account of defective titles. The man who had hurried across the mountains and without much reflection staked out a claim on the central Kentucky plateau stood an excellent chance of losing his labor and his land, because as likely as not the parcel of which he fondly believed himself the owner in some part lay within the boundaries of another claim or unknown to him would be overlapped by the preemption of a later arrival. By contrast, the broadcloth gentry had proceeded more deliberately to secure land and when questions of title arose called upon expert legal counsel to protect their interests. As a colony of England, Virginia had doubtful authority to supervise the settlement of Kentucky in the face

of the Proclamation of 1763, which specifically reserved the
tramontane region to the Indians. With the Revolutionary
War in progress, Virginia in 1777 and 1779 passed legislation
intended to end the confusion but neglected to provide for
orderly surveys, with the result that the disputes went finally
to the courts for adjudication. Both the ignorant pioneers and
the transplanted aristocrats were often victimized by unscrupu-
lous speculators and arrant rogues, but in the courts the well-
educated settlers stood the best chance of clearing their titles.
The eminent jurist George Robertson leaves no doubt that the
prolonged disputes occasioned by the defects in the Virginia
land law worked to the disadvantage of the pioneers: "These
anomalous rules and doctrines operated unjustly to individuals
and injuriously to the prosperity and peace of Kentucky. They
produced vexatious and protracted litigation involving, for
many years, most of the original titles—and that litigation generally resulted to the loss, and often the ruin of the early
appropriators, who had neither craft nor the foresight necessary
for eluding the legal net woven by the avaricious or unskilful
legislators, cunning lawyers, and metaphysical courts. Many,
perhaps most, of the advance guard who rescued the country,
were supplanted by voracious speculators."[44]
Whatever the ultimate justice of the claims of a class often
too ignorant or too negligent to comply with the land laws,
the development of the Kentucky frontier followed a familiar
pattern: farsighted speculators secured control of the best
land by various devices[45] but at the same time spoke for
equality, liberal suffrage, and proportionate representation to
lull the suspicions of the equalitarian, anarchic element which
sprouts in new ground and is invariably brought subtly under
control and then as likely as not expelled. Armed with grants
and warrants of one kind or another or with money sufficient
to repair the lack, men with no stomach for the privations of
the frontier but with a keen appetite for fertile soil gradually
wrested the hard-won land from the first settlers, who commonly failed for one cause or another to secure their claims

against legal chicanery or neglected to crop their properties with minimum care. The intelligent eastern planters who relinquished their own eroded acres for the new land in Kentucky are not to be indicted out of hand for reaping the golden harvest earned with blood and sweat by the pioneers, for the majority risked their own capital and acted no less than honestly to protect their investments. Often justice was divided, the first settler having met all the conditions of the law except registration and the affluent planter having purchased in good faith. The latter had obvious advantages when the question of title came to the courts, as the cloud of legal vultures which early invested the Garden of the West protected those with means.

Eager to foreclose a mortgage or to press a weak claim, the lawyer earned the everlasting hatred of the poor after the Revolution, and nowhere more than in Kentucky found a use for his dubious talent. The reputation of the legal profession seems not to have improved with the progress westward, to judge from the candid observation of a hunter on the Missouri frontier: "I seed the country warn't a going to be worth living in, and so I left the Gasconade Caywnty and comed here, for you'll mind that wherever the lawyers and the court-houses come, the other varmint, bars and sich like, are sure to quit."[46] Lawyers or no lawyers, pioneer no less than Indian life was doomed to extinction wherever the land was rich enough to tempt men possessed of wealth and intelligence. A few like James Harrod and Benjamin Logan, who were careful about business affairs, managed to retain large estates, but the colorful Indian fighters in the main died in poverty. Boone and Kenton, who were usually as careless about the surveys which they managed for others as about their own, eventually lost all of their thousands of Kentucky acres and moved perforce to other frontiers.

Before many years, however, legend reversed the courts and restored the frontiersman to the garden, where in the American imagination he yet roams, hunting the elusive deer and skirmishing with the subtle braves of Blackfish, the Shawnee chieftain. While the shadow of the buckskin warrior lengthened, the aristocrat who dammed the streams flowing with milk and honey dwindled into the absurd colonel, an obese hedonist in broadcloth lolling on his spacious veranda and straining mint julep through his preposterous whiskers. Thus, to the confusion of historians devoted to the literal truth, the collective fancy has reworked the tapestry of the western expansion, creating idols larger than life, warriors who embody the qualities associated with the heroic age, the period of racial adolescence after which men yearn. Regarded as a symbol of a way of life, the legendary Kentuckian, if not the abused guardian of the forts, is a complex figure, his significance varying according to diverse conceptions of the ideal state of mankind.

5 The Buckskin Hero

"I have no doubt that had these pioneers lived in other ages, they would have ranked with the deified heroes of antiquity."—AUTOBIOGRAPHY OF REV. JAMES B. FINLEY

THE KENTUCKY frontier proved briefly for land speculators a source of quick and easy profits, but for writers an inexhaustible treasure hoard of story, as hundreds of travelbooks, histories, sketches, and novels attest. Since Filson's *Discovery, Settlement and Present State of Kentucke* (1784), with the *Adventures of Col. Daniel Boon* appended, few years have passed without the publication of some extensive relation of pioneer life below the Ohio. That the Kentucky drama remains eternally fascinating ought to occasion no surprise, for the setting is paradisiacal and the action utterly heroic. If all forms of warfare possess an element of color, none other matches in appeal the mortal hand-to-hand contests of individual heroes and fearfully savage foes over control of valuable properties. In all likelihood, Filson first perceived the heroic quality of the struggle for Kentucky, and he patently supplied both inspiration and matter for many frontier sketches and novels. Yet men with historical perspective in Europe and America could not long have remained insensible of the epical dimensions of the conflict in the western wilderness and certainly not during such a period as the Romantic, when Scott and Byron in particular revived interest in heroic story and Thomas Campbell with *Gertrude of Wyoming* (1809) drew attention anew to the literary possibilities of Indian warfare. Inevitably then, writers seized upon the Kentucky frontier scene. That they wrought unimpressively was no fault of the material, than which perhaps no richer has as yet been exploited in this country.

Whenever in the course of migration the human stream encounters a very nearly insuperable obstacle and churns blood red in passage, strong men rise to the critical occasion and by their deeds plant themselves in the collective imagination. Circumstances favoring, such a spot of time may prove completely heroic and thus furnish a platform enabling a few intrepid individuals to leap into the skies. Since conditions in neither Virginia nor Massachusetts were entirely propitious, Captains John Smith and Miles Standish for all their valor remain entombed in the pages of colonial history, save in their inconsequential experiences with women largely forgotten. In truth, not one authentic epic hero arose during the century and a half after the founding of Jamestown, although Indian warfare enveloped the migrant stream all the way from the Atlantic to the Appalachians and provoked heroic actions beyond count. By contrast, the twenty-year struggle for Kentucky raised up the indomitable frontiersman who, individualized frequently as Boone, achieved epic stature within a relatively short period. The reason was not so much that Indian fighters of the seventeenth century were lacking in skill or courage as that conditions were something less than suitable in the East.

Emigration, hardship, and conflict in combination may produce a heroic age, heroes, and subsequently heroic literature, provided that the emigrants while breaking decisively with the main body of the race yet preserve their identity and meet the challenges of the new and perilous environment without major compromises. A heroic situation was wholly unlikely—Indian warfare notwithstanding—so long as colonists clung to the seaboard or to the valleys below the falls lines of the rivers emptying into the Atlantic and thus preserved rather close connections with Europe. Conditions in the Shenandoah trough

in the third quarter of the eighteenth century appear to have
been much more favorable, for the residents were in the main
a grim and hardened lot who had matured on the frontier. By
the standards of the East no sufficient mark of gentility showed
in these people, but they possessed the qualities calculated to
create a heroic society in the tramontane region. While assuredly not absolute masters of their environment, the settlers
who departed for Kentucky from the Block House in the Holston section and Redstone Old Fort on the Monongahela had
made a largely successful adjustment to primitive surroundings.
Although several generations closer to Europe than the population of the East, they seem actually to have slipped to a lower
cultural level, in the process losing whatever affectations of
dress and manner polite society valued in the period. A few
decades of regression under the impact of the frontier returned
them to a condition which with qualifications may be described
as adolescence, an ideal state—in contrast to either savagery or
sophistication—for heroic accomplishments.

The influence of the wilderness—red man and rigorous nature
—upon the early emigrants produced substantially heroic conditions, first in Kentucky and Tennessee, and afterward at
nearly every stage of the march to the Pacific. By this construction, the heroic period of American history extends from
the settlement of Harrodsburg and Boonesboro (1775) to
sometime before 1880, when, in Turner's opinion, the frontier
vanished;[1] or, determined with reference to the careers of the
heroes, from Boone's first visit to Kentucky in 1769 to the
death of Wild Bill Hickock in 1876. Nearly all of the sensational exploits of those frontiersmen important for legend fall
within a period of a century, and few of the heroes actually
lived beyond the upper limit. That genial old charlatan of the
"big top," Buffalo Bill Cody, who slaughtered far more bison
than Indians, lasted until 1917, but it is doubtful that he rightly
belongs in the frontier pantheon.

Quite properly it may be objected that by no means all of
the early settlers of Kentucky were cultural adolescents, as

the aristocratic society erected in the Bluegrass implied education and taste. Nor were they. The state developed much according to the preconceptions of men of culture and wealth —Virginians in the main. The gentry, however, absented themselves from the front of the emigration, leaving to the simple backwoods folk the task of wresting Kentucky from the Indians. During the interval between the first settlement and the imposition of orderly governmental processes, de facto if not de jure control of the region belonged to that class loosely denominated pioneer, a group eminently qualified to win a paradise but not to hold it against legal chicanery. These buckskin-clad warriors were the authors of the heroic age, and from their ranks alone arose the western heroes. Whatever the merits of the aristocratic minority, which generally was lacking in neither courage nor sagacity, legend has favored none of them. Yet this hierarchy accelerated the maturation of frontier society and accordingly blunted tendencies which in earlier times proved the glory of other races in other lands.

Mature enough to plan and execute but not to reflect, adolescents create heroic ages out of their passion for everlasting fame among their own kind. They seek out occasions, no matter the cost, to display uncommon might and skill. Men of a heroic society must verify their manhood by acts of ultimate courage. By strength and daring they assert their worth and in accordance lay claim to land, women, and chattels. Understandably, hunting and fighting are not only duties but opportunities. Warfare functions in heroic societies as social and commercial interplay in mature ones, taking the measure of men according to fixed values. Warfare, the severest of all tests, not only separates the able from the unfit but provides the best of all scenes for strong and fearless individuals to obtain maximum growth and to create by their deeds sagas of enduring pride to their people. Whatever the cost in life and substance, heroic periods evoke heroic acts which become monuments to racial greatness. All races treasure such moments of ancient glory and appear to derive from them strength to meet present distresses.

The literary history of heroic ages is the history of individuals who realize in themselves to a very high degree the qualities esteemed by their peoples. Insofar as the intrepid warrior embodies the aspirations of his race, he may be said to serve the collective interest; but his real concern is personal renown. To become fit to die through martial works and then to die in a blaze of glory—the hero asks little more. Utter savages may be only faceless servants of the common good—the question is unimportant in this context. Civilized men recognize the efficacy of group action and indeed behave more confidently in company than alone. In contrast, the folk hero, by definition adolescent and egotistical, refuses to share the glory of victory over whatever monsters, dragons, tyrants, or common villains threaten his race. Heroic poetry from the *Iliad* to the *Nibelungenlied* is largely a record of single combats, as men of the temperament of Achilles and Siegfried are scarcely amenable to conventional military discipline. Even when engaged in actions involving thousands of men, the warrior of renown, like Roland at Roncesvalles, fights with little immediate reference to the whole, though by his success against one after another of the enemy proving an inspiration to his comrades. The traditional hero is a self-sufficient person and a unified military instrument, prepared to fight one or many and if need be to die without complaint.

Death to the epic hero is not so much a penalty for defeat as an inevitable termination of his career by powers beyond his control. The gesture of fate may not be anticipated with delight, but it certainly occasions no sleeplessness. The chief concern of the warrior is to die with his boots on in some action which will enhance his prestige, preferably a desperate encounter against superior forces. The greater the odds, the greater the opportunity for fame. Since man in a heroic society acknowledges the obligation to prove himself deserving of the esteem of his tribe in those matters which count most, a sudden and violent departure from the world is commonplace and cause for only momentary lamentation. The manner of the warrior's going provokes far more interest than the fact.

An existence which evokes manliness alone and provides occasions in abundance to test man's strength and fortitude powerfully offends at close range the sensibilities of sophisticates. Men subjected constantly to hardship and danger and at the same time denied most of the amenities of civilization tend to become reckless, violent, frank, boastful, and markedly rude of manner. The warrior in a severe milieu is hard because no other condition will serve to keep him alive. He preserves his sanity by acting rather than meditating, fighting rather than worrying. His view of death is fatalistic, his reaction to the trials of life stoical. Given heroic conditions, the warrior class inevitably comes into being, and out of this group spring immortal heroes. Poets of the olden time, meaning to serve the spiritual needs of their peoples, canonized secular heroes through mitigating their faults and magnifying their virtues. Accordingly, Achilles, Hector, Aeneas, Ulysses, Siegfried, Grettir, Dietrich von Bern, and Hildebrand are held in memory not as symbols of the barbarian menace but of the primeval greatness of their races.

Less fortunate thus far than Hellenic and Germanic heroes or even Celtic, the legendary Kentuckian has yet to be framed in literature of classic dimensions. For reasons presently to appear, he generally subserves alien ideologies in frontier romances and even in dime novels, and cannot therefore attain complete growth, although everywhere intimating his heroic character. In sketches, anecdotes, tall tales, and more or less true relations, however, the Kentuckian enacts a role less affected by irrelevant standards. If not the complete epic hero, for lack of a literary vehicle of proper magnitude, he is unmistakably the child of a heroic society—violent, boisterous, and mischievous. This formidable figure, in contrast to the serious

and purposeful Leatherstocking type familiar to the early
novels, seeks mainly to demonstrate his superior quality in
combat with man or beast, and he is little concerned with
abstract issues. The informal literature of the frontier rather
better than the romances supports the judicious portrait of the
Kentuckian drawn by Godfrey T. Vigne, a London barrister:
"The inhabitants of Kentucky may be called the Gascons of
America. They have a humorous, good-natured, boasting,
boisterous peculiarity of language and manner, by which they
are known to all parts of the Union. To a stranger, they are
courteous and hospitable; but amongst themselves, they quarrel
and fight, like the Irish, for fun; or merely to see which is the
best man, without any provocation; and they evince great
partiality for their own state—which they familiarly denom-
inate 'Old Kentuck,'—perhaps more than the inhabitants of
any other in the Union."[2] A heroic society produces such men
as Vigne described. Competent in matters which count—
securing food and repulsing enemies—they are nonetheless
overgrown children, not, like the Leatherstocking sort, philosophical gentlemen of the forest.

Failure to secure game no less than the failure to repel
intruders proves fatal to men of a heroic age. The frontier
Kentuckians, like the Indians, grew some of their food, notably
corn, but depended considerably for perhaps two decades after
the settlement upon buffalo, deer, bear, and lesser animals.
Their fine marksmanship, understandably exaggerated, was
owing as much to sheer need as to the excellence of the Kentucky rifle. With this weapon they achieved a high degree of
skill and accordingly a saving of powder and ball. A term
familiar to U. S. Army parlance, *Kentucky windage,* acknowledges even yet the uncanny ability of these backwoodsmen to
make offhand allowance for cross winds. Christian Schultz
commented in 1810 upon the precision shooting of the Kentucky hunters, and Captain R. G. A. Levinge at a later day
pronounced them "capital rifle shots," able to hit a squirrel in

the eye at sixty yards.[3] Charles Wilkins Webber, writing at some distance from the frontier period and obviously persuaded by fabulous stories, paid an extravagant tribute to their marksmanship: "To drive a nail is a common feat, not more thought of by the Kentuckians than to cut off a wild turkey's head, at a distance of a hundred yards. Others will bark off squirrels one after another, until satisfied with the number procured. Some, less intent on destroying game, may be seen under night snuffing a candle at the distance of fifty yards, off-hand, without extinguishing it. I have been told that some have proved so expert and cool, as to make choice of the eye of a foe at a wonderful distance, boasting beforehand of the sureness of their piece, which has afterwards been fully proved when the enemy's head has been examined!"[4] The last sentence Webber surely borrowed from John James Audubon, who, though a fairly trustworthy ornithologist, was often a whimsical chronicler of the frontier. Audubon probably saw Boone "bark" a squirrel, as he maintained, but judging from his description of Daniel as "gigantic," absolute veracity was not his major concern.[5]

Anyone disposed to believe that Boone and his kind could drive nails and nick turkey necks consistently at a hundred yards scarcely needed a larger gullet to swallow the most improbable shooting yarns recorded in frontier literature. When Cooper fashioned Leatherstocking, with suggestions from Filson's portrait of Boone, he endowed him with a remarkable eye for shooting, the equal of which even the boastful Mike Fink would not have claimed for himself. In the *Pioneers* (1823) Leatherstocking killed a pigeon on the wing with a rifle shot, and in the *Pathfinder* (1840) he hit two gulls with one ball in the split second when their lines of flight intersected. Robin Hood never shot so well, nor even the fabulous Trojan archer Eurytion, who, according to Virgil, sent an arrow through a dove on the wing. Cooper's public, however, exhibited a gratifying willingness to suspend disbelief, and as

the nineteenth century wore on developed a keen taste for
western fables.

For a time after the frontier period all Kentuckians to some
extent bore in the popular imagination the mantle of the
legendary marksmen of the wilderness. In consequence, the
hero of any shooting yarn was as likely as not to be called a
Kentuckian and as likely as not to enact the role without conspicuous modesty. So identified, he was privileged—indeed,
expected—to perform miraculous feats with a rifle. According
to a tale printed in the Paulding, Mississippi, *Democrat*, November 18, 1846, a Kentuckian serving as purser on an American ship possessed the skill to make extraordinary shots and
the effrontery to call them as well. While ashore on the island
of Malta, he was invited by the commander of a British frigate
to try his marksmanship against a picked group of six Englishmen. The Kentuckian watched his opponents fire unsuccess-
fully at a piece of paper the size of a dollar from a distance
of seventy-five yards. Pronouncing the performance "no shooting at all," he asserted his superiority in unmistakable terms:
"I'll bet a wine supper for all hands . . . that I'll make three
shots, every one of which will be better than any yet made,
and each succeeding one better than the first." The bet covered, the Kentuckian proceeded to make good his boast; and
then, adding insult to injury, he retreated forty yards, and
after laying his first shot a hair from the target, with the second
drove the nail holding the paper.

One of the most extravagant of the tall tales reflecting the
myth of Kentucky marksmanship appeared in the *Arkansas
Advocate*, December 23, 1836. A Kentuckian one day attended
a shooting match in England. The targets were pigeons and
the arms shotguns. After a time, the visitor, who like Leatherstocking despised shotguns, offered to try a few shots with his
Kentucky rifle, which quite by chance he had brought along.
The best one of the trapshooters agreed to a test with the
American; each was to shoot at six birds with the rifle and

the winner to enjoy a dinner at the other's expense. The Englishman fired first, missing all six of his shots. The American's version of his own shooting follows:

I took the rifle—the first bird flew slant-wise in so singular a manner that I could not bring the sight to bear,— after raising my piece to my shoulder I lowered it again, and allowed the pigeon to escape without firing. You know the Kentucky rule—"Never shoot till you are sure." The second bird served me in the same manner, and I again lowered my piece. The by-standers manifested signs of disappointment and dissatisfaction, and I—I must confess, felt the very reverse of comfortable. The third pigeon was loosed, and she flew straight a-head: and when at the distance of 70 yards at least, a rifle ball whistled through the air and—she fell. A loud shout proclaimed my success. Another I succeeded with, and at a greater distance. The people were literally delighted, for they positively understood nothing about rifle shooting. "Now," said I, "if I kill the next I will not fire at another—but let any other gentleman try that pleases." I said this, because I did not wish to risk the missing of either of them, if I pulled the trigger, that is, if I could possibly avoid it. A dead silence ensued, now and then only interrupted by the audible whispers of "American"—"an American"— "Well, it is extraordinary. . . ." I felt as if I were shooting for the honor of my country—that sentiment nerved and steadied my hand and eye, and gave me hopes of victory. This, the last bird, flew upwards—but straight a-head, and in a second or so, fell, having received the ball at a still greater distance than the other two. The applause was tremendous, and I was regarded as a prodigy by all around—while I felt quite cool upon the business, as you know that amongst Western hunters, it would have been merely considered "pretty fair shooting"—but nothing wonderful.

Kentucky hunters were not entirely dependent upon the rifle, but when occasion demanded could operate on wildlife with cold steel and even with fang and claw. The Reverend James B. Finley, a great hunter himself, related the story of a settler who confronted a bear though armed only with an ax. The beast wrested the weapon from the man and lacerated his left arm. Thereupon the resourceful Kentuckian caught the bear's nose in his teeth and proceeded to gouge out its eyes before help came. Some years later, this rough-and-tumble fighter was asked how the bears made out with him, and he replied: "They can't stand Kentucky play. Biting and gouging are too hard for them."[6] According to a story printed in the *Missouri Republican*, June 21, 1827, and attributed to the New York *Courier*, not even a Florida alligator could endure Kentucky gouging:

A Kentuckian belonging to a surveying party, under an officer of U. S. Engineers, swimming in St. Johns' River, was seized by a large alligator and taken under the water. In a short time the Kentuckian and the alligator rose to the surface, the latter having the right leg of the former in his mouth, and the former having his thumbs in the eyes of his antagonist. The officer immediately gave orders to his party, who were in a boat a few yards from the combatants, to go to the relief of their comrade, but the Kentuckian peremptorily forbade any interference, saying, "give the fellow fair play." It is needless to add that the gouger obtained a complete victory. Having taken out one of the eyes of his adversary, the latter, in order to save his other eye, relinquished his hold upon the Kentuckian's leg, who returned to shore in triumph.

The gougers were little remarkable by comparison with a fabulous Kentucky hunter whose speed and bottom enabled him to run down large game. Neither James Ray, who distanced a party of Shawnee near Harrodsburg, nor John Coulter, who ran an entire tribe of Blackfeet into the ground, ever attempted to overtake a herd of elk. First printed in the St. Louis *Reveille* and later collected by J. M. Field, the story of the elk runners is elaborately authenticated.[7] Two young men were employed during 1818 as hunters by the Missouri Fur Company and stationed at Fort Lisa, below Council Bluffs— one a Kentuckian, identified as John Dougherty, "a fine daring fellow, with a frame of iron, the speed of the ostrich, and the endurance of the camel"; the other, a redoubtable halfbreed called Mal Boeuf. As the hunters whiled away one July evening in gambling, their employer approached and took them to task for failing to supply the post with fresh meat. The next morning they set out and after traveling some five miles sighted a herd of sixteen elk. The Kentuckian proposed a

maneuver that would enable them to obtain fair shots, but
Mal Boeuf, disgruntled by his gambling losses, replied sourly,
"I don't kill elk with my *gun,* but with my *knife.*" The Kentuckian accepted the implied challenge. They approached as
near as possible to the herd and then raised the war whoop,
which sent the animals flying. After a twenty-mile run, the
hunters managed to turn the herd; but the elk were not yet
winded and raced on many miles more. Exhausted finally and
maddened from thirst, the animals plunged into a prairie pond,
utterly indifferent to their enemies. The Kentuckian and Mal
Boeuf, close behind, quickly cut the throats of all sixteen,
dragged the carcasses from the water, and prepared them for
transportation. They then raced back to the fort for packhorses
and arrived running neck and neck, but utterly exhausted,
having covered a distance of seventy-five miles in eleven hours.
The Kentuckian eventually recovered from his ordeal, but the
halfbreed, having given himself up to dissipation, died not
long after the great hunt.

Kentuckians during the frontier period were probably more
successful as hunters than as fighters, but the hunting exploits
of warriors never arouse such enduring interest as their raw,
man-to-man combats. Hunting in a heroic society is secondary
to fighting, a mere substitute for what is, by the view of cultural adolescents, the manliest of all exercises. Since they
neither delve nor spin, warriors inevitably rust without military use. Though justly celebrated as hunters and marksmen,
the early Kentuckians understandably have been memorialized
in frontier literature primarily as fighters. Hell on mules and
women, life around the forts while the Shawnee prowled offered men occasions aplenty to display the "true grit" and to
win undying fame in saving their scalps from indefatigable
collectors of hair. Not surprisingly, tradition has caught up
a larger number of heroic episodes from the Kentucky scene
than from any other in America of comparable area.

As deep though poorly buttressed salients in the Indian
country, the early settlements of central Kentucky throughout

the period of the Revolution attracted the attention of the formidable Ohio braves. For appearing to stand forlorn against the savage menace, the defenders of Harrodsburg, Boonesboro, St. Asaph's, Bryan's, and other stations aroused the interest of romantic chroniclers and through their aid speedily entered into legend. Kentucky came to be regarded as the proving ground of western heroes, and whoever participated even briefly in the conflict with the Shawnee and Delaware was certified forever afterward as a warrior par excellence. Admittedly, many a hardy frontiersman hunted game and fought red men in Kentucky before moving west to an equally heroic life on the plains, though Emerson Hough in classifying a majority of the far western scouts, explorers, trappers, and Indian fighters as Shenandoah-Kentucky stock probably consulted legend as well as records.[8] His claim, however, suggests the value of a Kentucky connection, which, perhaps in fact as well as in fiction, brought the possessor an unearned increment of reputation. An even more impressive tribute to the region as the incubator of western heroes is the frequent identification of Davy Crockett as a Kentuckian, especially in the almanacs. Levinge so named the Tennessean and placed him at the head of the Kentucky frontiersmen, whom he regarded as "the roughest of all the inhabitants of the United States."[9] In an almanac anecdote, Davy plainly asserted his Kentucky origin when calling upon two dueling congressmen to stop and desist or suffer his wrath: "Gentlemen . . . I'm Davy Crockett, the darling branch o' old Kentuck, that can eat up a painter, hold a buffalo out to drink, and put a rifle ball through the moon."[10] Apparently to improve their hero's credentials, the shameless fabricators of the Crockett pseudomyth substituted Kentucky for Tennessee, even though the settlers of the latter state won laurels enough in Indian warfare, especially against the Creeks.

Tennesseans deserved major credit for humiliating Pakenham's regulars in the Battle of New Orleans, yet received no mention in perhaps the most notable literary memorial of the battle—*The Hunters of Kentucky*. The Kentucky contingent of 2,200 men under the command of Major General John Thomas and Brigadier General John Adair arrived virtually weaponless in New Orleans on January 4, 1815, four days before the British attack. When the fighting commenced, perhaps no more than half of the Kentuckians possessed arms even of an inferior sort. Understandably, they failed as a group to bear themselves with as much distinction as the more numerous Tennesseans, although their conduct was considerably more gallant than Andrew Jackson ever allowed. Inexperienced recruits in the main and markedly inferior to the old pioneers of fact and legend, they were nevertheless chosen over their betters for immortality. Samuel Woodward, the author of *The Old Oaken Bucket,* represented the Kentucky troops according to the heroic pattern and by implication awarded them the palm of victory in the stirring song *The Hunters of Kentucky, or the Battle of New Orleans.* The second stanza supports the general impression of the piece that the New York composer actually had in mind the legendary Kentuckian:

> We are a hardy freeborn race,
>   Each man to fear a stranger,
> Whate'er the game, we join in chase,
>   Despising toil and danger;
> And if a daring foe annoys,
>   Whate'er his strength and forces,
> We'll show him that Kentucky boys
>   Are "alligator horses."
> O Kentucky, the hunters of Kentucky.
> O Kentucky, the hunters of Kentucky.

Noah Ludlow, a well-known actor of the ante bellum South, introduced the song to New Orleans in early May, 1822, and the mixed audience of Creoles and rivermen received it with wild enthusiasm.[11] About a month earlier, a brother had clipped the song for him from the New York *Mirror,* and the actor decided to use it on his benefit night. After the completion of the scheduled play, Ludlow appeared on the stage dressed in buckskin and an old hat and carrying a rifle. The

garb, the subject, and the melody proved so compelling that
he was forced to grant two encores the first night and willy-
nilly to sing *The Hunters of Kentucky* wherever his company
appeared for months afterward. Notwithstanding the excellence of the melody, which Ludlow believed taken from the
comic opera *Love Laughs at Locksmiths,* the popularity of the
piece was owing in some part to the spreading fame of the
legendary heroes of the Kentucky wilderness.

At least one Kentuckian in the Battle of New Orleans recalled the tall men of the frontier, to judge from a British
officer's vivid account of the marksmanship of E. M. Brank of
Greenville. A member of Pakenham's staff, this officer perceived through his field glasses a singular personage towering
above the American breastworks: "But what attracted our
attention most, was the figure of a tall man standing on the
breastworks, dressed in linsey-woolsey, with buckskin leggins,
and a broad brimmed felt hat that fell round the face, almost
concealing the features. He was standing in one of those
picturesque graceful attitudes peculiar to those natural men
dwelling in forests." The Kentuckian spotted the British staff
moving forward on horseback and with painful deliberation
proceeded to pick off one after another at extreme range. The
survivor's estimate of the effect of Brank's firing, though doubtless exaggerated, deserves consideration: "We lost the battle;
and to my mind, the Kentucky rifleman contributed more to
our defeat, than anything else; for while he remained in our
sight, our attention was drawn from our duties; and when, at
last, he became enshrouded in the smoke, the work was complete; we were in utter confusion, and unable, in the extremity,
to restore order sufficiently to make any successful attack."[12]
This testimony had no demonstrable influence on the Kentucky
legend, but it is evidence of the reputation of Kentucky
marksmen.

The legendary Kentuckian probably assumed definite form
as early as the third decade of the nineteenth century, but
year by year, at least until the Civil War, sketches, anecdotes,

and novels added detail to his portrait. Though certainly the prototype, Filson's Boone is by no means identical with the perfected Kentuckian, whose shaping owed a great deal to writers far more sensible than Filson of the violent and mischievous nature of the real frontiersmen.[13] Unlike Timothy Flint, the usual observer felt no obligation to excuse the conduct of a class who by repute commonly issued such a rude greeting as "Stranger, will you drink or fight?" The tradition of violence was fertilized by travelers like William Faux, whose account of an atrocity told him by Richard Flower of Illinois is representative: "I knew a party of whites who last year in Kentucky roasted to death, before a large log fire, one of their friends, because he refused to drink. They did it thus:—Three or four of them shoved and held him up to the fire until they themselves could stand it no longer; and he died in 20 hours after."[14] A New Orleans editor protested violently against "every two penny English tourist" who titillated his countrymen with accounts of assassinations, Bowie-knife fights, and lynch-law jurisprudence in America. It is inconceivable, however, that the horrific instance which he cited could have been written in earnest, although credulous readers may have swallowed it:

I was once travelling in the State of Kentucky. It was summer, and the heat of the sun is so great there at that season, that blacksmiths dispense altogether with coal, and heat their iron by a few minutes' exposure to its rays. Well, I took shelter under the shade of an umbrageous tree, in the vicinity of which a quiet and peaceable family of the name of Coon was temporarily sojourning. The father's name was Richard; but with their usual ignorance of correct English and their improper pronunciation, they abbreviated it, and instead of calling him Ric, called him *Rac* Coon. I had not been long under the tree, when a stalworth [*sic*] Kentuckian approached, his eyes glaring like the revolving lamps of a light house. When within a few yards of me, he levelled his large double-barrel rifle, and I at once concluded my days were numbered. I could know of no cause for this anticipated attack, except the naturally sanguinary disposition of the people. . . . He fired, and Mr. Coon, who happened to be taking his *siesta* in the tree right over my head,

though I was not aware of his presence, fell dead at my feet. . . .
The murderous Kentuckian seemed to be no more concerned on
the occasion, than one of our sportsmen would at taking down a
snipe on the wing.[15]

Whether the editor detected the humbug—if, indeed, he did
not originate it—is less important than the implication of the
piece for the development of the Kentucky character.

The gentlemanly Boone strain, while never actually obliter-
ated, struggled increasingly with less refined elements in the
anatomy of the Kentuckian, elements which early travelers
perceived or imagined and which popular writers flagrantly
magnified. Responsibility for filling the veins of the Kentucky
type with sulfuric acid and saltpeter seems to have been
divided. The average foreign traveler in all likelihood had been
persuaded before setting out of the violent nature of the western Americans, and understandably often discovered what he
had been led to expect. At the same time, American writers
seem deliberately to have pandered to the universal taste for
violence, embroidering their accounts of the backwoods with
as much gore as Victorian sensibilities could tolerate. It is
apparent that the legend of Kentucky barbarism flourished in
the nineteenth century from purposeful cultivation by native
novelists and journalists as well as from the mendacious accounts of Europeans.

William Alexander Caruthers introduced a Kentuckian into
the misnamed *The Kentuckian in New-York* (1834) for display,
not for use. This sentimental novel has nothing essentially to
do with the backwoods or with backwoodsmen, though obviously in need of color to heighten the commonplace plot. Montgomery Damon, a Kentucky yeoman, merely ornaments the
novel by his swaggering manner and bold speech, as there is
no organic function in an elegant social setting for a person
who represents himself as a nonchalant butcher of savages:
"I think no more of taking my jack-knife, and unbuttonin the
collar of a Creek Injin, than I would of takin the jacket off a
good fat bell-wether, or mout-be a yerlin calf" (ch. 2).

Caruthers' use of Damon, however reprehensible on aesthetic grounds, probably enhanced the general appeal of *The Kentuckian in New-York*, for this character, though actually performing only mild comic service, recalled the incredible accounts of Bowie-knife surgery emanating from the barbarian fringe of America. Ante bellum newspapers printed, in addition to the political and diplomatic staple, horrific narratives of rough-and-tumble combats, in which Kentuckians figured prominently. Accordingly, Damon, though not called to display his physical prowess, suggested heroic capacity to a public widely familiar with western legendry.

Caruthers' audience in all likelihood identified Damon with the type of the ferocious, though cheerful, alligator-horse of Kentucky like Bill Sedley, who "feared no shape of man or beast."[16] Sedley fought a truly epic battle in 1822 in Mother Colby's hotel in New Orleans. At the time, the saloon and gambling rooms of the hotel were rented to two Spaniards from Vera Cruz, Juan and Manuel Cortinas. Gambling alone with the brothers, Sedley lost steadily. He finally detected Manuel cheating and proceeded to denounce the brothers in unmistakable terms: "I'm a Salt River Roarer. . . . You mustn't play me for a spring chicken, you d——d greaser, you. I'm a cross of a cock-eyed alligator and a red-hot snapping turtle. Give up that money, you thief, or down goes your tabernacle." Juan barred the door, as Manuel shot Sedley through the left arm. Persons outside heard Bill assault Manuel physically and verbally: "I'm the catamount of the Cumberland. . . . I'm the painter's (panther's) playmate. Here's at you—you greaser, you nigger!" As the fight progressed, Sedley warmed to his murderous work: "Come on both of you. I'm the ring-tailed squealer. I'm the man on the pale horse—whoop—try it again. I'm the terror of the wilderness." In due course, the door to the room opened: Bill Sedley stood bleeding from two pistol wounds and half a dozen knife wounds, although not mortally hurt. Manuel lay dead and Juan dying.

Yet in the role of a common brawler—biting, gouging, dirk-

ing, and emasculating his own kind—the Kentuckian neither
in fact nor in fiction could achieve truly heroic stature, for the
issues which provoked his anger were entirely too trivial and
his methods much too bestial. Against the Indian, however,
he fought as an agent of the common interest, clearing the
wilderness of primitive man in order that civilization might
root and flourish. Accordingly, killing Indians became the
noblest activity engaged in by the Kentuckian and the activity
which more than any other recommended him for literary
treatment. Hunting Indians was, besides, incomparably more
exciting than hunting wild animals, as the frontiersman Adam
Poe candidly admitted: " 'I've tried all kinds of game, boys!
I've fit bar and painter (panther) and catamount, but,' he
added regretfully, and with a vague, unsatisfied longing in the
plaintive tones of his voice, 'thar ain't no game like Ingins—
No, sir! no game like Injins.' "[17]

Western society placed a high value on the ability to master
the red enemy and consequently intensified in the white warrior class a desire to collect scalps, a practice which many
backwoodsmen seem to have approved as wholeheartedly as
the savages. Atrocities doubtless produced many a so-called
Indian hater like Colonel James Hubbard of East Tennessee,
who in cold blood killed one Indian fishing from a river bank,
another perched on a platform at a lick waiting for game, and
a third innocently participating in a shooting match;[18] but the
white man's desire for fame possibly took as many Indian lives
as his passion for revenge. The Indian was the finest instrument of the hero's ambition, for notable deeds wrought against
him earned the adulation of the public. Lovers of the Indian
there were from the period of the first settlements on the
Atlantic, though always a minority until the removal of the
tribes beyond the Mississippi, after which sentiment increased
to close the season on Adam Poe's favorite game. The public
tended to rationalize the slaughter of the aborigines in the
name of progress and privately reveled in the bloody work
of the frontiersmen as recorded by journalistic writers.

The appetite for Indian narrative did not of course decline in the 1830's with the removal, nor has it been completely satisfied even to this day, to judge from the westerns issued by Hollywood. In 1832 John A. McClung published *Sketches of Western Adventure*, a collection of ostensibly true, though unquestionably embroidered, relations of frontier combats. Born in Mason County in 1804, McClung had some opportunity to assimilate Kentucky legendry from firsthand sources, though he obviously made considerable use of Bradford's *Notes on Kentucky*.[19] First issued in Maysville, his book was reprinted elsewhere six times before 1855, and revised and enlarged in 1872.[20] It proved popular through no lack of seriousness in the author, a Presbyterian minister of wide if not deep learning. Although esteeming Scott, Byron, and Moore (romancers all), he quite modestly proposed to write neither romance nor epic but a true relation of frontier tales in an orderly and dignified manner. If McClung sometimes failed to give the Indian his due, he clearly perceived the heroic character of the frontiersman's ordeal. Epical rather than romantic in spirit, his sketches pay a quiet but worthy tribute to the Indian fighters of the Ohio Valley frontier. McClung's book, though by no means exhaustive, is a substantial compendium of heroic exploits during the Indian wars, containing most of the familiar experiences of Daniel Boone, Simon Kenton, and Benjamin Logan, among others less well known, and brief accounts of the major engagements. A majority of McClung's heroes were Kentuckians by adoption, and Kentucky is more often than not the scene of action. The book directly strengthened the Kentucky legend and significantly influenced later fictional treatments of the frontiersman.

"It is much to be regretted," McClung wrote, "that the materials for a sketch of Boone are so scanty. He has left us a brief account of his adventures, but they are rather such as one would require for the composition of an epitaph than of a biography."[21] The truth was, as the minister must have

known, that Daniel's actual accomplishments in the role of
frontier warrior poorly supported his towering reputation;
Lady Fame, as Horace observed long before, bestows her
favors capriciously on military figures. Many a Kentuckian
engaged in much more heroic actions with the Shawnee than
Boone but unfortunately lacked a Filson. McClung managed
to spread his sketch of the legendary hunter· over forty-two
pages only by including material of dubious relevance. There
is slight evidence that Boone ever knowingly killed an Indian
and no record of a violent hand-to-hand combat, although,
according to W. H. Bogart, during the siege of Boonesboro
he shot a renegade Negro dead at a distance of one hundred
seventy-five yards.[22] Aside from this battle and the daring
rescue of his daughter Jemima and Betsey and Fanny Callaway
from the Cherokee chief Hanging Maw and a few Shawnee,
Boone seems to have dealt with the Indians by avoiding or
placating·them. If he hated Indians, as Thwaites implied,[23]
the Shawnee were insensible of the fact, releasing him un-
harmed in 1769 and actually adopting him early in 1778, a
few months before the attack on Boonesboro. As John Bakeless
observed, "there was always a faintly chivalrous note in Daniel Boone's warfare with the Indians."[24] It was indeed fortunate
that Daniel had acquired no taste for scalps, or Blackfish would
have subjected him not to a ceremony of adoption but to a
ceremony of execution—black paint and slow broiling.

Alexander McConnel, according to McClung, killed more
Indians in five minutes than Boone killed in fifty years.[25] Early
in the spring of 1780, McConnel shot a deer near Lexington,
and returned home for a horse to carry the game. Meanwhile
a party of Indians found the fresh carcass and awaited the
hunter's return. After capturing McConnel, who had small
opportunity to resist, the savages proceeded leisurely toward
the Ohio, good naturedly allowing their prisoner considerable
freedom of movement. The evening before the party expected
to cross the river, McConnel set about devising some means of

escape. After cutting his bonds with a knife carelessly left within his reach by the Indians, who had fallen asleep, he sat by the fire seeking some alternative to flight, which would have been futile.

After anxious reflection for a few minutes, he formed his plan. The guns of the Indians were stacked near the fire; their knives and tomahawks were in sheaths by their sides. The latter he dared not touch for fear of awakening their owners; but the former he carefully removed, with the exception of two, and hid them in the woods, where he knew the Indians would not readily find them. He then returned to the spot where the Indians were still sleeping ... and taking a gun in each hand, he rested the muzzles upon a log within six feet of his victims, and having taken deliberate aim at the head of one and the heart of another, he pulled both triggers at the same moment.

Both shots were fatal. At the report of their guns the others sprung to their feet, and stared wildly around them. McConnel, who had run instantly to the spot where the other rifles were hid, hastily seized one of them and fired at two of his enemies, who happened to stand in a line with each other. The nearest fell dead, being shot through the center of the body; the second fell also, bellowing loudly, but quickly recovering, limped off into the woods as far as possible. The fifth, and only one who remained unhurt, darted off like a deer, with a yell which announced equal terror and astonishment. McConnel, not wishing to fight any more such battles, selected his own rifle from the stack, and made the best of his way to Lexington, where he arrived safely within two days.

Whether McConnel actually killed four Indians with three shots is unimportant for a study of the legendary Kentuckian, but it should be remembered that the hero of a class of traditional narratives on occasion kills all of an opposing band of enemies but one, who escapes to bear the ill tidings to the next of kin. Like most frontier chroniclers McClung was not greatly concerned with separating truth from fiction.

A few years before the admission of Kentucky to the Union, a woman acted as principal in an Indian episode even more spectacular than McConnel's. Disturbed one night by the barking of his dog, John Merril of Nelson County opened the

door of his cabin to investigate the cause of the disturbance
and immediately received the fire of six or seven savages,
whereupon Mrs. Merril closed and barred the door. Her husband seriously wounded, she alone chopped up four Indians
as they attempted one after another to force the door. Two
others then mounted the roof and descended the chimney, but
providentially the lady had anticipated this maneuver by laying her feather bed on the fire, thus creating a blazing reception. Smoke and flame rendered the Indians easy marks for
Mrs. Merril's ax. She then ran back to the door in time to
fetch the seventh and last savage a severe cut on the cheek.
Like the survivor of the McConnel affair, this Indian withdrew
and returned hastily to Chillicothe with a sensational report
on the prowess of a "long-knife squaw."[26]

If the Shawnee had fallen in such numbers as frontier
sketches suggest, few indeed would have remained in the
period of the relocation. In truth, the Ohio Indians were
usually more than a match for the settlers and apparently lost
significant numbers only in large-scale actions, to which they
never became entirely accustomed. Even so, formal campaigns
against them were not always successful, as witness Crawford's,
Harmar's, and St. Clair's. The American victory in the Battle
of the Thames (1813) over Tecumseh and his British allies,
moreover, owed as much to superior force as to superior fighting quality. None of the Kentucky frontiersmen seems actually
to have killed a great number of Indians, and not many survived a close acquaintance with them. Among only a very few
backwoodsmen, Simon Kenton dealt fairly successfully with
the Indians, and even he suffered frightfully at their hands.
Unlike Boone, who had reached middle age before coming to
Kentucky to settle, Kenton actually matured under the most
difficult frontier conditions, having fled west at sixteen with
the mistaken notion that he had fatally injured his successful
rival for the hand of a Fauquier County, Virginia, girl. In 1775,
the year of the first permanent Kentucky settlement, he turned
twenty, already a seasoned frontiersman. Four years earlier

with John Yeager, who had lived for some time as an Indian captive, and George Strader, Kenton (or Butler—his alias after his flight from home) had voyaged a considerable distance down the Ohio River, looking for the fabulous garden land of Kentucky, which Yeager remembered from his captivity. Unsuccessful in their somewhat desultory search, they had turned back to the Great Kanawha and trapped until March, 1773, when Indians attacked, killing Yeager and putting the others to flight. Without provisions or weapons, Kenton and Strader had barely managed to extricate themselves from the wilderness. In 1775, after his fifth trip down the Ohio, Kenton settled on the edge of the great canebrake lying inland from Limestone and there with Thomas Williams raised a crop of corn. For many years thereafter fighting Indians was his chief occupation. During a skirmish before Boonesboro in 1777, Boone received a disabling wound and lay helpless before a savage with upraised tomahawk, whereupon Kenton, according to tradition, shot the Indian and bore Daniel into the fort. As Edna Kenton observed in connection with this event, Simon seems continually to have been placed in positions requiring rapid shooting to forestall savages about to fire on friends or on himself.[27]

Kenton's progress through Ohio as a captive of the Shawnee required more strength and courage than the death march of the survivors of Bataan; no other frontiersman ever endured so much punishment and survived.[28] Under orders of Colonel John Bowman, Kenton with Alexander Montgomery and a young man by the name of George Clark set out in September, 1778, for Chillicothe to spy on the Shawnee, who were at that time causing the settlements great distress. The requisite information about the activities of the Indians obtained, the party had no further business in the region and might have returned unmolested to Kentucky. Apparently Kenton had come prepared with salt and halters to steal whatever horses came to hand,[29] and, despite the danger, he rounded up a string of seven, though not without the knowledge of the

Indians, who methodically took up his trail to the Ohio River. The unwillingness of the animals to cross the river, exceedingly rough at that time, occasioned a delay during which the Shawnee arrived. Montgomery was scalped and Kenton run down. Clark swam the river safely.

The Indians started Simon north tied hand and foot and mounted on an unbroken three-year-old. Following a necessarily hectic journey to Chillicothe, he entertained the exultant Shawnee by twice running the gauntlet. After due deliberation, during which the captive made some recovery, the tribe decided to burn him at the stake in the village of Wappatomika, forty miles away on Mad River. En route, he ran the gauntlet for the residents of Piqua and again for those of Machachack. In the last instance he broke the line of screeching braves and squaws and sped into the woods, or rather into the midst of a party of Shawnee under Blue Jacket, come to see the famed Kentuckian roasted. For his pains Simon received a terrible head wound from a tomahawk wielded by one of the warriors who rode him down. Under other circumstances he would certainly have escaped, as no Indian, according to tradition, could match his speed and bottom. The battered Kentuckian was marched to the council house and bound. Blackfish, Boone's father by adoption, arrived soon after and delivered the captive a lecture on the evils of horse stealing. Intending to insult Simon, an old squaw sat on his face and promptly received a bite to her screaming discomfiture and the amusement of the braves. His sorry predicament notwithstanding, Simon defied the Shawnee and won their respect; but he again ran the gauntlet and received another scalp wound. The renegade Simon Girty, an old friend of Kenton's, came forward in time to save him from the stake. Unfortunately, a war party arrived about three weeks later from Virginia in a sullen mood on account of heavy casualties and not surprisingly demanded a retrial. Girty failed to persuade the council to let Simon live but managed to have the burning transferred to Sandusky. Although suffering a broken arm and a broken collarbone en route, the captive attracted the attention of Logan and received a promise of aid from the great Mingo chief. But he had to run the gauntlet again—the ninth time. The stake was prepared for him at Sandusky, however, and burning would surely have been his fate except for a cloudburst, which extinguished the fire. Shortly after, Pierre Druillard, an Indian trader and interpreter for the British at Detroit, induced the reluctant Shawnee for a price to hand Kenton over to be questioned. In time the Kentuckian recovered and with the assistance of American sympathizers at the British post escaped in the company of Jesse Coffer and Nathaniel Bullock.

Simon Kenton in real life seems to have possessed those qualities—generosity, strength, cunning, bravery, and even ferocity—which anciently raised warriors to the skies. Far from dreading the formidable Ohio savages, he deliberately courted their hostility by scalping their fallen slain and stealing their horses. In contrast to Boone, this tall, big-boned frontiersman from all accounts took uncommon pleasure in Indian fighting. On the other hand, he regarded hunting as a chore. Like Beowulf he was a lazy youth; unlike Beowulf he was a lazy adult, once remarking that he had never done a full day's labor. As a warrior, however, he shone more brightly than any other defending the settlements. When occasion demanded, he plunged fearlessly into the Indian country above the Ohio, for days skulking about Shawnee and Delaware villages, eating as opportunity permitted, and in the end returning to Kentucky with valuable information and Indian horses besides. When a party with supplies for the troops at Fort Washington was attacked between Lexington and Limestone and the leader James Livingston borne off, Kenton raised a force immediately and set out in pursuit of the Indians. Half a day north of the Ohio the savages became aware of the pursuit and broke into three groups to foil the settlers. Examining the separate trails, Kenton rightly judged that Livingston accompanied the middle group. Two miles farther on, this party split, and Kenton again made a correct judgment. The following day the pursuers overtook the fleeing Indians and liberated the captive.[30] For Anthony Wayne's successful campaign against the Indians of the Old Northwest culminating in the Battle of Fallen Timbers (1794), Simon organized a contingent of one hundred able backwoodsmen, who, left much to their own devices, rendered important service by infiltrating enemy territory and spying out the movements of the Indians. The Shawnee made no mistake in placing a high value on this Kentuckian's military prowess; they erred in not killing him out of hand when the opportunity offered.

Far more than most pioneer Kentuckians, Simon invited apotheosis, as he embodied those special traits which heroic societies prize and wrought as impressively as a hero ought. From the year of the first settlement until the elimination of the Indian threat, Kenton continually engaged the Ohio tribes both as an individual and as a member of expeditions, and he achieved unequaled renown as a scout or spy. No other looms so large in McClung's frontier pantheon, although legend has been far kinder to Boone.

Boone and Kenton, though towering heroes in the romantic literature of the frontier, figure insignificantly in formal history. While occasionally acknowledging the contributions of the frontiersmen, Mann Butler, the first substantial Kentucky historian, concentrated upon the political record and major military actions, regarding the forays of the irregulars as more sensational than effective.[31] Butler's position may hardly be assailed, for the handful of really expert scouts cannot be said to have acted a decisive role in the Indian wars. Whether the type of the peerless warrior has ever accomplished single-handedly exploits of transcendent importance to his race cannot really be determined; but whenever competent annalists have reported campaigns, military executives rather than individual warriors have received credit or discredit for the results. A passion for frontline leadership has sometimes seized modern generals like George S. Patton, who apparently achieved a degree of success as a swashbuckler; but others—Thomas B.

Hood, George A. Custer, and William F. Dean—have succeeded largely in jeopardizing the safety of their commands, in the end winning fame though not battles. Achilles, it may be recalled, slew Hector and many another Trojan champion, but a wooden horse toppled the lofty towers of Ilium. Nonetheless, people apotheosize fighters, not executives. Though chronicled extensively, Alexander and Caesar have yet less glory than Achilles and Aeneas, not merely for lacking a Homer or a Virgil but more importantly for distinguishing themselves as strategists rather than as invincible warriors.

The popular imagination feeds no more eagerly on the national issues of war than on the careers of military planners and directors. Emotion inevitably leaches out of original provocations, and recollections of even the most fateful battles become progressively dimmer. Little feeling now inheres in the American Revolution, and that little relates to George Washington as eponymous hero. There remains today no burning interest even in the Civil War except among a group of southern partisans, who have invested the conflict with profound spiritual meanings and thus created a provincial mythology of uncommon appeal. None but the specialist clearly perceives the complex issues in the struggle for the Ohio Valley; in the mind of the generality, poor but noble settlers fought bloodthirsty Indians for the possession of land which the Lord somehow intended exclusively for Anglo-Saxons. The names and achievements of the numerous colonels, captains, and lieutenants who campaigned with Wayne and Harrison are held in memory mainly by those among their direct descendants with a passion for genealogy. For all his heroic quality and uncommon sacrifices, George Rogers Clark is now only such a memory as hard stone can perpetuate. The injustices of history occur through no evil intent to slight deserving personages; the fault lies with the deep-seated need of humanity for images of epic figures. Whatever the truth about ancient heroes, all have been assimilated to a common pattern— the invincible warrior against a multitude of the wicked. Of the several classes of men who participated in the Kentucky settlement, the frontiersman alone developed a completely heroic character according to ancient prescriptions, and he alone flourished in the cultural stream. Tradition thus supports most movingly in the frontier scene the type of the legendary Kentuckian stalking the wily savage in the primeval garden.

Traditionally, the epic hero, necessarily larger than life, embodies all desirable qualities in full measure. Whatever his historical reality, time transforms him into a symbol mediating between past and present; in the ancient hero, a wish figure and therefore ideal, a race satisfies its longing for power and fame and uninhibited self-expression. Whether today, as Dixon Wecter has argued, Boone and his kind are only "static heroes," lacking the appeal of the Founding Fathers and the greater Presidents,[32] they have nevertheless lodged in the popular imagination and, to judge from the past, ought to endure longer than executives and legislators. The frontiersman needs only a fitting literary memorial to fix him securely in the skies, as Flint recognized long ago: "But although much has been said in prose, and sung in verse, about Daniel Boon, this Achilles of the West wants a Homer, worthily to celebrate his exploits."[33]

No American writer of the nineteenth century had the gifts necessary to translate the frontier type to a large national context and to express through him the spirit of the westward movement. Daniel Bryan attempted to do for Boone what Homer had done for Achilles, but his *Mountain Muse* (1813), a blank-verse epic in seven books, transforms the old hunter into a preposterous Miltonic hero and sets him alongside an improbable romantic plot. Even had Bryan possessed vastly greater powers, he would probably have failed, for epic literature of finished quality seems never to have sprung immediately from heroic situations. Homer stood at a very great distance from the Trojan War, and the *Beowulf* poet, a product of the rich Latin culture of northern England in the seventh and eighth centuries, sang the deeds of continental warriors who lived two hundred years earlier. The rude minstrels of heroic societies have probably always composed celebrative verses soon after important events, and these traditional poems, often altered and elaborated in oral transmission, the perfected artist has sometimes synthesized years later. Epic material of extraordinary richness had accumulated in the Ohio Valley by the third decade of the nineteenth century. A heroic age had come and gone, leaving behind the towering buckskin warrior and a full book of his exploits against the Indians. Already grown a legend and a symbol too, the Kentuckian awaited in vain the transcendent genius who could dramatize his stand against the forces of savagery and eloquently spell out the implications of his way of life.

6 The Playful Savage

"And if a daring foe annoys, / . . . We'll show him that Kentucky boys / Are 'alligator horses.'"
—THE HUNTERS OF KENTUCKY

EPIC WARRIORS become totally admirable only after time has painted over the blemishes in their portraits. Though doubtless fascinating even at close range, the Kentuckian gave cause for offense in many things. If from one angle of vision a hero in buckskin opposing the common enemy, he was from another an utter terror and by his own admission "half horse, half alligator." In the latter role the Kentuckian is to be discovered chiefly in the tales and sketches of travelers and journalists,[1] seldom in novels. Responsible romancers had little use for a character who by word and deed set law at nought and threatened to shatter the social and political foundations of the state. Barbarously comical although not a buffoon, the alligator-horse was by the long view a sinister figure, embodying brute force and animal cunning—a symbol in fact of murderous and lustful anarchy. As drawn by fanciful humorists, he obviously stood at some distance from reality; but society nevertheless recognized him as a familiar disturber of the peace. Flint acknowledged the existence of the alligator-horse strain in the real Kentuckian, though without indicating its implications for civilization: "Accustomed to see the steamboat with its prodigious and untiring power, breasting the heavy current of the Mississippi, the Kentuckian draws his ideas of power from this source; and when the warmth of whiskey in his stomach is added to his natural energy, he becomes in succession, horse, alligator, and steam-boat."[2] This statement explains nothing, nor was meant to. While somewhat blinded to the horrific reality of the frontier by the garden myth, Flint, as every other preacher with firsthand experience, well knew the disruptive effect of the alligator-horse, who in obeying simple impulse by his own preference and by leave of the sentimental primitivists behaved mightily like a predaceous monster of the prime.

The alligator-horse recalls Greek myth and the violent, lascivious centaur, a creature half human and half horse, though his begetting owed nothing to antiquity. American humorists found the essential character, if not the outlandish appearance, on the real frontier and exploited it with great success. Like Emile he had been free to realize his natural quality and had done so, though with unforeseen results. Neither Rousseau nor any other eighteenth-century social philosopher anticipated the rise in the American West of this gross caricature of the noble savage. While amusing enough in the formless, lawless West of the imagination, the alligator-horse yet symbolizes whimsical destructiveness and tends as he is viewed as an approximation of reality to evoke anxiety rather than laughter. Thus, the roaring boy bodied forth with impossible imagery in the *Cincinnati Chronicle*, January 13, 1838, can be contemplated with composure only so long as detached from social and political contexts:

I'm very like a whale, with a little shade of the big elephant, and a slight touch of the wild catamount; I'm a real catastrophe—a small creation, Mount Vesuvius at the top, with red-hot lava pouring out of the crater and routing nations; my eyes are two blast furnaces —tears red-hot melted iron—and every tooth in my head a granite pillar; my feet are Virginia plantations—legs,—branch rail-roads of whalebone—fists, Rocky Mountains—and arms, Whig liberty poles, with cast-steel springs. Every step I take is an earthquake—every blow I strike is a clap of thunder—and every breath I breathe is a tornado: my disposition is Dupont's best, and goes off at a flash;

when I blast, there'll be just nothing left but a hole three feet in circumference and no end to its depth. My gig is a wild-cat, with hoopsnake wheels—my team a tandem of sea-sarpents with rattle-snake reins, and four roaring lions for a body-guard; and I advance and retreat like a hurricane.

Taken at his own Crockett-like estimate, such a being has no more objective reality than a Cyclops; the fancy is clearly his proper sphere. His nominal field of action, remote in space and indefinite as to time, has no apparent connection with the here and now; and his colossal offenses against reason, prob-ability, and humanity, because at wide variance with the norm, excite only laughter, much as the grotesqueries of *Gargantua and Pantagruel.* Conventional judgments on manners and morals are clearly inappropriate in the irrational universe of giants, ogres, and miscellaneous monsters. When, however, the giant follows Jack into the rational world at the foot of the beanstalk, he appears in an entirely different perspective, no longer a droll creature of fiction but a present menace to law and order. While in the latter view less awesome than his self-portrait suggests, the roarer of the American West had yet means to inspire terror. Captain Levinge, though titillated by the rumor of Kentucky barbarism and eager to collect horrific yarns, yet recoiled in alarm from the spectacle of the living and breathing alligator-horse on a voyage from Buffalo to Cleveland: "There were a number of Kentucky men on board; they were dressed in blanket coats of green, crimson, and all colours. They were perched up on one of the paddle-boxes, eating cabbage swimming in vinegar, lumps of which they were thrusting down their capacious throats with their bowie-knives, assisted by an occasional shove from their huge fore-fingers, cursing and swearing between each mouthful. They had a number of tumblers of gin-sling, cocktail, & c., before them, the effects of which were soon apparent in a general row; till the conductor of the boat was obliged to interfere. We were rejoiced to land in Ohio, and get clear of such accumulated horrors."[3] Levinge's easy escape was not possible to western society, which constantly faced the problem of keeping this anarchic element under control and only partially succeeded.

Kentucky during the frontier period was a favorable, if not a perfect, milieu for the natural man, as the restraints on conduct were negligible. Whatever the formative influences on the "half horse, half alligator," civilization cannot be reckoned as important among them. While the arts and sciences illuminated the central Bluegrass, only the "light of reason," which the Enlightenment made accessible to men of all conditions, shone in the surrounding wilderness; and the backwoods folk were in no way corrupted by the luxurious mode of the aristocracy. Their innate virtue notwithstanding, noble savages on the prod performed spectacular feats of violence and established a tradition of barbarism. Travelers generally assumed responsibility for perpetuating the notorious, if colorful, conception of Kentucky, reporting fact and fabrication indiscriminately. Less tolerant than most, Faux confessed to only unfavorable impressions of the inhabitants and by his own admission crossed over the Ohio to Indiana with considerable relief: "At sun-rise I left Louisville . . . well pleased to turn my back on all the spitting, gouging, dirking, duelling, swearing, and staring, of old Kentucky."[4] Not to be outdone by earlier visitors to the Garden of the West, Levinge rode his imagination without saddle or bridle. Yet he described the inhabitants with a fine sense of their dramatic quality and usually with a sense of humor lacking in Faux: "They all carry knives, generally *Arkansas toothpicks*. The blades, being longer than the handles, allow only three parts to be shut; over the point a scabbard is carried, which, when in expectation of a row, they take off, and begin picking their teeth with the point, preparatory to opening the full length of the blade, which is only resorted to should the row become a general one."[5] While obviously fascinated by the handsome Kentuckians and truly appreciative of their elan and mastery of weapons, Levinge was no less convinced than others that these people were something less

than civilized. At the same time he was less concerned with
the simple truth, which was grim enough, than with the colorful libels. Yet the portrait of the wild Kentucky roarer which
emerges from the fabrications of Levinge and others is not
inconsistent with a heroic age.

While willing to fight fair or rough and tumble, the alligator-
horses, to judge from sketches and tall tales, much preferred
the latter and more grotesque exercise, which indeed produced
results nothing short of devastating. Inasmuch as neither claws
nor fangs were barred, no contestant could rightly expect to
emerge unscathed; it is to the credit of the Kentuckians that
they cheerfully accepted their losses and took satisfaction in
whatever trophies fate granted them. Adlard Welby recalled
the story of a badly mutilated Kentuckian, who rejected all
sympathy and triumphantly exhibited an eye scooped from
the head of his opponent.[6] Charles Sealsfield learned on his
trip down the Mississippi that Battle Island at the mouth of
Wolf River just below Chickasaw Bluffs took its name from
a rough-and-tumble fight between two Kentuckians. According to report, a certain captain obligingly held his boat at the
island while the antagonists stepped ashore and locked in
martial congress for half an hour, at the end of which period
both were ready to resume the voyage—one without nose, the
other without eyes.[7]

It is needful to remark as a foreword to a truly horrendous
instance that rough-and-tumble play was quite familiar to the
backwoods of Virginia long before the Kentucky settlement;
and it is to be suspected that the Scotch-Irish in Ulster and
in the Lowlands earlier used comparable tactics. There is,
interestingly enough, classical precedent in the *Metamorphoses,* a work scarcely more extravagant than the Kentucky
yarns. At the marriage of Pirithoüs and Hippodamia, according to Ovid, a drunken centaur, Eurytus, seized lecherously
upon the bride, thereby precipitating a great brawl between
the Centauri and the Lapithae in which the devices of the
alligator-horses were employed. The fanciful Roman poet

would have relished the account of a Kentucky free-for-all growing out of a shooting match staged to determine which of several alligator-horses should have the pleasure of debauching himself with a gallon of whisky. While all participants seem to have behaved like beasts of prey, the narrator, one Billy Hardyarn, and a no less improbable character called Arthur Leven-ribs apparently performed most spectacularly, and they were assuredly engaged longest in the melee:

We commenced fighting about ten o'clock in the morning, and fit like all wrath till sun-down. I begun to get awful tired, and was afraid that if Leven-ribs didn't soon gin in, that I must; and while I was thinking what I had best do, my old woman, who had heard what was a goin' on, come a tearin, and as soon as she got within hollerin distance, she begun: "*Hooraw, my Bill!*" As soon as I heard her, I knew that if I got whipped, she would think she had just cause and provocation to leave my bed and board, as the sayin' is. So, I made up my mind to whip that fellow, or die, right thar. So, I gathered all the little strength I had, and I socked my thumb in his eye, and with my fingers took a twist on his *snot-box,* and with the other hand, I grabbed him by the back of the head; I then caught his ear in my mouth, gin his head a flirt, and *out come his ear by the roots!* I then flapped his head over, and caught his other ear in my mouth, and jerked that out in the same way, and it made a hole in his head that I could have rammed my fist through, and I was just a goin' to do it, when he hollered: "Nuff!" My old woman then jumped up on a stump, and hollered out: "If any feller in this here crowd says that ain't Bill Hardyarn's whiskey, jest let him trot his wife out, and I'll use her a darned sight wuss than my old man has done Arth Leven-ribs, and if he's got no wife, I'll pull him through!" But none of 'em dared to take er up, and after comparing notes a while, every fellow started for home, thinking he had seen a fight as was a fight.

Billy admitted to having lost all of his hair in the fight; how others fared can be judged from his assertion that on the following day a two-bushel basket was filled with ears, noses, and eyes at the scene of the battle royal.[8]

Sensible of the spreading fame of the "half horse, half alligator," civilized Kentuckians abroad in the ante bellum period sometimes acted, or threatened to act, as expected and accordingly received the trembling respect due warriors of an invincible and unpredictable kind. At a Washington Birthday dinner in a Havana tavern, a sterling son of "Old Kaintuck" represented himself to a credulous Englishman as a consummate exemplar of barbarism. It is not extravagant to assert from his relation that he would have proved a fit companion for Rabelais' peerless Friar John of the Funnels and Gobbets, who set upon an entire army with a sorb-apple staff and accomplished ingenious and revolting offenses against flesh and bone. Having one eye light blue and the other dark hazel and a small wart on the bridge of the nose near the corner of the right eye, the Kentuckian presented a sinister appearance indeed. Feeling his whisky, he determined to play upon the Englishman's obvious anxiety and turning to an acquaintance at the table remarked having seen that day a man with whom he much desired to continue an old quarrel.

"Perhaps you don't know all the circumstances of that fight," said the other, drawing himself up, rather proudly. "The way it began, you see, was rather queer. That man's cattle used to get into dad's pasture, and one day I caught"—

. . . .

"One day I caught a favorite Durham short-horned bull, cut off its tail and right fore-leg, tarred and feathered it, and sent it home, in all its glory."

The eyes of the Englishman were fixed upon the narrator with a glassy stare. The Kentuckian continued his tale.

"There were three brothers of them; two came to me the next day to give me a flogging. I killed one, by throwing him three rods over a stone-wall with a pitch-fork. The other run and jumped into a horse-pound, where I pelted him to death with squashes. The jury acquitted me, on the ground that I had merely acted in self-defence. A few days after, the third brother—the one now in Havana—and myself, went out a-training, and fought until we were completely tuckered out. When we got thro' we compared notes. He had got my right eye, and I had chewed off both of his ears, and we made an even swap; that was the way I got my eye back. A celebrated eye-doctor came along a day or two after, and fastened my eye into my head again. Do you see that?" (pointing to the black wart in the corner of his eye) "that is the head of the screw by which he fastened the eye to my nose, in order to hold it!"

The Englishman could stand no more and hastily left the tavern, but he was not to escape so easily. The Kentuckian raised the war whoop and pursued him for a considerable distance down the street.[9]

Although famed as a warrior from the time of the first settlements, the Kentuckian evolved into a roaring, bucking, comical anarch only after the commencement of extensive river trade. When the Indian menace abated about 1790, backwoodsmen of the roughest and most venturesome sort took to the keelboats, the operation of which required greater strength and endurance than men have often been compelled to display. Possessed of a gross sense of humor and a sublime contempt for danger, they both amused and abused the inhabitants of river towns from Pittsburgh to New Orleans for four or five decades. It is quite true as V. L. O. Chittick argues, that the "ring-tailed roarers" came into prominence at many points on the inland waterways,[10] but to judge from the anecdotal literature they were associated in the popular imagination with Kentucky. Legend located some of the escapades of Mike Fink, the greatest keelboatman of them all, in Kentucky, and Emerson Bennett intimated this connection in the novel *Mike Fink* (1848), probably to enrich his hero's credentials: "I'm nobody less nor Mike Fink, at your sarvice; half land, half sea dog, with a touch o' the Kaintuck war-horse, the snapping turkle, and Massassip alligator" (ch. 1). As previously suggested, a Kentucky origin increased the stature, though not the reputation for gentility, of both real and fictitious heroes.

From his tour of 1807-1808, Schultz reported that on the lower Mississippi the inhabitants of the Ohio Valley were indiscriminately called *Kentuckians*—with no compliment intended.[11] The connotation of the term *Kentuckian* in ante bellum Louisiana can be fairly judged from Sealsfield's report that the Kentuckians eagerly accepted and flagrantly abused the hospitality of the gracious Creole planters, first drinking themselves to a roaring pitch on the rum and brandy served by their hosts and then through enacting the role of the "half horse, half alligator" creating an unspeakable impression: "These people are the horror of all creoles, who when they wish to describe the highest degree of barbarity, designate it by the name of Kentuckian."[12] Unlike the Goths who cascaded upon the Campagna di Roma in the twilight of the Empire, the boatmen proposed to trade rather than to loot, but like the Goths they were filled with the sudden passion and intolerable arrogance of men forged and filed according to the harsh specifications of a heroic society. The genteel Latins of the Delta country were grateful indeed for the cargoes of tobacco, hemp, flour, and livestock which floated out of the north on the spring rise, but their pleasure was much abated by the antics of the handlers of the boats. From his tour of 1818-1820, James Flint arrived at what appears to have been the usual estimate of the boatmen: "I have seen nothing in human form so profligate as they are. Accomplished in depravity, their habits and education seem to comprehend every vice. They make few pretensions to moral character; and their swearing is excessive, and perfectly disgusting. Although earning good wages, they are in the most abject poverty; many of them being without any thing like clean or comfortable clothing. I have seen several whose trousers formed the whole of their wardrobe, and whose bodies were scorched to a brown colour by the rays of the sun."[13]

Natchez-under-the-Hill provided the first relief from the desperate circumstances of a voyage down the Mississippi, and in the brothels and gambling dives of this unmentionable cellar of the aristocratic old cotton town, boatmen forgot the miserable food and the back-breaking labor of the past weeks. Their play was no less strenuous than their employment.

Schultz recorded a colorful dispute which he overheard one night in Natchez between two boatmen, each having much the same carnal designs on a Choctaw damsel:

One said, "I am a man; I am a horse; I am a team. I can whip any man *in all Kentucky,* by G—d." The other replied, "I am an alligator; half man, half horse; can whip any *on the Mississippi* by G—d." The first one again, "I am a man; have the best horse, best dog, best gun, and the handsomest wife in all Kentucky, by G—d." The other, "I am a Mississippi snapping turtle: have bear's claws, alligator's teeth, and the devil's tail; can whip *any man,* by G—d." This was too much for the first, and at it they went like two bulls, and continued for half an hour, when the alligator was fairly vanquished by the horse.[14]

Between Natchez and New Orleans the boatmen floated into a world largely foreign to their experience. Nothing in the Ohio Valley prepared them for the topography, the atmosphere, or the culture of the Latin kingdom spread along the lower Delta—a low-lying, fertile, and slightly fetid land of miasmic cypress swamps strung with ghastly Spanish moss and populated with alligators and cottonmouths, mosquitoes and scorpions, panthers and wildcats; a land of vast cotton plantations tilled by aboriginals dug out of the heart of the Dark Continent and ruled by a polished and decadent aristocracy faithful to the traditions of the *ancien régime.* By the time their boats touched the foot of Canal Street, the alligator-horses were completely intoxicated with the lush paradise, and they strode across the levee full of ardent spirits and reckless curiosity.

For the French, the boatmen represented the barbarian menace descended upon them out of the wilderness, although with commodities of great price. Yet the Vieux Carré had means to exhaust the energies even of barbarians, and, if not, Recorder Joshua Baldwin's court stood ready to administer appropriate chastisement. Then as now, however, New Orleans took a Continental view of sin and generally allowed guests to mingle freely in the bistros with ingenious trollops and beady-eyed gamblers. Henry Bradshaw Fearon testified to the relative freedom of these noble savages: "It is said, that when the Kentuckians arrive at this place, they are in their glory, finding neither limit to, nor punishment of their excesses."[15] A passage in Winston Churchill's *Crossing* between a porter at the Convent of the Ursulines and one of the minor characters of the novel accurately represents the feeling of the French population toward the Kentuckians. Nick Temple, in company with Davy Trimble, jestingly offers a bribe to the porter to let the two of them enter the virginal precincts after dark, whereupon they are deluged with a stream of Gallic curses and decisively repulsed: "*Bon Dieu!* . . . you are Kentuckians, yes? I might have known that you were Kentuckians, and I shall advise the good sisters to put glass on the wall and keep a watch" (ch. 11). The reputation of the Kentuckians in New Orleans considered, it can only be regarded as unfortunate that an exceedingly courteous gesture by one of them should have produced an untoward result: "A first rate 'Mississippi snag' from Kentucky, meeting a powdered French dandy in the streets of New Orleans, on horse back, as he passed the equestrian Monsieur near a puddle, the boatman made a sweeping bow, pulling off his hat at the same time, and giving it a low swing, at which the mettled steed, not fancying such grace, took fright and left the Monsieur to make a pedestrian retreat out of the mire. With a national characteristic of his urbane country, he returned the salute, but could not refrain from exclaiming, 'saire, you are a little too d——nd polite, saire.'"[16] The Frenchman's rueful observation contains a profound truth, for the Kentuckians characteristically erred on the side of excess, whether in courtesy or violence.

Observers mindful of conventional social values found little in the boatmen to admire; humorists nonetheless exploited the rumor of their ferocious brawling with uncommon success. Whether admired or deplored, the alligator-horses met the challenge of their hazardous calling so recklessly and exuberantly as to attract the attention even of Europe.[17] The special quality of these men owed a good deal to the terrible conditions of river transport, although they were eminently suited by breeding and upbringing for the hard life of the waterways. As L. D. Baldwin maintains, the keelboatmen were toughened frontiersmen and many of the early ones Indian fighters as well.[18] On the rivers they caught the attention of the public, though perhaps disclosing no excess of mischievousness or bestiality not wholly familiar to the backwoods. This is not to say that the circumstances of river trade were less arduous than generally supposed. No man with experience of the comforts of civilization could have brought himself to contend with mere bone and muscle against the inexorable rush of water through the treacherous Mississippi system.

Much the worst of the work fell to the keelboatmen and bargemen, for they had not only to manage their heavy vessels on the downstream trip to New Orleans but also to pole and pull them back to their points of origin on the tributaries of the Ohio and Missouri. When running with the current, the boats required little attention for long stretches, but there were nevertheless moments of great distress, as Timothy Flint observed: "The descent, if in autumn, has probably occupied fifty days. Until the boatmen had passed the mouth of the Ohio, they must have been in some sense amphibious animals, continually getting into the water, to work their boat off from shoals and sandbars. The remainder of the descent was amidst all the dangers of sawyers, sandbars, snags, storms, points of islands, wreck heaps, difficulty and danger of landing, and a great many anomalous dangers. The whole voyage is a scene of anxiety, exposure and labor."[19] It was no mean task to control a keelboat loaded with from twenty to thirty tons or an even heavier barge, particularly in swift water; only the cunning of the patroon and the sheer strength of the crew preserved the cargo from a multitude of more or less concealed hazards. To judge from Mark Twain's *Life on the Mississippi*, there were difficulties enough for steamboats, which, of course, had power to break the hold of the current. Their cargoes unloaded in New Orleans, manufactured goods taken on, and themselves satiated with wenching, drinking, and brawling, the crews had then to reflect on the return trip—a thousand miles against the current at a mile an hour, fifteen miles a day. While sails occasionally lightened the work, keelboats and barges were moved in the main by poles and cordelles. When the water was too deep or the current too swift for poling, there was no alternative to hauling a boat forward at the end of a long rope, no matter what trees, underbrush, rocks, and other obstacles cluttered the shoreline. More arduous work than cordelling can scarcely be imagined. The circumstances of upstream travel considered, it is not surprising that keelboats required crews of ten or more and barges between forty and fifty—and those of the hardiest. To Marryat is owing a brief but uncommonly graphic description of the incredible conditions under which the alligator-horses lived: "After a hard day's push they would take their 'fillee,' or ration of whisky, and having swallowed a miserable supper of meat half burnt, and of bread half baked, stretch themselves, without covering, on the deck, and slumber till the steerman's call invited them to the morning 'fillee.' "[20]

Much the greater part of the upcountry produce moved to market in flatboats, or, in western parlance, "broadhorns." By contrast with the keelboats and barges, these crude, unwieldy vessels—fifteen feet wide and forty to a hundred feet long—were intended only for downstream transportation, being broken up and sold as lumber at their destinations. The crews returned home on foot or horseback over the Natchez Trace, which in consequence of a heavy infestation of highwaymen was no less perilous than the river. In time, the steamboats provided an easier and decidedly safer means of return for the flatboatmen, though insufficient protection from professional gamblers. Steam came increasingly to dominate the Mississippi and Ohio, but the flatboats, because economical, continued in use well into the 1840's. Moreover, the keelboats, for having

120 The Frontier Mind

a shallow draft, operated profitably in small streams closed to steamboats. Some indication of the traffic can be gathered from Flint's report of observing between two and three hundred descending craft, mostly keelboats and "flats," on a trip from Pittsburgh to Natchez in the fall of 1826.[21] The importance of the river trade to the Ohio Valley can scarcely be exaggerated; while perhaps only ginseng was worth the carriage across the mountains to the eastern markets, the surplus of the major crops found a varyingly satisfactory outlet on the Mississippi.

Manual transport during the ante bellum period used men up with distressing rapidity; yet life expectancy was low under any circumstances, and there were obvious compensations for the boatmen, though in high adventure rather than wealth. To survive in the boat trade was to flourish. Where all endure relatively equal stress, there is no middle ground between success and failure. Accordingly, proven boatmen knew themselves a superior sort and wore their distinction with understandable pride. Filled with a strong sense of their uncommon strength, stamina, cunning, and ferocity, these men by demeanor and gesture intimated a challenge to all. They fought out of lust for battle and also to win the esteem of their fellows. Evolved in a world ruled by force, these frontier amphibians displayed courage and daring as casually as civilized men acted the part of courtesy. The elemental world about, crowded with forces hostile to mortal existence, constantly tested their manhood. Under the circumstances, survival was tantamount to triumph, and the alligator-horses no more than the conqueror of Grendel could forbear proclaiming their ineffable quality. Whether from the influence of wide spaces and colossal natural phenomena or from a native gift for language, they commanded idiom and metaphor adequate to describe their accomplishments and potentialities. Beowulf was the soul of modesty by comparison with the ring-tailed roarers, who not only claimed exceptional human endowment but also arrogated to themselves the destructive energy of great natural forces. The life of the river generated a vast legendry, much of it clustered around Mike Fink, the peerless keelboatman, and much of it involving the Kentuckian without more specific identification.

As a social being, the Kentuckian, whether of the river or of the forest, acknowledged no superiors and, despite his profession of republicanism, very few equals outside the ranks of his own kind. Fully informed of the rights and privileges appertaining to the condition of citizenship though only vaguely of the obligations, he asserted his own essential worth in the face of the gentry and demanded to be heard. It ought to be remarked that the Kentuckian in whatever role—epic hero, agent of progress, noble savage, or alligator-horse—displays nothing of Leatherstocking's servility in the presence of genteel personages. Even the romancers, whose preconceptions were normally upper class like Cooper's, usually honored the tradition of Kentucky independence and equalitarianism and refrained from placing the frontier heroes in servile postures. William Alexander Caruthers used Montgomery Damon for comic effects in *The Kentuckian in New-York* without, however, despoiling him of his dignity. Though not completely sympathetic toward the backwoods, this Virginia author paid due respect to Damon as the type of the sturdy yeoman: "Our Kentuckian was no quiet man; but, like most of his race, bold, talkative, and exceedingly democratic in all his notions; feeling as much pride in his occupation of drover, as if he had been a senator in Congress from his own 'Kentuck,' as he emphatically called it" (ch. 2). To Simon Kenton is attributed a convincing demonstration of the real Kentuckian's extreme sensitivity to degree. McClung's *Sketches of Western Adventure,* though enthroning the old warrior in the frontier pantheon, aroused his indignation from imputing to him undue civility. Asked of the accuracy of McClung's portrait, Simon replied: "Well, I'll tell you . . . not true: the book says that when Blackfish the Ingin warrior asked me, when they had taken me prisoner, if Col. Boone had sent me to steal their horses, that I said 'No sir.' I tell you I never said *sir* to an Ingin in my life: I scarcely ever say it to a white man."[22] This laughable reaction has yet a sad implication, for the pioneers were so determined to allow nothing to rank as such that they tended to deny superior merit altogether and especially if associated with high social position and education.

The hostility of the backwoodsmen toward rank was not deeply rooted in abstract principle, for individually they sought titles even of the meanest sort. A term as magistrate conferred upon the incumbent the permanent title of squire, whether he had broad acres and blooded horses or not. The brief and ineffectual forays of the Kentuckians against the Ohio Indians created captaincies, majorities, and colonelcies, sufficient to staff a modern army. Even after the abatement of the red menace, county militias mustered annually, largely, it is to be suspected, to permit the officers, usually political appointees, to show their quality before the homebreds. While no family in the West can pretend to the kind of distinction recognized by patriotic societies without a sheaf of old commissions, the possession of them is not proof of gentle beginnings; they were available to men of unimpressive background like Daniel Boone and Davy Crockett, colonels both. Indeed, neither occupation nor previous condition seems to have been an insurmountable barrier to a wide variety of titles, as a witty report in the Brandon, Mississippi, *Disseminator,* of February 8, 1845, suggests: "Jacob Klepser of Delpha, Indiana, publishes a notice of the elopement of his wife (the mother of three children,) with one George W. Mazwell, who is a blacksmith by trade, was Col. in the Militia, a Justice of the Peace, a Master Mason in the Masonic Fraternity, and a Class leader in the Methodist church. He has taken his Commission as Colonel and Justice, and a certificate of his good standing in the lodge with him. He has also left a wife and children behind." Where titles of one kind or another come easily, social status necessarily hinges on additional values. Acres, educa-

tion, and descent were of no less account in Kentucky than
military renown, and a high-sounding title alone had small
trade value.

Yet a meaningless Kentucky title enabled one Jack Cole to
play a magnificent role in France, if S. P. Avery is to be
credited. With the appointment to take the 1850 census in
Frankfort, Jack received a commission as marshal, which he
later used at a ball in the Hôtel de Ville in Paris and on other
occasions not merely to claim parity with but actually pre-
cedence over *maréchals de France*. When informed of the
matter, John Young Mason, the American minister, "allowed
that Jack was doing a large business on a very small capital."[23]
Another Kentuckian, with even less capital than Jack Cole,
faced down the captain of a French boat running between
Lyons and Avignon and got for himself service reserved for
nobility. According to the account printed April 3, 1848, in
the *Western Citizen*, this bold son of the Garden of the West,
after having vainly besought the captain to provide him with
dinner, sometime later discovered that worthy in the act of
setting an excellent meal before a "tallow-faced Russian count."
He thereupon stated his own claim to equal treatment as
strongly as truth allowed:

"I thought you had told me that you did not furnish passengers
with dinner?"

"Pardonne, Monsieur, dis be not one eber-body passenger; he
be one grand Russian count."

"And what the hell if he be!" said the Kentuckian, who was as
ardent as western sun could make him; "if he be a *count*, I'm a
Kentuckian; I'd like to know which should rank higher?"

"Pardonne, Monsieur," said the captain, "you be a Kent—what?—
dat be title one noble Anglaise, eh?"

. . . .

"No," said the Kentuckian, bluntly, "that is the title of an American sovereign."

"Ah," said the little French captain, shrugging up his shoulders,
and bowing his head, "ah, excusez, Monsieur—pardon, I did not

know you be one gran nobleman; but now I get you dinner tout suite," and in due time the dinner was brought, to which, with the addition of a bottle of sparkling hock, the young Kentuckian did ample justice.[24]

While often the butts of practical jokes in the humorous literature of the frontier, the French generally fared better than other alien groups exhibiting marked national or sectional differences. There were in the migrant stream numerous Huguenots, who, if less effectual in the wilderness than the English and Scotch-Irish, commanded respect enough. The Westerners jollied the French for their fastidiousness, credulity, and linguistic eccentricities, though usually without any trace of animus. These people doubtless benefited from the fragrant memory of Lafayette and also from the tolerant reports of French travelers, who seem as a group to have appreciated western manners rather more than the British. The Germans, consistently spoken of as Dutch, figure only occasionally in anecdotes and then usually as dupes. It was for the Catholic Irish, even more than for the Yankees, that the West reserved its deepest resources of hostility and contempt; nothing good is spoken of these people either in the newspaper sketches and anecdotes or in the romances. Crèvecoeur thought them least likely to succeed on the frontier because of their love of liquor, propensity to quarrel, and ignorance of farming;[25] whether for these reasons or not, they were indifferent pioneers. Though admittedly comical, the "bog-trotting" folk by common consent deserved precious little respect and received none.

The shrewd, parsimonious, prudential Yankee of legend was hardly the type to appeal to the West, nor the real Yankee, who opposed the War of 1812 and threatened in a fit of petulance to secede from the Union. Moreover, New England peddlers—the "tin wagon, pit-coal-indigo, wooden nutmeg, and wooden clock missionaries"[26]—earned for their section of the country an enduring reputation in the backwoods for flagrant dishonesty. Fordham declared, "A Kentuckian suspects nobody but a Yankee, whom he considers as a sort of Jesuit."[27]

By the second quarter of the nineteenth century and thus well before the Civil War, there had generated in the Ohio Valley strong "damnyankeeism," reflected in tales of trickery, theft, and sudden departure without settlement of accounts. The boatmen played upon the dislike for the Down-Easters by greeting queries from the shore as to their lading with the infuriating reply, "Pit-coal indigo, wooden nutmegs, straw baskets, and Yankee notions."[28] Unluckily for the reputation of Kentucky, Faux encountered this prejudice in crossing the Ohio at Maysville. Taken for Yankees by the boatmen operating the ferry, Faux and his party were forced to pay seventy-five cents per horse, instead of the customary twenty-five, and apparently a dollar for each person. There is no difficulty in reconstructing the amusing incident from the author's sour report: "'We will not,' said the boat-man, 'take you over, for less than a dollar each. We heard of you, yesterday. The gentleman in the cap (meaning me) looks as though he could afford to pay, and besides, he is so slick with his tongue. The Yankees are the smartest of fellows, except the Kentuckyans.' Sauciness and impudence are characteristic of these boat-men, who wished I would commence a bridge over the river."[29] There was no disposition in the West to underrate the Yankees, who, to judge from legendry, consistently demonstrated the superiority of brain over brawn; but there was never any disposition to admire them either.

Western story attributes to the Kentuckians of the "half horse, half alligator" strain a broad sense of humor and a wonderful gift for involving themselves in humorous situations. In real life, moreover, they were quick to perceive the ridiculous and unaccountably patient in enduring a joke, if Fordham judged rightly.[30] Barbarous, intolerant, and arrogant though he was, the Kentuckian following the War of 1812 leaped onto the stage as a comic type beside his mortal enemy Yankee Jonathan, of wooden nutmeg notoriety. Constance Rourke argued stoutly for the ideological kinship of the Yankee and the frontiersman, alleging a common racial and religious back-

ground and a similarity of manner.[31] Both of these comic
figures assuredly came of British stock with a perceptible
Calvinist bias, but these points of resemblance can hardly
smooth over the fundamental differences between the crafty,
enigmatic Down-Easter and the expansive, exuberant alligator-
horse. They were perhaps equally individualistic and equally
determined to dominate their environment, though otherwise
quite different. The Yankee, sprung from thin, ungenerous soil
and reared in an unfriendly climate, images the parsimonious,
mercantile soul of New England. In contrast, the frontiersman
embodies the spirit of the wild, anarchic West; his is a universe
of license and abundance, reckless living and sudden dying.
Whatever his faults, there is nothing prudential or petty in
his character. While sometimes guilty of trickery and gross
insult, he is not disposed to "slope" like Jonathan but characteristically remains to answer for his offenses.

Colonel Nimrod Wildfire, the hero of Paulding's *Lion of the
West* and the preeminent representative of the Kentucky frontier on the ante bellum stage, was known to Miss Rourke only
by report; until the discovery recently of a copy in the British
Museum, the play was thought to be irretrievably lost.[32] When
Paulding wrote this two-act farce is uncertain, but in 1830
it won a prize of three hundred dollars offered by the actor
James H. Hackett for a comedy presenting an American
character in a leading role. Produced the next year in New
York, the *Lion of the West* appears to have been immediately
popular and to have remained so for many years; Hackett was
playing the part of Wildfire as late as 1862. The popularity
of the farce was owing not to its essential dramatic excellence
but to the antics of the colonel, who was regarded as a likeness
of Davy Crockett and assuredly exhibited the most striking
qualities of the alligator-horse Kentuckian. Paulding may have
had some knowledge of the *Pedlar,* a three-act farce written
by Alphonso Wetmore for the St. Louis Thespians and published in 1821. Though incredibly poor, this piece presents
the Yankee peddler and several frontier types in comic roles.

The humor of the Old Southwest, though perhaps not as indigenous as sometimes thought, has a lasting appeal, in contrast to the now insipid matter of the prominent nineteenth-century humorists exclusive of Mark Twain. The appeal, however, is far from universal, as not all can well enter into the spirit of the amoral, chaotic sphere of the alligator-horses, where civilized values count for almost nothing. Indeed, whoever takes delight in the type of the barbarous Kentuckian, or for that matter in the Norse prankster Loki and Rabelais' fabulous creatures, doubtless nourishes an inclination toward an uncircumscribed condition without hindrance to the expression of impulses of every elemental kind. This state of affairs revolts individuals of delicate sensibility, and admittedly the rights and persons of the meek and the gullible suffer outrageously from the antics of boisterous anarchs like Davy Crockett, Mike Fink, and the Salt River roarers. Ethical justification is obviously not to be sought for their behavior, as they stand quite above or beyond the law. Yet the civilized imagination is to a considerable extent accountable for the playful savages caught up in western humor, for their creation appears to owe quite as much to the dark, irrational content of the metropolitan unconscious as to the physical frontier; psychologically, they image man's rebellious self gleefully setting aside the whole structure of convention by which society lives. While the real frontiersmen largely sloughed off the trammels of civilization and abandoned themselves to a life of maximum liberty, it does not follow that they originated any large number of the stories representing them. If, as seems altogether probable, the best of western humor is new wine in old bottles, that is, Old World motifs adapted to the American scene, it reflects the urban as well as the frontier mind. Consideration of this vexed question may well be deferred, but it is pertinent to observe here that ante bellum newspapers served up the portrait of the barbarous frontiersman for the enjoyment of an educated and ostensibly refined public.

Like comic creations of all times and places, the Kentuckian provokes mirth by departing egregiously from the norm; unlike many others, however, he misses the mark very often out of plain intent and thus implies contempt for standards binding on the generality of mankind. He is clearly not only an object of detached amusement like the classic comedian but also a wish figure embodying anarchic tendencies. While often involved in ridiculous situations, he is seldom himself the object of ridicule, normally proving superior to circumstances in consequence of sheer power, supreme audacity, or animal cunning. A Kentuckian debarking from the *Harry of the West* with plunder in one hand and five dollars in specie in the other had the misfortune to tumble off the gangplank into the Mississippi but recovered his peculiar dignity as soon as he could swim ashore. Having lost three of his dollars and suffered a thorough wetting, this alligator-horse was fully aroused, the more so because the passengers had witnessed his discomfiture. Throwing himself into a belligerent posture, he reviewed his experience and then issued a brazen challenge to the boat: "I've got five dollars in this here bundle, two dollars in my hand—have just been ducked—stand five feet ten in my stocking feet—tolerably stout for my age—rayther mad—and dog my cats ef I can't flog any man on that boat, far fist-fight or rough and tumble! Who'll say yes? Whoop! whoop! hurra for old Kentuck!"[33] Similarly, admiration as well as amusement is excited by the portrait of a "half horse, half alligator" who upon viewing a circus for the first time offered to bet the owner that he could whip his lion together with all his monkeys, while a zebra kicked him now and then.[34] Taking life as a series of challenges, the roarers had constantly to test their manhood. While to fail was sometimes to "go under," the thought of success and heightened reputation spurred them on against formidable obstacles.

Ever mindful of his dignity, the Kentuckian endured repulse and discomfiture with the greatest distaste. It is not surprising that he somehow rose to most occasions, though seldom in a socially creditable way. Levinge records the story of an alligator-horse who conceived a violent passion for a strange beauty at a party but upon being refused a dance exerted himself to find an offensive rejoinder: " 'By Jams! that gal's worth spoons, so I guess I'll dance with her.' On the conclusion of the set, the *gentleman's* self-introduction ran as follows;—'Miss, will you dance with *me?*' On the young lady's declining, he exclaimed, 'Well, you're not so handsome but what you *might;* and if you have got a friend or a brother in the room, I'll whip him, by ——!' "[35]

A flatboatman had deposited his goods in New Orleans and returned home with a check for $8,000 on a Lexington bank. Having taken no pains after the long journey to repair the damage to his clothing and person, he understandably aroused the suspicion of the cashier of whom he requested payment. The prudent banker questioned the rough boatman, who answered, however, as impudently as needful to indicate his contempt for the other's distrust: " 'My friend where did you come from?' To which he replied, in a surly manner, 'I came from the moon.' 'You came from the moon, did you?' says the cashier, 'pray, how did you get down?' 'Why,' answered he, 'I slid down on a rainbow.' "[36]

The Lexington banker was not the last to cause himself embarrassment by judging an alligator-horse's financial condition from his appearance. The red jeans and rough manner of a tall, gaunt Kentuckian who one day strode into an Ohio bank were a poor index to his wealth, as the teller soon learned. He asked to exchange some notes issued by Ohio banks for the equivalent in Kentucky money. The teller, thinking the Kentuckian had only a few dollars, replied patronizingly that he had nothing smaller than notes of $500 denomination, whereupon his uncouth customer, who had just sold a drove of hogs for $15,000, took his entire supply, consisting of twelve or fifteen notes, and to the other's further discomfiture demanded more.[37]

As an anarch of a particularly obstreperous kind, the Kentuckian could not well be expected to mingle with his fellows in cheerful amity. In the terms of social psychology a poorly integrated personality, he was on occasion as blunt as a sledge hammer, as cutting as a meat cleaver, and as impudent as a crow in a corn patch. Moreover, retaliation on his tanned hide was not to be thought on by the meek in spirit. An innocent Cockney by the name of Sniggens sat down to dinner on board a Mississippi steamboat expecting no untoward event, least of all in consequence of the calm person across the table, who, however, happened to be an unusually forthright "Red River Kentuckian."

"Stranger, I don't want to hurt your feelings, but you are the ugliest man that was ever turned out of the workshop of creation!" a salutation which he concluded by a thump on the table that set the dishes and cutlery in commotion.

"Sir-r-r!" sputtered the gentleman in wrath and confusion, "if you mean to insult me—."

"By no means," quoth the son of Red River, with a gracious nod; "but the thing was on my mind, and I couldn't help telling you so."

Somewhat mollified, Sniggens took the prudent view that the Kentuckian's rudeness was owing to the American addiction to bantering.[38] Another Kentuckian, by his spectacular—indeed, asinine—rudeness to one of his neighbors in the Ohio Valley, amused the passengers on a Mississippi boat and gained their everlasting gratitude as well. A Hoosier from the Wabash had taken passage on the *Indiana* for New Orleans. Fancying himself no mean fiddler, he played constantly, much to the annoyance of his captive audience. All efforts to induce this backwoods virtuoso to discontinue his concert proved unavailing until a strapping Kentuckian seated himself by his side and commenced braying like an ass. This maneuver forced the fiddler into retreat, to the vast relief of the passengers. Unfortunately, the Kentuckian debarked during the night, and the next morning the Hoosier proceeded to take his revenge. At the first screeching of the fiddle, a Frenchman of delicate ear shouted desperately: "Vare is he? Queeck! Queeck! Mon

Dieu! Vare is Monsieur Kentuck, de man vat play on de jackass?"[39]

A Dutch innkeeper of Pennsylvania had reason to be thankful that a provoked guest from Kentucky assailed him with gross wit rather than with his fists. Having suffered outrageously from bedbugs during the night, the Kentuckian determined to score a point on his host; and when the time came for settling up, he loudly demanded the price of beef.

"De price of beef!" responded the half frightened and half wonder struck tavern keeper.

"Yes, what is beef a pound in your village!"

"Why tish, let me see—tish six pence de pound."

"Here then," said the Kentuckian, "take that"—at the same time throwing down on the counter a silver dollar.

"Dat! and vat ish dat for, Mynheer sixfooter?"

"Half of it is for my bed and board—and half to purchase beef!"

"Beef for vat?"

"For the d——n hungry bugs in your beds—they came nigh eating me up alive—look here—and—here"—said he, at the same time showing the bites and marks of blood on his face, arms and legs.

"Do you mean to insinuate that my beds are buggy?" said the landlord, stepping around in a great passion.

"Buggy! to be sure I do—and that you are but one door off from being a murderer—had it been a thin consumptive fellow that had slept where I did last night, instead of me, he would have been a dead man before morning—and to guard against such a catastrophe, I make a present to you of that money—buy beef with it, and feed your bugs every night before putting any body in your beds."[40]

Inexperience sometimes led Kentuckians into spectacular errors of judgment, but even on those occasions they proved as frightening as laughable. Doubtless willing to abide a joke, they were dangerously inclined to fall back on force when involved in a confusing situation. A piece attributed to the St. Louis *Pennant* fairly estimates their quality: "In fighting they are equal to Hercules—for fun, the rivals of Momus—for the *oddity* of their blunders up to an *Irishman* in his *best days*." The writer supported his generalization by relating an anecdote concerning a party of nine alligator-horse Kentuckians on a tour of St. Louis. Their leader, one Isaac, who controlled the exchequer, had some experience of the town, though, as subsequent events proved, by no means enough. He decided to stand his robust friends to a dinner in a fine tavern, the like of which none of them had ever seen. At Isaac's insistence, they drank bottle after bottle of wine and devoured, in addition to the main course, cheese, oranges, raisins, and finally oyster pie. Isaac called for the bill. The waiter, thinking they were not yet finished, handed him the bill of fare. Though innocent of French, he could read the prices well enough and, under the impression that all the amounts indicated were owed by his company, proceeded to add the columns of figures. Since wine alone totaled four hundred eight dollars, Isaac and his companions decided to fight out the whole. The Kentuckians confronted the barkeeper, who, seeing the joke, kept them in suspense for a time. When there was some danger of his being beaten, he explained to Isaac that a bill of fare was not a "fair bill," which in this instance came to only twenty-five dollars.[41]

A group of Kentuckians gathered in 1838 to see the play *William Tell, the Heroic Swiss* performed by a traveling theatrical company showed themselves disconcertingly unfamiliar with dramatic illusion. All went well until the climax, when the evil viceroy Gessler chose an exceedingly small apple for Tell to shoot from the head of his son. The spectacle of the hapless father pleading for a somewhat larger apple that the test might not be utterly impossible was more than the Kentuckians could stand. Several leaped upon the stage, one confronting Gessler and exclaiming: "Give him a fair chance! I vow to snakes it's too mean to make him shoot his son! 'spose I let him shoot one of my niggers; or if that won't do, I'll let him have a crack at me, provided he puts a pint cup on my head instead of that cursed little apple."[42]

Western humor, it may be allowed, generally supports the previous assertion that the alligator-horse though comical is in no sense a buffoon. To laugh at him is in some degree to envy his freedom from restraint and his utter self-sufficiency. Accordingly, the portrait of the Kentuckian as a cockalorum, bodied forth most fully in Bird's *Nick of the Woods,* arouses suspicion. Where this author found the likeness of Roaring Ralph Stackpole is unclear. Albert Keiser has stated that Bird, who twice visited Kentucky before writing his novel, drew the character in part from real life; but C. B. Williams thinks that Mike Fink was the model.[43] Some credit is surely due Cooper, for in the *Prairie* he displayed the Kentucky bee hunter Paul Hover in one of the absurd postures affected by Stackpole: "The first act of Paul Hover, on finding himself the master of Ishmael's citadel, had been to sound the note of victory, after the quaint and ludicrous manner that is so often practised among the borderers of the West. Flapping his sides with his hands, as the conquering game-cock is wont to do with his wings, he raised a loud and laughable imitation of the exultation of this bird" (ch. 16).[44] Such foolishness as this is completely out of keeping with Paul's character, though not with Ralph's. Whatever his motive, Bird made Stackpole as absurd as he made his Indians hateful: "He was a stout, bandy-legged, broad-shouldered, and bull-headed tatterdemalion, ugly, mean, and villainous of look; yet with an impudent, swaggering, joyous self-esteem traced in every feature and expressed in every action of body, that rather disposed the beholder to laugh than to be displeased at his appearance" (ch. 3). As if simian features were not degradation enough, Bird dressed Stackpole like a scarecrow and called him a horsethief. He attributed to him a certain renown as a fighter, though actually endowing the bloody Quaker Nathan Slaughter with much greater might. Ralph describes himself as a "ring-tailed squealer" from Salt River, but none of those roarers ever had so little dignity or ever prepared for battle with so much inane posturing: "He flapped his wings and crowed, until every chanticleer in the settlement replied to the note of battle; he snorted and neighed like a horse; he bellowed like a bull;

he barked like a dog; he yelled like an Indian; he whined like a panther; he howled like a wolf; until one would have thought he was a living menagerie" (ch. 3). There is nothing of frontier realism in this portrait and nothing of the legendary Kentuckian either. Far from existing in real life, Ralph Stackpole gives every indication of belonging to the company of the braggart soldiers with Plautus' Pyrgopolynices and Shakespeare's Falstaff. Although not permitted by Bird to engage in foolish wooing like most of his kind, he appears nonetheless to be the classical military dupe disguised as a backwoodsman. Later novelists borrowed many things from *Nick of the Woods*, one of the earlier and better Kentucky romances, but not Ralph Stackpole.

To tax Bird with violating the dignity of the Kentuckian is not at all to imply that the figure represented in ante bellum newspapers is wholly true to life. While it may be readily granted that many a Kentuckian was in fact formidable and —at a distance—barbarously comical, the reality at most only generally supported the fabrication. Some of the humorous matter lodged in the newspapers doubtless originated in the wilderness, but many of the anecdotes and tall tales involving the alligator-horse are traditional narrative structures cleverly translated to the frontier. Suspicion falls hard on American journalism inasmuch as a large percentage of frontier stories, to judge from the attributions, actually appeared first in the East. While it can never be proved that this matter was not drawn out of oral tradition, to argue that backwoods folk refitted Old World motifs in accordance with circumstances in the West is to endow the illiterate with uncommon powers. Once assumed, the inventiveness of the folk has been seriously questioned of late. In any case, it is unlikely that the bulk of frontier humor, including the Davy Crockett and Mike Fink yarns, actually originated on the frontier. Many problems in this connection remain to be solved, but numerous western tales were assuredly planted in the West through the agency of eastern newspapers.[45] All things considered, it is reasonable to regard the "half horse, half alligator" of Kentucky as an approximation of reality and as a projection of the metropolitan imagination into the forest. On both counts he has serious implications for society.

The grotesque alligator-horse suggests an image in a crooked mirror held up to reality. Something of a caricature he may be and yet an embodiment of the brutal, amoral content of primitivism; he is in fact the idealized Kentuckian, the child of nature, stripped of his a priori endowment of natural virtue. The alligator-horse is obviously symbolic of power directed toward the satisfaction of egotism and appetite; in him act follows impulse in a straight line without reflection. Untouched by institutions and innocent of standards save those meaningful in a chaotic universe, he represents barbaric individualism. The alligator-horse, in many things abhorrent, has yet a terrible fascination for possessing so superbly the qualities suited to the actual state of nature. Untroubled by scruples and unweakened by luxury, he stands able and eager to meet force with force. As being simplified to fang and belly, he is utterly competent to secure life, liberty, and the pursuit of happiness for himself if not for others. He is accordingly an ideal figure for that part of the metropolis which acknowledges the "call of the wild." Many a social idealist, taking civilization as the source of evil, failed to perceive that the alligator-horse, not the noble savage as projected, was the true antitype of institutional man and that institutional man yet longed after his antitype because subconsciously harboring his image. The error may have been of no more than academic concern for Europe; but in America, which had to deal with the alligator-horse as a social being, the false assumption about the noblemen of nature caused unending difficulties.

III *The Forest and the City*

7 The Agent of Progress

*"The work, which long he in his breast had brew'd /
Now to perform he ardent did devise; / To wit, a
barbarous world to civilize."*— CASTLE OF INDOLENCE

THE IDEA OF the possibility of unlimited human and institutional progress fell on exceptionally fertile soil in late eighteenth-century America and germinated in a variety of more
or less coherent programs for the development of the rich new
country and especially for that part lying beyond the mountains. The manifest abundance, the relative freedom from
traditional authority, and the quick rewards of enterprise every
day contradicted religious pessimism and confirmed the optimistic forecasts of social philosophers in Europe during the
century past. Although paradisiacal visions filled the westering
masses, the occupation of Transappalachia was officially conceived in a rational framework and the destruction of the flora,
fauna, and indigenes justified by reference to civilization and
Christianity. The tremendous energy unleashed by various
forms of the myth of progress first against the Ohio Valley
and afterward against the whole West produced a spectacle
of rapid and sweeping change unequalled before or since in
this hemisphere. In return for their prodigious efforts, settlers
confidently anticipated a new life conspicuously free of the
defects of the old and lacking in no desirable thing.

By the view of most nineteenth-century writers, who as a
group signally failed to discriminate the several types of social,

political, and religious thinking represented in the emigrant stream, the pioneers served the nation as agents of conservative, upper-class progress, destined to lay the foundation for yet another extension of Western civilization. That they accomplished something of the sort may be granted, but not their special concern with that noble purpose. The progressivism of the early settlers, irrational rather than philosophical, assumed immediate personal satisfactions, and their frenzied and generally destructive descent upon the garden land followed directly from that expectation. Understandably, the motives and acts of the reckless individuals who conquered the West were not much inquired into by later and increasingly nationalistic generations of Americans. In *Wooing and Warring in the Wilderness* (1860) the novelist Charles D. Kirk stated the view of the pioneers and their achievement which the sentimental and progressivist upper-classes officially accepted: "Their destiny is one of peace—to conquer nature with the arms and arts of husbandry—to soften the wild features of the wide West—to plant flowers and reap harvests, and create home and happiness. No bugle blast heralded their approach —no measured tread gave notice of their march. There were no banners waving—no swords gleaming—none of the pomp and circumstance of glorious war. It was the tramp, tramp, steady and slow, but sure, of the advancing hosts of Civilization and Christianity" (ch. 6).

It was through no misconception that Kirk included religion in his image of the expansion. The very idea of progress had been evoked in the seventeenth century by anxieties of a fundamentally religious sort, and the elaboration of it during the Enlightenment, while mainly secular in reference, was not without significance for religion. By the period of the Transappalachian emigration, the Western world had been substantially reoriented by progressivism and man resolved of all those heavy doubts which had arisen with the final collapse of the Middle Ages under the impact of the new science. The concept of progress—a linear theory of history and in contrast to the cyclic essentially optimistic—had largely filled the void left by the destruction of the Scholastic synthesis of the medieval church, which had provided man with a reconciliation of reason and revelation, a unified view of the cosmos, and a safe hope of heavenly reward. Philosophical pessimism diminished as men recovered from the Copernican revelation and realized that nature stood in no immediate danger of decay and that there was place for divine as well as natural law in the new cosmology. If God were less free to interfere with His eternal design and man himself less certain of the hereafter, all signs foretold steady progress to an earthly state of universal contentment.

The subrational and exclusively religious counterpart of progressivism was millenarianism, a doctrine long regarded as heretical in the Roman church but widely accepted by the radical sects incubated in the Reformation and by a multitude of Protestants in the seventeenth century and after. Many of the poor and persecuted who fled to America in the eighteenth century treasured the millennial hope, and it eventually produced systematic programs among the Shakers, Mormons, and Millerites. The evangelical sectaries—Baptists, Presbyterians, and Methodists—who preceded these groups into the West were possibly no less confident that the Great Day approached, although poorly comprehending the implications of the doctrine.[1] With the general improvement of conditions in the nineteenth century the West tended to favor postmillennialism, a kind of secular compromise postulating a gradual betterment of conditions before the millennium, in contrast to the cataclysm of premillennialism.

The philosophy of progress and the millennial illusion, though having discrete origins and postulates, somewhat resemble each other in orientation and content and have probably interacted to a degree. Lately the proposition has been advanced that the success of the idea of progress was directly contingent upon the acceptance by Protestantism of the likelihood of the world's gradual improvement instead of degenera-

tion.[2] While Calvinist sectaries never composed their differences with humanists over the nature of man, by the end of
the seventeenth century religion generally had taken a for-
ward-looking turn in the direction of the dominant secular
movement. Significant contributions to the theory of progress
were made by a group of Anglican ministers, including John
Edwards and Edmund Law, who found in patristic writings
what they regarded as ample warrant for a progressivist conception of history and an optimistic view of man's moral and
spiritual growth.[3] At the beginning of the eighteenth century,
progressivism stood in an altogether favorable position.
Descartes had enthroned reason, Newton had placed natural
law beyond doubt, and the third Earl of Shaftesbury was pre-
paring to endow man with an innate moral sense. It was no
great task for sanguine philosophers to prove shortly that
"social evils were due neither to innate and incorrigible dis-
abilities of the human being nor to the nature of things, but
simply to ignorance and prejudices."[4] Obviously, the millennium awaited only the correction of error. The mind of the
Enlightenment was swept by strong philosophical crosscurrents, but such was the optimism, notwithstanding, as to still
most doubts and fears and to assimilate to a progressivist
context even regressive tendencies like primitivism, which in
one way or another influenced most social idealists of the
century. Although the theory of degeneration lingered on, the
climate poorly suited pessimism of any kind.

The easy solution of the world's ills reached by eighteenth-
century visionaries nowadays occasions sardonic laughter, and
there is an increasing tendency to regard man, with Thomas
Hobbes, as a creature governed by the pleasure-pain test, reluctant to serve the general interest on account of preoccupa-
tion with his own. It is well to remark, therefore, that the great
immigration to these shores after 1700 occurred in an atmosphere of optimism, an optimism no whit abated even among
those who suffered terrible privations in settling the West.
As Ralph H. Gabriel has observed, the importance of the

individual and the likelihood of progress were articles of faith along the frontier.[5] If programs for the development of the nation varied fundamentally among yeomen, utopians, and aristocrats, all provided for conditions meant to produce general contentment. The Declaration of Independence and the Constitution assume the moral character of men in general and their capacity for intelligent judgments. Jefferson planned according to enlightened European thought and, though envisaging a deserving aristocracy for leadership, concerned himself nonetheless with the rights and privileges of the yeomanry. The growth of America may today be described in cynical terms as a rape of nature, a contest among rogues for wealth and fame, or a struggle between classes for domination; but the eighteenth-century view was cheerful and hopeful. It is significant of the temper of the expansion that for decades following the Revolution, Pope's *An Essay on Man* was exceedingly popular,[6] as this philosophical poem superficially assimilates diverse systems to an optimistic ethics and ontology, with unmistakable deistic overtones. Arguing from the premise, "Whatever is, is right" in relation to the whole, Pope vindicated the ways of a beneficent God to man and forecast widespread happiness when society had fathomed its nature and applied right reason to error.

Although not without regret for the sacrifice of nature, the Indian, and the frontiersman, writers concerned with the West generally accepted the article of progress together with the corollary that the fabled land beyond the Appalachians was intended for the occupation and the enjoyment of civilized whites. They dramatized the expansion according to progressivist doctrine, often intimating a conflict between the forces of light (civilization) and the forces of darkness (savagery). The version of progressivism ordinarily received (and, curiously enough, only occasionally questioned) constituted a suitable rationale for an expanding economy and for class discrimination based on wealth and education. The actual circumstances of frontier life, mirrored in the glass of upper-class thought, were inevitably distorted, though hardly out of an evil design to falsify history. In literature, the symbolic meaning of the backwoods hero varied according to the requirements of the western scene as visualized by the literate minority. Represented as an agent of progress during the civilizing process, the uncouth frontiersman very conveniently for his betters reverted to a primitive role when the work of conquest had been completed. There was understandably no place in romantic fiction for the bald truth, that the pioneer was stripped of a hero's rewards by the broadcloth gentry, who meant to transform the garden of the Indian into an Athenian state; and there is some doubt that he would have much enjoyed living in the Ohio Valley under such conditions as Samuel L. Metcalf described: "Here civilization and the arts are fast advancing to perfection, and here genius, nurtured by science and philosophy and enriched by the improvements of former ages, is to shine forth in all the splendor of intellectual power."[7] It is apparent that without wealth, breeding, and education the backwoodsmen fitted little better than the Indians and varmints into such a setting. Nor was it intended for them, as Mann Butler tacitly admitted in commenting upon Boone's willingness to brave the wilderness: "Yet while these difficulties deter the quiet and industrious, they only stir the blood and string the nerves of the enterprising and the restless. Both characters have their appropriate periods and sphere of social utility."[8] By the third decade of the nineteenth century, when Butler wrote, the age of refinement had arrived; the squirearchy occupied the garden, busily engaged with the arts and sciences, fast horses, and corn liquor.

The genteel residents of the seaboard during the eighteenth century regarded the rude folk of their own backwoods with a feeling of contempt mingled with fear; but as the frontier receded beyond the mountains and the buckskin warriors gallantly repelled the savage menace, the national debt to this class of men was increasingly acknowledged. Moreover, distance lent considerable enchantment to the frontiersmen and to the drama which they enacted in the Ohio Valley. At the same time, it was apparent that the ordinary Indian fighter who roamed the most advanced line of the frontier, cropping very little and hunting a great deal, and seldom lingering to gather his fruits, consorted badly with progressivist ideology. While allowing this uncouth individual his primitive ways, writers had necessarily to implicate him in the horrendous assault upon the West in order to piece out the myth in which the expansion was framed. Cast as an agent of progress, the frontiersman acted in the general interest, clearing the wilderness of the enemies of civilization; but as a congenital nomad, he conveniently stepped off the stage at the end of his scene. That the real wanderer of the forest in all likelihood cared nothing about progress or refined ways and keenly resented the encroachment of gentry upon his hunting grounds deterred imaginative writers not at all. They simply created a hero to fit a preconceived pattern—the myth of progress.

Daniel Boone became the prototype of western heroes as a consequence not of folk tradition but of literary. Filson represented him as a homely philosopher of the backwoods, content to live in solitude and resigned to the will of Providence, but nonetheless conscious of his exalted function—"an instrument ordained to settle the wilderness."[9] Boone in old age is supposed to have relished the "instrument" idea, but more importantly writers seized upon it as a means of reconciling the frontiersman as a type with the doctrine of progress. This is not to say that every hard-bitten squatter in the Kentucky paradise became in consequence an apostle of culture, for, as Cecil B. Hartley remarked, writers often represented the common garden variety of pioneers as indolent savages.[10] In the *Deerslayer* (1841), Cooper distinguished unmistakably between Henry March, the brutal and treacherous backwoodsman, and Natty Bumppo, the most famous of Boone's numerous progeny. It is noteworthy that Daniel, except in the dime novels, seldom enacts a truly ferocious role, though always intimating his capacity for great military feats. Filson's portrait encouraged the conception of a high-minded, humane person, possessed of native wisdom and instinctive faith in God. Years afterward, Frank Triplett translated Filson's suggestions into concrete terms: "If we take Boone as the type of the Kentucky pioneers, we find in him united the philosophy of the stoic, the courage of the demi-god, the firm purpose of the statesman, and the humanity of the Christian."[11] Of course, most writers regarded him as superior to the type, though concurring in these attributes. W. H. Bogart, the author of a popular life, described Boone as a "mild but firm conqueror."[12] Little more than thirty years ago, Constance L. Skinner solemnly insisted that he was law abiding and peace loving[13]—doubtless an accurate observation but significant nonetheless of the continuing inclination to shape the old hunter in the image of the natural man as conceived by the Enlightenment, a man good and wise from perceiving through uncorrupted eyes the laws of nature.

Daniel Bryan, author of the *Mountain Muse,* failed dismally as a poet, but he placed the kind of construction on the struggle for the Ohio Valley that admirably suited the middle-class soul of the times. His Boone as an agent of progress has the active support of angels of the Lord, who talk, interestingly enough, like eighteenth-century philosophers concerned with spreading the benefits of the Age of Reason into the darkest corners of the world. For a leader of the forces of light, the angelic powers require not so much a backwoods stoic as a man of feeling, overflowing with Christian virtues:

> But let the chief on whom our choice alights,
> Be one, in whose expanded breast are found,
> The great, ennobling virtues of the soul;
> Benevolence, Mercy, Meekness, Pity, Love,
> Benignant Justice, Valor lion-like,
> And Fortitude, with stoic *nerves* endow'd. (I.727-32)

That this incredible portrait of himself revolted the real Boone is not surprising, but no less a man would have served to accomplish the heroic mission ordained by God in His curiously modern Providence—to transform the garden into an ideal state according to the rational visions of the Enlightenment:

> Upon his [Boone's] *Fancy's* pictured tablet, shone
> In splendid tints, a thousand varied scenes;
> Embellishing a dark Barbarian World!—
> Refinement's golden file with smoothing sweep,
> Reducing swiftly from the savage mind,
> Its heathen incrustations—kindling light
> And splendor, where investing glooms and rust,
> The Indian's intellectual treasures spoil'd.
> A thousand valorous, soul-ennobling feats
> Attendant on the patriotic enterprise,
> Grandly preparing, an expanded sphere
> For Commerce, Wealth, and all the brilliant Arts,
> Where they before had never cast a beam,
> In brilliant prospect warmed the Hero's soul. (II.78-91)

The resemblance of Bryan's Boone to the middle-class Knight of Arts and Industry may be a coincidence, but it is altogether probable that the *Castle of Indolence* (1748) by the Scottish poet James Thomson was known to the author of the *Mountain Muse,* if not to Filson. Like Boone, Thomson's knight came of humble parents—a poor hunter called Selvaggio and Dame Poverty—and like Boone he proposed a transformation of the primeval garden according to a progressivist formula:

> The work, which long he in his breast had brew'd
> Now to perform he ardent did devise;
> To wit, a barbarous world to civilize.
> Earth was till then a boundless forest wild;
> Nought to be seen but savage wood, and skies;
> No cities nourish'd arts, no culture smiled,
> No government, no laws, no gentle manners mild. (II.xiv)

Bryan's portrait of Boone possessed no more reality than the Knight of Arts and Industry, but an important segment of the public was nonetheless pleased to accept it. Boone the frontiersman, as an acknowledged agent of progress, sanctioned the civilizing process, whatever the cost to the Indians and to his own kind, and thereby put a happy face on a matter which somewhat troubled the American conscience. In truth, Daniel Boone played a relatively minor role in the early history of Kentucky; Simon Kenton engaged the Indians far more audaciously, and George Rogers Clark wrought with incomparably greater effect as a leader of the despondent pioneers. If, as Thwaites remarked, Boone's "career possesses a romantic and even pathetic interest that can never fail to charm the student of history,"[14] the reason is that the American imagination seized upon the simple hunter as a much-needed symbol and cloaked him with appropriate legends. Boone, the "superman guiding his generation and future generations across the mountains," a conception despised by Alvord,[15] served his country best not as a reality but as an epic hero enthroned in eighteenth-century rather than classical myth. Having accepted Boone in this role, the public could approve such flights as Charles Wilkins Webber's: "The Romulus of Saxon blood, he was founding a new empire, and, greater than he—was fed, not upon the 'wolf's milk'—but upon the abundance of mild and serene nature—upon the delicious esculence of her forest game, and fruits of her wild luxuriant vines."[16] The transformation of old Daniel from a rather ordinary backwoodsman into a heroic agent of progress owed something to a desire to conceal the unpleasant reality of the expansion and something also to cultural idealism.

Following the frontier breed into Kentucky were men of manifest culture—eastern planters, lawyers, physicians, and merchants—who, if not of worshipful origin, sprang from well-regarded families of some means and education. A number of this small but influential group had previously been leaders in Virginia, particularly in the Valley, though perhaps only George Nicholas originally possessed sufficient social standing to occupy a pew in Bruton Parish Church with the stately Carter kin or to dance the night away at Westover beside the James. Yet theirs were in the main Tidewater ideals, and the society which they erected in the Bluegrass, while never so brilliant or intellectual as that of Williamsburg, was similar and quite as exclusive and internally consistent. Although far from equalitarian by conviction, this burgeoning aristocracy displayed no marked inclination to assume the prerogatives of feudal lords and never after the fashion of Colonel Richard Henderson. Through military and treasury warrants, grants, preemptions, and purchases, they gathered to themselves much of the best land and, as Indian hostilities subsided, instituted a coherent political and social system. By the period of admission, control of the state had largely passed into their hands, the heroes of the settlement having died, emigrated westward, or fallen into relative obscurity.

Owing to the libertarian temper of the majority, the new commonwealth in the wilderness developed much according to a democratic pattern, though not without exception and not without dissent. The constitution under which Kentucky entered the Union in 1792, influenced by the corresponding Pennsylvania document, provided for free white manhood suffrage, equal representation, popular control of the government, and religious freedom, in short, for rights especially desired by the yeomanry, Jefferson's adopted children. Whether the fears of the lower classes were entirely justified or not, a loud outcry against aristocracy arose as the time approached for electing delegates to the constitutional convention of 1792, perhaps with the consequence that the great landholders lacked a majority, though capably represented by such leaders as Alexander S. Bullitt, John Edwards, Richard Taylor, Matthew Walton, and Robert Johnson. A compromise resulted, for in the interest of the large planters the constitution sanctioned slavery, provided for an electoral college to choose the governor and senators, and enabled the legislature to appoint the Court of Appeals, the supreme judiciary of the state. In a sense, the triumph of the lower classes was illusory, as documents are not proof against the machinations of an intelligent and determined minority, but the keen political interest and independence of judgment displayed by the people as a whole both before and after the convention unquestionably blunted certain aristocratic tendencies imported from Virginia. Fordham stands witness to the proneness of Kentuckians to quarrel fiercely about politics and to their congenital hostility toward all forms of Toryism, and his testimony is supported by the controversies which flamed through the pages of the *Kentucky Gazette* and other newspapers during the crucial formative period.[17]

The Tidewater was for the Bluegrass at the end of the eighteenth century what the English court had once been for the Tidewater—a shining model. Virginia, of course, originally had no aristocracy, but only an upper crust of shrewd traders of English middle-class origin who in time accumulated enough wealth and tradition to affect the precious manner of the Cavaliers and, more significantly, to cultivate polite learning. Their learning, if not profound, was commendably extensive, and their taste, while founded on European criteria, was expressed as magnificent Georgian mansions, with simple but rich exteriors and geometrically patterned grounds, and elegant dress and manners commensurately genteel. The example of gracious living set by the First Families figured importantly in the ambitions of Virginians who sought their fortunes in the West. Clearly the Kentucky gentry meant to emulate their betters. While turning the wild garden into woodland pastures and crowning their estates with impressive dwellings, they cultivated belles-lettres and debated the burning issues of political and moral philosophy. Whatever the Bluegrass lacked of the genteel tradition, Colonel David Meade supplied in 1796 when he removed from Virginia to Jessamine Creek and there proceeded to erect Chaumière du Prairie—a mansion and an aristocratic way of life. The accumulation of wealth from hemp and tobacco enabled others to affect the grand manner of Colonel Meade, and an agrarian aristocracy assumed perceptible form. Unified by common interests and by the hostility of obstreperous levelers, the Kentucky aristocrats acted cunningly to perpetuate their social order. Whether from

democratic tendencies or from a judicious appraisal of the
backwoods temper, they seem not as a group to have pressed
for the privileges so irksome to the lower classes in the East
before the Revolution, but they secured much of the rich blue
limestone triangle and the right to own slaves, without which
a truly gentle condition could not have been sustained during
the frontier period.

Gentlemen in and around Lexington—the "Athens of the
West"—prided themselves not only on their blooded stock
and well-kept acres but also on a knowledge of language and
literature, philosophy and natural science. Their learning may
not have been deep, and yet, as in the case of the Puritans,
succeeding generations proved by no means as erudite. The
emphasis from the outset on classical studies is significant of
the desire—certainly strong through the first quarter of the
nineteenth century—to conserve in the Garden of the West the
spirit and substance of the European heritage. Educated men
and women wrote serious and inevitably stilted verse after
the Neoclassical fashion of Alexander Pope, and occasionally
a Kentucky virtuoso set his hand to classical meters. They
assembled in literary and debating societies with the very best
intentions of improving themselves and society. Their activities culminated in the Transylvania University of President
Horace Holley's administration (1817-1827); the school, while
destined for ultimate mediocrity, achieved during this period
national prominence as an intellectual center.

The books advertised for sale in 1795 by John Bradford,
editor of the *Kentucky Gazette,* suggest that by the time the
Indians surrendered Kentucky a respectable culture had been
planted in the Bluegrass. Bradford offered not only practical
works on law, medicine, surveying, agriculture, public speaking, accounting, and grammar but also the best of eighteenth-
century English fiction, books of travel, classics, collections of
sermons and poetry, weighty philosophical treatises, the essays
of Thomas Paine and Oliver Goldsmith, the *Tatler* and *Spectator, Gil Blas,* and *Don Quixote,* among others no less com-

mendable. To judge from the newspapers of Kentucky—indeed of the whole Mississippi Valley—during the first half of the nineteenth century, the literate possessed exceptionally wide interests. Editors liberally varied local and national news with articles on foreign affairs, society and fashions, literature and drama. Exceptions granted, the Bluegrass squirearchy before the Civil War took culture seriously and acted not altogether ineffectually to plant the arts and sciences and elegant manners in the new state.

A rich culture presupposes a flourishing economy, and a flourishing economy presupposes the exploitation of human or natural resources or both; for without material support and leisure, creative genius dies on the vine. Old World instances from Athens to Tuscany are too familiar to require enumeration. The intellectual and artistic life of ante bellum Kentucky depended ultimately on the fertile soil and manufactories of the central plateau, the trade of river towns, and slavery. Outside of Louisville and the Bluegrass, wealth was usually insufficient to support a broadcloth and crinoline aristocracy devoted to philosophy and the arts, horseracing, and fox hunting. To judge from the rapid increase of industry, many an early arrival in the Garden of the West shared the commercial foresight of Cooper's Marmaduke Temple. The existence of the "Kentucky Society for the encouragement of manufactures" as early as 1789[18] is significant of the concern to balance western agriculture with industry in order to free the region in some measure of economic dependence on the East. How well the program of the society succeeded may be estimated from the multiplication during the next twenty years of cotton, hemp, flaxseed oil, paper and powder mills, furnaces and forges, nail factories, tanneries, and whisky distilleries. Meanwhile, Bluegrass planters poured tobacco, hemp, flour, and livestock into the economic stream, and with the mounting profits indulged themselves in fast thoroughbreds and stately mansions. Louisville became the first commercial city in consequence of the trade made possible after 1815 by the steamboat, but Lexington remained the center of culture.

Such was the progress of the knights of arts and industry that Henry Bradshaw Fearon could report in 1817 that several sections of the "dark Barbarian World" described by Daniel Bryan had been illuminated and "modes of luxury which might rival the displays of London and Paris" instituted where not long before only the beasts and the savages roamed.[19] Foremost in Fearon's mind was the Bluegrass, by the third decade of the nineteenth century an orderly park occupied by a society which, however middle class its origins, affected manners and tastes commensurate with the richness of the land. If little of enduring value resulted, the squirearchy yet set an example of abundant living and exhibited commendable arrogance in the face of rude levelers and narrow moralists. The Virginia aristocrats, whose conception of the proper organization of the Kentucky paradise prevailed for a time, need not be censured unduly for imagining that Greek Revival architecture, classical learning, and Ciceronian eloquence constitute a Periclean civilization. At the same time, the cost of the experiment in human values ought not to be minimized: Negro slaves hewed the wood and drew the water for the privileged class, the luxurious mode of Bluegrass society engendered lasting and politically consequential resentment in the yeoman farmers of the surrounding hill country, and finally the pioneers as well as the Indians were expelled from the fabled garden. These results may have been inevitable, though there now seems small cause for the exultation expressed in the *Banks of Elkhorn,* a poem contributed to the *Kentucky Gazette,* March 3, 1826, by a poetaster who identified himself as "Oscar":

> The savages far to the Westward are banish'd,
>   Their manners and habits terrific, are gone;
> The Buffalo, wild Deer and Bear all have vanish'd
>   And we, undisputed possessors, remain.

No longer the yell of the savage alarm[s] us,
  Industry, and Arts too, our country adorn;
The Sun, which for ages, has ceas'd not to warm us.
  Vast changes has seen on the Banks of Elkhorn. (st. 3)

Without troubling about the matter, Oscar assumed that the cultural end justified the means. More sensitive progressivists deplored the incidental consequences of their program but usually reassured themselves with varyingly specious arguments. Accordingly, the deprivation of the Indian and even of the frontiersman was accomplished not without reasons regarded as good and sufficient by the public. In the sixteenth century, Europe had conceived two views of the Indian—one idealistic, the other derogatory—and these were held alternately during the next three centuries according as the red man aided or obstructed the progress of civilization and Christianity. The Virginia colonists appear to have had some hope of civilizing the aborigines, but after the terrible massacre of 1622 tended to regard them as a menace to be removed. The Puritans of New England took a comparable position for much the same social and economic reasons and, moreover, invested the Indian with a satanical character, a conception which obviously influenced the *Mountain Muse*. Nevertheless, attempts were made periodically to trace the Indians to the Lost Ten Tribes of Israel, of which the most extensive and ostensibly learned was James Adair's.[20] Largely founded on imagined similarities of language and custom, the Hebrew hypothesis sprang from no scientific motive, but, in the opinion of R. H. Pearce, from a desire to find an honorable place for the Indian in Christendom.[21] Whether a bronze Israelite or not, the Indian found small sympathy among the western settlers, who with few exceptions took a dim view of savage life. As Theodore Roosevelt doubtless realized, the concept of the ignoble savage best agreed with Manifest Destiny.[22]

Although the seizure of Indian land and the mistreatment of the red race occasioned the American conscience some pain, the penetration of the continent proceeded no less rapidly on that account. Wherever possible, desired tracts were procured under the color of purchase, usually after settlement had actually commenced. It is a credit to the intelligence of the Indians that they ordinarily recognized that no choice was really involved and accordingly accepted the trifling offers of cutlery and fabrics and then retired. Pretexts were by no means lacking for these larcenous dealings. In *L'Histoire de la Nouvelle France* (1609), Marc Lescarbot had advanced the opinion that the children of God possessed a divine right to the land of the Indians, and this justification appeared in one form or another until the West was won. Daniel Bryan stated the Christian argument without reservation:

> No portion of this Earth
> To nurture Hell's infernal grisly brood,
> Was by its holy Maker e'er design'd;
> Or to remain a dark and frightful waste,
> When wisely furnish'd for the residence
> Of rational, humane and polish'd Man. (I.351-56)

Sometime later, the Kentucky lawyer William Ross Wallace in a commemorative poem on Boone even more plainly coupled the doctrine of use to divine right, expressing precious little Christian charity for "that Indian race / Whose lease to this majestic land, misused, / It hath pleased God to cancel."[23] Lest Wallace's view be thought peculiarly American, it ought to be recalled that the saintly Thomas More three centuries earlier granted his Utopians the moral right to wage war against a people who "holdeth a piece of grounde voyde and vacaunt to no good nor profitable use, kepyng other from the use and possession of it."[24]

By the first quarter of the nineteenth century, according to Pearce, the theory of savagism had hardened in the public mind: as a being fundamentally different from and inferior to the Caucasian and as a serious obstruction to progress, the Indian faced certain and probably necessary destruction.[25] Lacking the ability and the desire to adopt the ways of the whites, he could find no place in the progressive system. In the *Pathfinder* (1840) Leatherstocking expressed Cooper's own sense of the impassable gulf between the two modes of existence: "I tell the Sarpent, that no Christianizing will ever make even a Delaware a white man" (ch. 8). How far rationalization blinded the West to the rights of the Indians may be gathered from Mann Butler's amazingly sophistical appraisal of the Treaty of Fort Stanwix in 1768, extinguishing the Iroquois claim to Kentucky: "The most interesting aspect of the treaty is, that whatever may have been the weakness of the Iroquois title, still its extinction was required by humanity and forbearance, which should characterize the intercourse of superior and civilized nations, to their inferior and barbarous neighbors. Such has, most honorably to this republic, been *its* conduct to the Indians. The history of dependent nations does not, in any age of the world, exhibit such magnanimity and equity, as the general intercourse of the *United States* with the native tribes."[26] Thus, the Anglo-Saxons of the eighteenth and nineteenth centuries, having been endowed with benevolence by sentimental philosophers of Europe, glossed conquest over with rhetoric, whereas the old Germans, an unsubtle folk, had been concerned only to make the edge and point of their argument clear.

The doctrine of progress doomed the frontiersman no less than the Indian, though the former was spared the hatred and abuse lavished upon the latter. All savages, whether red or white, suffered from civilized processes, and all were savages who resisted the blessings of civilization. The predicament of the Boone species was cloaked by the romantic folds of primitivism. As a noble savage or child of nature, the Indian fighter had no desire for such rewards as delight men of culture; he sought only the pleasures of the primeval forest. The myth of Boone's atavism, in part a product of the mechanics of rationalization, seems not to have been examined critically—and no wonder, since it relieved the public of a sense of guilt. Cooper thought more deeply about the subject than most and frankly conceded that, however deserving, the white warrior of the wilderness—even his idealized Leatherstocking—could not claim under existing circumstances the rewards and rank of knights of old. He recognized Ishmael Bush, the rude frontiersman of the *Prairie* (1827), as the sort who in early periods led the onslaught of civilization against barbarism but at the same time noted important distinctions between the knight as anciently conceived and the Bush type: "Both might be called without restraint, the one being above, the other beyond the reach of the law—brave, because they were inured to danger—proud, because they were independent—and vindictive, because each was the avenger of his own wrongs. It would be unjust to the borderer to pursue the parallel much further. He is irreligious, because he has inherited the knowledge that religion does not exist in forms, and his reason rejects mockery. He is not a knight, because he has not the power to bestow distinctions; and he has not the power, because he is the offspring and not the parent of a system" (ch. 6). Cooper's is a thoughtful analysis of a problem which confronted every romancer who sought to exploit the western epic.

What the peerless warrior won by force of arms during the heroic stage and to some extent during the feudal he normally held in the same manner, though not without occasional recourse to political intrigue. While recognizing an overlord, whether king or noble, and rendering appropriate homage and service, he exercised complete authority over his domain and looked to his own defense. His title to land and folk, conferred originally as rewards for military achievement, rested somewhat on precedent but mainly on power measured by the number and excellence of the fighting men who would follow him out of loyalty or plain expectation of glory and loot. Capitalism and the modern state radically modified the old power formula and accordingly the status of the warrior. With the transfer of real wealth from land to trade, industry, and hard money, and loyalties from the provincial lord to the crown as symbol of national solidarity, the rewards for military prowess declined perceptibly. The distinctions of rank, nominal salaries, and appeals to patriotism increasingly procured after the Middle Ages what formerly required promises of substantial spoils. During the last four hundred years military honors have varied considerably in real value but have not often been convertible into great wealth. It scarcely needs saying that during the western expansion in America material benefits generally fell not to the Indian fighters, although they often claimed great tracts of land, but to the executives, the Marmaduke Temples. The frontiersmen were instruments of but not partners in the socioeconomic system, having neither the training for getting and managing wealth nor the social and educational advantages of those who did. What the buckskin warriors accomplished against raw nature and the Indian they accomplished not in the context of a heroic society but of a modern one. As the executors only, they had to share the rewards with the conceivers, whose foresight and capital made conquest possible. The cultural structure erected in the wilderness was actually not of the pioneers' devising but of the capitalists', and it was intended to perpetuate the values of the ruling class of the East. Under the circumstances, the rude victors could not translate their land and military titles into meaningful economic and social currency or even use force to retain what they had won when questions of title to land arose.

The myth of progress permitted the exaltation of Boone and his kind as instruments of civilization and their dismissal after the Garden of the West had become safe for commerce and culture. But the expectation of an Earthly Paradise remained with the frontier folk and, as will appear hereafter, lived on among their descendants. Meanwhile, it is desirable to consider how romancers concerned with the conquest of the West dealt with an epic hero who wrought mightily and yet received negligible rewards for his labor.

8 The Romance of the Frontier

"Modern romance is the substitute which the people of today offer for the ancient epic."—WILLIAM GILMORE SIMMS

WRITERS CONCERNED with exploiting in fiction the conquest of Kentucky and other western regions faced in contemporary social and economic circumstances a problem for which a wholly satisfactory solution could not be found. There was simply no honorable or even definable place within the structure of nineteenth-century society for the poor, illiterate buckskin hero—the agent of progress. Land he claimed in enormous tracts, and during the perilous stages of settlement sometimes occupied important offices; but once the threat of hostilities diminished and astute aristocrats arrived from the East, the frontiersman suffered progressive loss of both land and influence. When Kentucky entered the Union in 1792, none of the great Indian fighters yet retained conspicuous authority, and much of the land they claimed was involved in ruinous litigation. Ulysses ruled Ithaca in old age and Beowulf the land of the Geats, but Boone and Kenton died relatively poor, the lords of not one square foot of Kentucky. The dwindling of the western heroes, while a difficulty for literature, was in no way strange. The conceivers and the executors of the settlement, as previously remarked, were different sets of men—the former educated, polished, and sagacious; the latter illiterate, rude, and reckless. While conditions were heroic, the con-

ceivers prudently stayed at home; when the Indians had been
expelled and society stabilized, they asserted their claims and
dispossessed the defenders of the forts. The transplanted
squirearchy instituted a social order from which the backwoods
type, for the lack of breeding and schooling, was necessarily
excluded. Creative writers had somehow to frame the heroic
society of the West according to the values of the civilized
East and to use the picturesque features of the former state
while asserting the preferability of the latter. However unlikely, this relationship alone suited the rather confused mind
of the reading public.

The shifts devised by James Fenimore Cooper and widely
imitated in the Kentucky romances left the Indian fighter only
a poor supporting role in the western drama, but writers were
thereby enabled to exploit the high adventure and raw experiences of the frontier without sacrificing prevailing upper-class
postulates—the sanctity of property, the desirability of material
accumulation, the inevitability of progress, the stratification
of society, the need for moral uplift, and the rule of the wisest
(that is, the aristoi). Almost nothing of the truth of the
expansion appears in the romances, but they are nevertheless
valuable social documents, chiefly for intimating, even though
behind a facade of exotic adventure, the whole structure of
cultural assumptions made by those who fancied themselves
aristocratic or who respected that condition. Assuredly, the
pattern imposed upon the western scene first by Cooper among
the novelists, while in part shaped by literary convention, owed
a very great deal to the preconceptions of the literate and
privileged minority, who desired progress in all good things,
though at no cost to traditional values.

There appeared early a tendency to view Kentucky legendry
as material for romance rather than for epic, although a few
writers attempted the latter form. While Timothy Flint demonstrably perceived the epical quality of the western struggle,
he yet thought of it in terms suggestive of the historical
romance, a genre become enormously popular in consequence

of Scott: "Indeed, the first settlement of the country, the delightful scenes, which it opened, the singular character of the
first adventurers, who seem to have been a compound of the
hero, the philosopher, the farmer, and the savage; the fierce
struggle, which the savages made to retain this delightful
domain, and which, before that struggle was settled, gave it
the name of 'the bloody ground,'—these circumstances, con-
spire to designate this country, as the theatre, and the time
of its settlement, as the period, of romance."[1] Flint's eloquent
representation of the western scene doubtless owed something
to the widespread fear after *Waverley* (1814) that America
possessed for the purposes of literature only mediocre historical
matter. While the concern over the usefulness of indigenous
materials was relieved by Cooper's *Spy* (1821), as late as 1854
James Weir felt some need to proclaim in the *Winter Lodge*
the richness of the Kentucky scene as compared with Scott's
settings: "It was a famed land to them all [Indian tribes], the
'disputed territory;' a kind of Castle Dangerous, where the
young braves went forth to kill the deer and the buffalo; and,
like the tilting border knights of England and Scotland, met
each other in bloody conflict. Hence, it became as dear to
them, and as famous, in their war songs and dances, as the
Holy Sepulchre to the Red Cross Crusaders. Every hill, and
dale, and valley, was known and fastened upon their memo-
ries by some bloody contest" (ch. 1).[2]

It is abundantly clear from the literature that like Flint and
Weir the generality of creative writers in the nineteenth century could not bring themselves to dissociate the frontier from
Scott and the romance. Some authors surely catered to popular
taste, but others may not have perceived the inappropriateness
of the romance form for western subjects. There is the possibility, moreover, that a good many writers labored under
the same misapprehension about the distinctions between
epic and romance which William Gilmore Simms disclosed in
himself. Simms asserted in all confidence: "Modern romance
is the substitute which the people of today offer for the ancient

epic."[3] Nor did he mean that the romance, in his opinion "a poem in every sense of the word," was one whit inferior to or substantially different from the epic: "Its standards are precisely those of the epic." The absurdity of Simms' notion should have been apparent to educated Americans, as classical literature occupied a large fraction of the curriculum; and in all likelihood the fundamental differences between the *Iliad* and *Ivanhoe* were apprehended at least dimly by the considerable public given to reading romances. Yet the view that romance served as well as epic had undeniable efficacy, for it lent support to the disposition of authors to treat a heroic society in terms of a mature one.

The struggle for Kentucky created conditions indisputably heroic, and backwoods heroes accordingly required an epical vehicle, but one managed by writers who were at once the heirs of folk tradition and of perfected native art, writers derived like their characters from the migrant stream and, in consequence, profoundly sensible of the accomplishments of their race. But the epic poet normally arises after his people have achieved a settled condition—often a matter of centuries— and only then provided that a high degree of cultural homogeneity has been maintained. England, for instance, produced little epic poetry after the coming of the Normans, and America for a variety of reasons has produced none of any importance. All things considered, Daniel Bryan was doomed to fail in his attempt to enthrone Boone in epic, though admittedly the wretched quality of his *Mountain Muse* (1813) owed quite as much to the author's inferior talent as to adverse external circumstances. Richard Emmons wrought even more dismally in the *Fredoniad: or, Independence Preserved,* an enormous epic in heroic couplets, lauding the frontiersmen among other objects of American pride. The first canto of this notorious example of what R. L. Rusk calls "blatant nationalism" appeared in 1822 and the complete epic—all forty cantos—first in 1827.[4] James Kirke Paulding set his hand to the western theme in the *Backwoodsman* (1818) but gained no distinction from the effort. While deploring the tyranny of European literary conventions and apparently meaning to set an example of revolt, he fashioned an uncommonly dull "knight of arts and industry" in the tradition of eighteenth-century progressivism. These poets did not—indeed, could not—comprehend the frontier period through bona fide folk heroes embodying the ideals and aspirations of the race which brought them forth, and their ambitious poems are therefore significant of nothing save the urbane view of the West.

The epic poet by tradition works out of an altogether serious purpose: he draws the great warriors of his people according to heroic scale, charges them with superhuman obligations, and powerfully reveals the spirit of the age through their fateful decisions. As Simms should have realized, romance, in contrast to epic, has never been intended as a severe, masculine record of ancient glory but as a narrative of lively adventure, a thing of entertainment suited to the refined court rather than to the mead hall. The writer of romance casts about for likely plots and settings, caring nothing that the materials are utterly exotic to his public. Although sometimes drawing upon epic, he cannot write epic, for standing at too great a distance —cultural rather than temporal—from the heroic situation which he exploits. That he cannot understand the spirit of his source causes no apprehension, for he is ordinarily a conscious modernizer. Thus, the issues of romance are meaningful for the author's own time and only accidentally express the ideals of the period with which he ostensibly deals. Moreover, the characters of romance are masqueraders; one kind of costume suits them as well as another. In most nineteenth-century romances of the frontier, the savages—red and white—have no particular reality and might be presented with equal justice as Patagonians or Mongolians. The civilized whites are usually not backwoods people but only white people sojourning in the backwoods. Some notable exceptions granted, the frontiersman as civilized or uncivilized man suffered gross misrepresentation in popular novels, many of which, it is fair to say, succeeded reasonably well as fiction. It is well to note, however, that the backwoods hero could not attain epic stature in the romance.

For conceiving the western struggle in the context of the upper-class version of progress, writers deprived themselves of much of the best literary material at hand. Pontiac and Tecumseh as leaders of a doomed race had the qualities of tragic heroes, but the Indian was so far debased as to be unacceptable in a magnificent role—Hiawatha notwithstanding. Frank Triplett as late as 1883 sharply criticized Cooper for allowing the existence of a mere handful of noble individuals in a race of "remorseless fiends."[5] Although enacting heroic roles according to fact and legend, the frontiersmen for falling short of the urban ideal of masculine excellence suited little better than the chieftains. In the preface to the *Mountain Muse* Daniel Bryan inadvertently confessed the refractoriness of frontier materials when treated in the frame of upper-class preconceptions: "But after commencing 'Boone's Adventures,' he [Bryan] soon found that it would be impossible to do any thing like justice to that subject without giving to it a much greater extension than was at first contemplated. Upon *this* course therefore, in consonance with the suggestions of his own judgment, and the persuasions of his friends, he determined. He thought it most advisable too, to interweave with the History of Boone the narrative of the 'Allegany Robbers and Lost Maid.'" By "extension" Bryan meant casting Boone into a Miltonic setting—angels and devils and all—in order to amplify his matter and further to cloak conquest with divine sanction. His addition of the story of genteel lovers needs little explanation: the nineteenth century was generally unwilling to accept the rustic in the role of romantic hero.[6] The romancers, including Cooper, who began to work the frontier lode after Bryan, dispensed with the improbable machinery and contented themselves with superimposing timeworn plots, especially abduction and rescue, on the backwoods scene. Although often relished by the proletariat, the romance is an

aristocratic genre, and authors both ancient and modern have
generally ordered their plots so as to pay proper respect to
class. By the traditional terms, persons of inferior origin, no
matter how worthy, could not properly be cast in leading roles.
Though compelled to use absurd shifts, Cooper no less than
his imitators abided by convention and set genteel heroes over
the frontiersmen.

Poets of the olden time encountered problems enough and
resolved them with varying success, but theirs was never the
curious dualism which plagued frontier romancers. The orientation of the epic poet's world was essentially military, and
warriors necessarily occupied the center of the stage. By their
martial deserving and courage to decide between conflicting
loyalties they found a rank in society. While fighting collectively to restore glorious Helen to Menelaus, the Greeks at
Troy individually sought eternal renown; and Homer praised
each according to his prowess. With the rise of the institution
of chivalry in the Middle Ages and the concomitant cult of
love, the traditional focus shifted. The chivalric code elevated
woman to an unprecedented position, and her service became
a worthy aim of the knight. As symbol of the new idealism she
replaced mere personal glory as the end of warfare. To serve
or to deserve a peerless fair a knight at arms in medieval story
rides forth against heathens, tyrants, dragons, and miscellaneous malefactors, everywhere righting wrongs and generally
behaving with consummate gentility. Very often the lady her-
self languishes in the power of a matchless villain, awaiting the
gentle knight who will punish her abductor and receive the
reward of valor. The tests of true deserving in the feudal world
are martial vigor, noblesse oblige, and fidelity to chivalric
forms. American novelists felt impelled to integrate the frontier scene with the romance form, even though chivalry, upon
which romance feeds, had no meaning in the elemental struggle
of red man and white. The whole apparatus had to be imported and in an alien setting functioned awkwardly. To put
the matter another way, the essentially heroic conditions of

the frontier simply could not be assimilated to the romance pattern, which developed out of very different social conditions. That Cooper and afterward the authors of Kentucky novels should have regularly attempted this impossible fusion was owing somewhat to literary influences and somewhat to social compulsion.

A proper understanding of the romances of the Kentucky frontier and of the ambiguous role of the buckskin warrior in them requires some consideration of the discrete traditions synthesized most successfully by Cooper. It is needful to deny in starting that his Leatherstocking Tales are what Carl Van Doren calls the "classic record of an heroic age."[7] Cooper may not be allowed to have recorded either the spirit or the particular truth of the frontier. His hero is ultimately Filson's Boone, and his Indians are the improbable Iroquois and Delaware of John Heckewelder's *Indian Nations* (1819). Cooper simply constructed romances somewhat after the manner of Sir Walter Scott and launched them on the tidal wave created by *Waverley*. The judiciousness of Alexander Cowie's estimate of him as "one of the great novelists in English" need not be questioned here,[8] but credit for achieving a classic representation of the heroic age of America he assuredly does not deserve. The merit of Cooper's and of most other frontier novels of the nineteenth century is the merit of romance, which has never accurately reflected the spirit of heroic ages.

Although inventing nothing, Cooper perceived more clearly than any of his predecessors or contemporaries the possibilities of frontier warfare for fiction, and he imposed upon the scattered materials available to him what was, in consequence of Scott's vogue, the most acceptable form. His Leatherstocking Tales, which fixed the pattern of nineteenth-century romances of the frontier, were the culmination of several independent developments: notably, the accumulation of information (often inaccurate) about the aborigines, the rise of the frontiersman as a type, and the revival and perfection of prose romance by Scott.

The Indian in the guise both of a bloodthirsty fiend and an innocent child of nature had maintained a precarious existence in literature since the seventeenth century. Perhaps as early as 1601 Antoine Du Périer had framed a bestial portrait in the novel *Les Amours de Pistion.*[9] The noble savage, incubated in travelbooks and enlarged in the essays of Montaigne and in novels such as *Cleveland* (1732) by the Abbé Prévost, reached maturity in Chateaubriand's *Atala* (1801). Without much doubt, Chactas, the hero of the last work, furnished Cooper with suggestions for Uncas, the last of the Mohicans. The first American story dealing extensively with Indians was Mrs. Ann Eliza Bleecker's *History of Maria Kittle* (1781, published 1793), which, compounded of both fact and fiction, stood between the true account of Indian captivity and the frontier novel. For a century and a half before the Leatherstocking Tales, the public had feasted on the autobiographical abduction narrative, which under the color of personal history produced many of the pleasurable effects of fiction. The specimens of this type read by the Puritans ordinarily illustrated the power of the Lord to deliver the righteous from the imps of Satan, as the title of the earliest suggests—*The Sovereignty and Goodness of God, Together with the Faithfulness of His Promises Displayed; Being a Narrative of the Captivity and Restoration of Mrs. Mary Rowlandson* (1682). Later captivity tales were often presented frankly as adventures, and without the artifices of fiction or the bias of religion lacked a substantial basis of appeal. But the usefulness of both noble and villainous Indians for fiction became abundantly clear with the appearance of the Leatherstocking Tales.[10]

Meanwhile, the lives and deeds of the Indian fighters grew a rich hoard of legendry. As previously observed, early attempts to exploit this material in poetry failed in every case. While Cooper did not actually succeed in bodying forth an Achilles of the wilderness, with Leatherstocking he capitalized on the growing interest in the frontier warrior as an epic hero. The public was generally inclined to accept Cooper's Indian

fighters and Indians—their unnatural poses notwithstanding—
because, set in plain opposition, they illustrated the prevailing
symbolical construction placed upon the struggle for the West
and at the same time assumed individual and undeniably
colorful form.

Sir Walter in the meantime perfected the historical romance,
succeeding, in contrast to his precursors, in animating personages of remote periods. The Waverley novels renewed the
popularity and improved the literary standing of the romance,
which after deteriorating during the Renaissance seems to have
passed very nearly out of view in the middle of the eighteenth
century. Scott set his plots on ostensibly firm historical foundations, and, although often sacrificing truth to art, allayed the
traditional suspicion attached to pure fiction and caught
thereby the widest possible reading public. His novels cast
a soft romantic haze over the whole country, but especially
over the South, and strongly influenced two or three generations of Americans. For the lack of a wide variety of suitable
historical matter, his imitators inevitably overworked the Revolution and the frontier, and yet they scarcely diminished the
enthusiasm for historical romance, which even now has vitality
enough. For over a century the public has proved willing to
pay good money to read under varying titles much the same
story of Indians and frontiersmen and gentle heroes and
heroines.

The success of the *Pioneers* (1823), the *Last of the Mohicans*
(1826), and the *Prairie* (1827) produced no immediate erup-
tion of Kentucky novels, although the heroic matter accumulated since the founding of Boonesboro and Harrodsburg sur-
passed in richness and variety the storehouse upon which
Cooper drew. Moreover, English novelists a quarter of a
century earlier had demonstrated in some part the exploitabil-
ity of the Garden of the West: Kentucky figures as the setting
for substantial portions of Imlay's *Emigrants* (1793), Eugenia
de Acton's *Disobedience* (1797), and George Walker's *Vagabond* (1799). In 1832,[11] however, James Kirke Paulding began

to assay the ore with *Westward Ho!,* a novel constructed around an utterly lugubrious love affair and marred by the author's classical allusions and impertinent witticisms, but memorable for the portrait of the backwoodsman Bushfield. William Alexander Caruthers introduced a Jeffersonian yeoman into the *Kentuckian in New-York* (1834) purely for decoration, but this character, though apparently a doughty Indian fighter, has affinities with the comical Yankee of the stage rather than with the Boone species. The first good romance laid in Kentucky was *Nick of the Woods or the Jibbenainosay* (1837) by Robert Montgomery Bird, a Philadelphia physician. Although his frontiersman, Ralph Stackpole, is not an offspring of Boone but a low-comedy type garbed in buckskin, Bird brought together with suggestions from Cooper the chief features by which the romance of the Kentucky frontier has been distinguished. Not a great novel to be sure, *Nick of the Woods* yet remains as readable as the Leatherstocking Tales.

The Kentucky romances appeared under a variety of intriguing titles, but "Wooing and Warring in the Wilderness," used by Charles D. Kirk in 1860, would suit most if not all of them.[12] Over half, moreover, depend in some part upon the time-honored motif employed with conspicuous success by Cooper in the *Last of the Mohicans* and by many others since the High Middle Ages—indeed, since antiquity, for abduction and rescue figure in the ten-year struggle of the Argives against Troy. That the short historical past of Kentucky was a rare treasure of such thrilling episodes as romance feeds upon goes almost without saying: frontier sketches and chronicles overflow with kidnappings of fair ladies by ferocious Indians, frenzied and sometimes successful pursuits, in addition to desperate hand-to-hand combats, violent assaults on weakly defended fortresses and upon hapless flatboats on the Ohio, horrible massacres, and barbaric executions at the stake. Novelists incorporated into their conventional frames the most sensational events of Kentucky story, with the result that the course

of genteel love runs through a primeval forest ringing with
the mortal conflict of slinking Indians, blackhearted renegades
like Simon Girty, monomaniacal Indian haters, and redoubtable frontiersmen. If civilization and love appear to hang in
the balance between the forces of good and evil, the reader
has no real cause to fear the outcome; the reliable Caucasian
Providence always unhinges the red heathen, leaving the
wilderness safe for culture and cultured lovers. The path which
the well-born lovers tread passes through the dark forest without becoming a part of it. Since the romantic plot and the
picturesque background are never actually integrated, two
organic spheres of activity exist side by side, not clearly in
opposition or in harmony, but their relations sadly confused.

In the *Pioneers* (1823), first of the Leatherstocking Tales,
Cooper drew a well-nigh impassable line between the wilderness and civilization and created an appropriate hero for each.
These two very different sorts of men, Natty Bumppo and
Oliver Effingham, between them possess the important qualities united in the knight of medieval romance, but neither is
a complete hero for lacking in some part the character which
distinguishes the other in his proper sphere—the court or the
forest. Like most of his imitators, Cooper introduced his
genteel hero to the frontier as an apprentice and had him
taught marksmanship and woodcraft, but for all that, he remains an intruder in an exotic milieu. The novelists at work
with the Kentucky frontier had no alternative within the conventional framework to Cooper's discrimination of types, for
to the extent that the civilized man accommodated himself to
the wilderness he declined from the masculine ideal of polite
society. The acceptable protagonist, whether represented as
hopelessly inept in the backwoods or as nearly the equal of
Boone, necessarily stands for a set of civilized values and
thereby reveals the condition whence he came and to which
he will return when the drama is over. It is not surprising
that from the frontier period to the present the quality of the

romantic hero has occasioned authors great difficulty, or that
none has found a satisfactory solution.

The improbably sentimental and refined sort of hero appears
most often before the rise of the dime novels in the 1860's
and seldom after 1900. In *Nick of the Woods* Bird frankly
granted the relative helplessness of his hero Roland Forrester
and placed him under the protection of the bloody Quaker
Nathan Slaughter. Similarly, Emerson Bennett put the reliable hunter Tom Sturgess in charge of the hero of the *Phantom
of the Forest* (rev. ed., 1868), one Harry Colburn, who, though
represented as a capable Indian fighter, practices landscape
painting between skirmishes and describes himself as an "en-
thusiast." It is now difficult to believe that Bennett's portrait
of this Virginian of refined sensibilities was entirely serious:
"yet the thin, well-chiselled nose, firm-set mouth, close, com-
pressed lips, and round, prominent chin, denoted unusual
strength of character, and, taken in connection with his broad,
noble forehead, and clear, soul-beaming eye, bespoke the high-
toned principles, resolution and courage of the innate gentleman—for indeed men are *born* gentlemen" (ch. 1). William
Bradford, the protagonist of Charles Kyle's *Pioneer Hunters of
Kentucky* (1874), is an even more astonishing personage but
probably no less satisfactory from the nineteenth-century view-
point. Taking leave of his lady love, he exclaims, "Most reluc-
tantly do I leave you, yet ere to-morrow's sun shall have arisen,
you will see me again" (ch. 1). Saved from pursuing Indians
by Simon Kenton and offered something for his health, Bradford reveals that he has preserved his morality as well as his
eloquence: "I seldom pollute my lips with the beverage, and
never was under its influence in my life" (ch. 3). Charles
Glenn, a gentle Philadelphian removed to the backwoods in
J. B. Jones' *Wild Western Scenes* (rev. ed., 1907) with volumes
of Shakespeare and Scott for comfort, explains to Boone in
extraordinarily precious language his romantic motive for re-
treating from civilization: "I had heard that you were happy

in the solitude of the mountain-shaded valley, or on the interminable prairies that greet the horizon in the distance, where neither the derision of the proud, the malice of the envious, nor the deceptions of pretended love and friendship, could disturb your peaceful meditations: and from amid the wreck of certain hopes, which I once thought no circumstances could destroy, I rose with a determined though saddened heart, and solemnly vowed to seek such a wilderness, where I could pass a certain number of my days engaging in the pursuits that might be most congenial to my disposition" (ch. 1). Driven to the frontier by disappointments in love, the desire to recoup their fortunes, false accusations of crime, or an alleged passion for raw adventure, such dull Byronic blades as these deserve to lose their hair but ordinarily obtain both fortune and love. Over such fellows Boone might well have shaken his head and sadly remarked the passing of the old order, but not a public which had wept over Werther, Saint Preux, and René.

After the middle of the nineteenth century, novelists tended to narrow the gap between the refined fugitive from civilization and the rude frontiersman, and in some recent romances the two are scarcely distinguishable. Nevertheless, there was in Cooper's time, if not now, a real need to emphasize the differences so that the buckskin warrior would not in any way appear to be a rival of the fashionable hero; for the two sorts were plainly drawn from worlds a millennium apart, the one from the Enlightenment, the other from the heroic age reinstituted in the West. The urban ideal, as developed in the eighteenth century, was a man decorous, philosophical, and sentimental by virtue of birth and education. If he engaged in military action, he did so out of unpleasant necessity and took no pride in slaughtering his enemies. Frontier romancers faced a difficult problem in endowing their heroes with sufficient cunning, aggressiveness, and woodcraft to insure their survival without at the same time repudiating the ideal. No gentleman ought to slither through the forest on his belly or close with a verminous savage in mortal combat. A compromise was the result: sentimental heroes fight Indians and white villains but with decorum and with sentiment. Thus, Theodore Lockwood in J. H. Robinson's *Neverfail* no sooner strikes down an Indian in the Kentucky wilderness than he would "willingly recall this red child of the forest back to that robust life which he inherited but a few moments ago" (ch. 2). This portrait of innate benevolence stands at the opposite pole from the casual barbarism of Adam Wiston, whom Emerson Bennett described in *A Desperate Encounter*, a tale included in *Wild Scenes on the Frontiers* (1859): "Adam was a large, powerfully built man, six feet in height, and well proportioned, with iron nerves and whipcord muscles, and, at five-and-twenty, regarded himself as the equal in physical strength and endurance of any human being on the frontier. . . . He was, moreover, supple, active, long-winded, and quick of foot." This frontiersman characteristically feels no pity for an opponent, yet acknowledges the other's merit according to the standards of heroic societies: "Adam, finding the savage was at last really dead, slowly gathered himself up, seated himself upon the body, wiped the blood and perspiration from his face, and, in a somewhat doleful, half ludicrous tone, complimented his late adversary by saying: 'You war the toughest old red nigger as ever Adam Wiston fou't.' "

European princes and their soldiery in the eighteenth century managed military affairs with unprecedented courtesy, limiting their objectives according to good taste and demanding no more of the vanquished than reason allowed, while in the Ohio country during a part of the same period the Adam Wistons waged utterly primitive warfare against the Indian, with claw and fang, scalping knife and tomahawk, and long rifle. The contrasting conduct of the antagonists at Braddock's debacle and even at the Battle of New Orleans sixty years later suggests the difference between the two modes. Obviously, a responsible author steeped in the ideals of the Age of Reason could not approve the methods of a class of warriors risen from the barbarian past except as they contributed to progress, and he could not under any circumstances permit a genteel hero, the fair product of civilization, to adopt their primitive tactics. A third party was needed to mediate between savagery and civilization and to fill the role of agent in the myth of progress, a man both doughty and benevolent. It can hardly be considered an accident that Filson chose Boone instead of Kenton for immortality or that Cooper preferred Leatherstocking over Henry March.[13] Cooper clearly sought in nature the counterpart of the urban ideal, as Captain Middleton's characterization of Natty in the *Prairie* suggests:

The man I speak of was of great simplicity of mind, but of sterling worth. Unlike most of those who live a border life, he united the better instead of the worst qualities of the two people. He was a man endowed with the choicest and perhaps rarest gifts of nature, that of distinguishing good from evil. His virtues were those of simplicity, because such were the fruits of his habits, as were indeed his very prejudices. In courage he was the equal of his red associates; in warlike skill, being better instructed, their superior. "In short, he was a noble shoot from the stock of human nature, which never could attain its proper elevation and importance, for no other reason, than because it grew in the forest." (ch. 10)

Assuredly the effect of this portrait was to soften the contrast between the dark forest and the city and to support the romantic view of the Indian fighter, but Cooper wrought more complexly than he in all likelihood intended.

At first glance, Leatherstocking seems to be a satisfactory compromise. He combines the heroic qualities of the frontier with the plainer virtues of civilization and thus intimates a tribute to the founders of the West with no cost to the ideals of the East. There are difficulties, however. Represented as a friend of those who would tame the wilderness (an agent of progress, no less, though Cooper slights the issue), he yet despises entrepreneurs like Judge Temple. Suspended between the classes represented by Ishmael Bush and Oliver Effingham, he is neither churl nor earl. Cooper denies him meaningful rewards—wealth, women, and position—by pretending that he has no interest in them and sends him stalking beyond the pale when the red enemy has been repulsed from one white salient after another. In the *Deerslayer* (1841), a late work, Cooper attempted an explanation of Natty's confused raison d'être, but it is not yet clear whether he is a Wordsworthian resting in the bosom of nature or a child of Rousseau descended to that blessed condition one stage above savagery. There is no apparent reason why he should spend most of his time succoring the civilized, since he affects distrust for that condition. In truth, Leatherstocking is probably neither fish nor fowl but like the legendary Kentuckian, a close relative, the embodiment of conflicting ideologies, to which Cooper understandably grants unequal emphasis. However useful as a bridge between savagery and civilization, he posed more difficulties than Cooper could well resolve; and as a philosopher in buckskin, moreover, he became exceedingly tedious. Leatherstocking is unquestionably more significant as a social symbol than as a character of romance, which has endured these last eight centuries from action, not talk. A wish figure wrenched by organic contradictions, he also mirrors the tension in the mind of the nineteenth century between the forest and the city, anarchy and conformity.

Moral and didactic after the fashion of authors of the Enlightenment, Cooper imposed upon western materials not only a traditional form, taken in the narrow sense of structure, but also a traditional philosophical pattern. If the literal truth of the frontier suffered in consequence, the Leatherstocking Tales became a comprehensive, though defective, statement of "a conservative, evolutionary, eighteenth-century kind of progress."[14] Although his argument is superficial, illogical, and sometimes incoherent, Cooper presented the case for civilization as opposed to savagery in a manner usually acceptable to his period, and most romancers of the century agreed to his premises. Whatever his multiple significations, the frontiersman of the Leatherstocking type has only one function in the plot proper: he furthers civilization generally by oppressing the Indians as symbols of savagery and particularly by protecting the fair flowers of culture—hero and heroine—sojourning in the wilderness. Although ordinarily expressing contempt for civilization, he is nonetheless an agent of progress. As an instrument mainly, superior to the Indians and border whites, yet inferior to broadcloth gentry, he occupies no definable social position for lacking social reality. This matter has occasioned authors considerable distress without producing a solution, and indeed there is none.

In the minds of Cooper and other apostles of culture there was, however, no question about the quality of the refined hero: he was well bred, well educated, and consequently well mannered,[15] as indeed have been the gallant knights of romance since the portrait of Lancelot flowed from the pen of Chrétien de Troyes toward the end of the twelfth century. In ascribing high lineage to their heroes the romancers merely followed convention, but convention founded in something deeper than social use and stronger than equalitarian sympathies. The "squire of low degree" was no more acceptable in romances of the allegedly democratic frontier than in *Guy of Warwick* or the *Talisman*. The proletarian hero is a comparative newcomer to literature and has yet to prove his worth except as the Horatio Alger type, who by definition becomes through industry and honesty the image of his betters. Antiquity recognized no such biological miracle as a churl's becoming an earl. The Homeric heroes are all well born and some the bastard progeny of the immortal gods of Olympus. Both Siegfried and Beowulf stand in royal lines, which in Teutonic genealogy usually stem from Woden. If the heroes of Kentucky novels may scarcely pretend to immediate descent from royalty, they are with few exceptions scions of aristocratic—usually Virginia—families and never the offspring of ordinary yeomen or mechanics. They are, moreover, formally educated, a qualification upon which modern romancers have generally insisted. In this matter authors reflected the widespread enthusiasm in America for the appearance if not the substance of education. While sentimental philosophers of the Age of Reason, like the third Earl of Shaftesbury, granted to men of whatever condition an innate moral sense and accordingly the capacity for natural nobility, they could not avoid the self-evident fact that even the finest diamond is lusterless in the rough. And indeed it would have been strange if the Enlightenment, primitivistic tendencies notwithstanding, had repudiated education, for the arts and sciences were central to the rational theory of progress.

However fascinated by the state of nature and the child of nature after the fables of the voyagers, Europeans were far from approving savagery. What they did approve was the idea of an unfallen son of Adam in a paradisiacal scene. Conceived without firsthand knowledge of primitive societies, their man tended to have the virtues of civilization with none of the defects, and their setting bore a strong resemblance to the Arcadia of the poets. It is significant that Mrs. Aphra Behn, who in some things anticipated Rousseau, extravagantly praised the life of uncivilized indigenes in her short novel *Oroonoko, the Royal Slave* (1688) and yet elaborately distinguished her hero, one of the first of a long line of noble savages in fiction, from his own kind. She bestowed upon Oroonoko not only superior lineage but also a European education, provided by a Frenchman at his grandfather's court. Furthermore, after calling him a Negro and painting him ebony, Mrs. Behn denied that he had any negroid features besides color. The resemblance of her character to Othello can scarcely be accidental. Oroonoko calls to mind another fictional hero masquerading as an aborigine. Chactas, the sentimental lover of Atala in Chateaubriand's celebrated novel, is and is not an Indian, as the author carefully explained in the preface to the first edition: "He is a savage who is more than half civilized, since he knows not only the living languages but also the dead languages of Europe. He should then express himself in a mixed style, suitable to the line on which he marches, between society and nature." These picturesque offcolor characters are hardly exceptional; primitivists have generally preferred their noble savages less savage than noble. Furthermore, while obtaining obvious advantages from exotic materials, Mrs. Behn and Chateaubriand had to satisfy a historic requirement of romance, to wit, a hero—no matter what his circumstances—shaped in the image of the masculine ideal of the author's own society.

Something more than the traditional respect for learning enters into the emphasis placed upon formal education in modern romance as contrasted with medieval. The feudal noble had no special need for instruction in the seven liberal arts, which suited the priestly calling rather better than the military. When not hunting or warring, he whiled away the time at court talking with his fellows or listening to professional entertainers. Romancers necessarily grant their knights appropriate training in jousting and courtesy but make little of the matter. With the wide extension of the benefits of education to the laity in the Renaissance, learning came increasingly to be a mark of gentility and ultimately a *sine qua non* of respectability. By his insignia—arms, hair style, and civilian dress— the knight proclaimed his calling and his rank. Since the Middle Ages, however, the external distinctions of class have tended to fade, and though attempts have sometimes been made to regulate apparel, men have increasingly been free to dress according to their purses. Virginia aristocrats in the seventeenth century wore brilliantly colored vests, knee breeches, long coats of various hues, silk stockings, ruffles, and shoes with silver buckles. By the period of the Revolution, gentlemen dressed with considerable regard for the equalitarian temper of the masses, among other alterations having replaced the powdered periwig with the powdered but less ostentatious queue. The gentry of Kentucky in the early nineteenth century affected broadcloth, solid-gold watches, and blooded mounts, but these were rather pale insignia by comparison with the splendid adornment of the old nobility, who dressed like peacocks and behaved no less arrogantly. Rather by the elegance of their speech and manners than by their clothing gentlemen on the frontier disclosed their quality; where all were strangers, any man could pretend to riches and gentle birth, but none could conceal the lack of Cicero and Virgil, Newton and Locke and Lord Kames. At a time when rifle and ax would procure a lordly estate for even a yeoman or a mechanic, education was the surest test of class, and it is therefore not at all surprising that romancers regularly conferred this emblem of progress upon their heroes whether it was much used or not.

Cooper's solution of problems raised by distinctions of class was all too plainly artificial. The ante bellum public seems to have been willing enough to accept such inconsistencies as were produced by the framing of the frontier according to the upper-class view of progress, but an improved formula was obviously needed, especially to draw rank and merit closer together and to modify that tertium quid Leatherstocking. Cooper himself suggested a means in the *Pathfinder* (1840) and the *Deerslayer* (1841), the last of the series; he pulled the heroines and the opposite of one of them nearer to Natty and represented him in each case as a candidate for matrimony. However, the men who win the ladies are neither buckskin nor romantic heroes. Another solution is evident in a good many Kentucky novels: the chief Indian fighter, while recalling Leatherstocking, is yet a simple epic warrior, and the hero of gentle birth, stripped of some of the accouterments of civilization, stands nearer the center of the forest. Thus Boone takes Indian scalps in Bennett's *Renegade* (1848) more jubilantly than benevolence allows, and in the dime novel *The King of the Woods* (1884), by Beadle's man Joseph E. Badger, Jr., he kills savages in truly heroic style. This is not to suggest that Filson's Boone vanished, as he certainly plays a fairly prominent role in J. B. Jones' *Wild Western Scenes* (rev. ed., 1907) and enters into Lucy Cleaver McElroy's *Silent Pioneer* (1902) for a period of meditation. During the last fifty years his role in frontier romances has been limited largely to occasional appearances—a familiar symbol lending color to the background. The rough, somewhat ferocious frontier type visible in James Weir's *Simon Kenton* (1852) and in Bennett's works grew into the indomitable heroic-age warrior of the dime novels. Although possessed of only homely wisdom by comparison with the brilliant rural philosophy of Leatherstocking, he talks less, acts more, and wears better. Romancers have perhaps been wise in preferring him over the other, less realistic character, who suited the myth of progress but not the frontier epic.

As for the romantic hero, novelists in this century have sought plausible ways of providing him with such training and experience in Indian warfare as the heroic situation in the West actually required. Thus, Winston Churchill sends David Trimble, the hero of the *Crossing* (1904) into Kentucky while a mere boy, there to be tutored by the bona fide frontiersman Tom McChesney and his kind wife Polly Ann. This son of a Scottish earl and a Charleston belle endures the most rigorous sort of conditioning with Clark at Kaskaskia and Vincennes, and by the time the author returns him to Virginia for legal training he is an accomplished buckskin warrior. Equipped with the indispensable education, Davy goes back to Kentucky and labors on behalf of the commonwealth. In New Orleans on a governmental mission, he comes down with yellow fever, but the recently widowed Vicomtesse d'Ivry-le-Tour nurses him back to health and eventually marries him. Davy receives the rewards appropriate to birth and education and assumes his rightful rank in society. Although the *Crossing* is not a work of major importance, Churchill must be allowed to have accomplished an adroit fusion of the prime qualities of epic and romantic heroes.

More recently, Hal G. Evarts has attempted in *Tomahawk Rights* (1929) a solution similar to Churchill's, although carrying his hero much deeper into the forest. Shawnee braves abduct Rodney Buckner, the infant child of aristocratic Virginians, and rear him as their own. He early comes to love another captive, a beautiful little white girl named White Fawn by the Indians. Buckner is a thoroughgoing primitive by the time a rich uncle takes him back to Virginia for educating, and he later returns to place his superb training in Indian tactics at the service of the settlers. Evarts demonstrates his hero's fitness for the usual rewards of civilization and then represents him as rejecting both genteel love and fertile land. With White Fawn and their young son, Buckner —in contrast to David Trimble—follows the frontier nomads westward out of Kentucky, thoroughly disillusioned with civilization as a consequence of the bitter litigation over the fabulous garden of the Indian. In the *Shining Mountains* (1948) by Dale Van Every, Matt Morgan goes west in the period of the Lewis and Clark expedition. Although provided with education, he has little need for this insigne of respectability in his roving life on the plains. The author eventually returns him to civilization, however, and provides him with a somewhat tarnished lady of no great social pretensions. Van Every modified the romance formula even more radically in the *Captive Witch* (1951). His hero is a Virginian but neither well bred nor well educated. Adam Frane, a truly formidable frontiersman, endears himself to two women who are poles apart—a beautiful Virginia widow of wealth and culture and an uncommonly shrewish but fascinating girl who had been reared by Indians after her aristocratic parents perished in the notorious Suck on the Tennessee River. In the end he acts like Rodney Buckner, rejecting the cultured Cynthia Wyeth on the threshold of the bridal chamber and returning to the wilderness cave where the "natural" woman awaits him. The shift employed in the *Crossing* to merge the two kinds of heroes Evarts and Van Every have carried to an extreme by assimilating the product of culture to the forest. *Tomahawk Rights* and the *Captive Witch* are much more satisfying aesthetically than the average frontier romance of the nineteenth century, but their excellence entails a considerable sacrifice of the civilized values which Cooper and his contemporaries carefully preserved.

The older American novelists were moral if anything. While meaning to entertain, they solemnly accepted the responsibility of upholding the values of the society which supported them, whatever the expense to art and truth. Although their eighteenth-century legacy included sentimental primitivism as well as the doctrine of progress, there was for them no alternative to treating the struggle for the West according to the latter. This is not to say that the earlier romances are free of primitivism, as nothing could be farther from the truth. Nevertheless, the forest as symbol of the world of primitive impulse is held clearly apart from the world of rational behavior. The representatives of civilization may venture into the wilderness to achieve the familiar objectives of romance but do so at no cost to their principles. In the end they return to that blessed state whence they came full of exotic experience though no whit declined from that degree of excellence which good breeding and education wrought in them. It is permissible to charge the authors of nineteenth-century romances of the Kentucky frontier with flagrant misrepresentation; yet no other construction of the frontier was possible within the limitations imposed by the canons of romance and by upper-class postulates. All authors who dealt with the West probably realized that the knights of arts and industry behaved scarcely less barbarously than the savages who stood in urgent need of light, and that the fair products of the Enlightenment who marched safely in the rear of the emigration displayed more avarice than benevolence. To have laid bare the spotted actuality of the expansion would have been to shock tender sensibilities in the East and to disturb the rosy optimism which sustained the march to the Pacific. Admittedly, none had the courage to ask if the means justified the end, but popular literature after all is scarcely the vehicle for scrutinizing the myth of progress.

Cooper, Bird, Paulding, Weir, Bennett, and James Hall went wrong in many things though not from lacking a rational view of the western scene. If they winked at inequities, they clearly perceived the ideal consequences of progress and regarded themselves as apostles of the greater good. By their preconceptions most of the frontier romances written in this century are, like the dime novels, lacking in serious purpose and national scope, and a number of them are subversive and immoral. For rejecting civilization the heroes of *Tomahawk Rights* and the *Captive Witch* would have been wholly unacceptable to Cooper, as no responsible American author seriously considered relinquishing the fruits of progress. His Leatherstocking, a querulous old anarch and congenital nomad, damns civilization, but he is not a product of aristocratic breeding and classical education and cannot therefore be expected to recognize beneath superficial blemishes the enduring glory of refined society. Furthermore, Cooper confers no rewards upon Natty but lets him grumble his way through the wilderness till death. The defects of the city provided no sufficient justification for taking to the woods.

By the nineteenth-century view, the exceedingly successful novel *The Big Sky* (1947), by A. B. Guthrie, Jr., is irresponsible. The author allows the hero Boone Caudill, an illiterate, barbarous warrior from Kentucky, to roam the plains fighting and fornicating as his bowels move him. Inasmuch as his career is not integrated with the tide of progress and he himself is not recovered at last from the state of savagery, the book has no sufficient moral basis by the lights of the progressivists. Decency required the older authors to restore to society all the amenable wanderers of the benighted outer world. Jasper Western of the *Pathfinder* and Paul Hover, the bee-hunting Kentucky frontiersman of the *Prairie*, though indifferently schooled and apparently satisfied in the wilderness, in the end prefer at Cooper's insistence fame and fortune within the pale. Juliet Alves' *Huldah* (1942) is susceptible to much the same criticism as *The Big Sky*. The heroine—there is no hero—of this excellently conceived domestic novel is an amoral but utterly fascinating redheaded shrew, who displays epic courage and extraordinary sagacity but actively opposes the apostles of arts and industry in Kentucky and even expresses contempt for the formality of marriage. Indeed, the easy sexual relationships of recent frontier novels suggests that authors have abdicated a responsibility which the moral censors firmly insisted upon in the last century. While fornication for the sake of fornication is no more reprehensible than violence for the sake of violence, the horrendous fighting which distinguishes the dime novels is a somewhat more heroic exercise, and it has historic sanction besides. Thus, in many things modern writers offend against the decalogue of progress, and perhaps chief among them is questioning the preferability of the state of grace in enlightened society over the state of unregeneracy in the dark world of primitive desire. Good preachers all, authors of the old style well knew that when black and white mingle, the resulting grayness leaves right and wrong in doubt.

The strong influence of European literary conventions granted, American authors yet produced in the nineteenth century the very kinds of books—generally uninspired and prudential—demanded by the reading public, and that public was self-righteous, class conscious, prudish, and sentimental. The ideas which America tended to accept from Europe consorted well with a robust Christian materialism and a morbid obsession with sin. However liberal the dominant minority may have been in the period of the Revolution, by the second quarter of the century after, when native writers began publishing in volume, Jeffersonianism was in decline, and the upper-class point of view allowed progressively less credit to deviationists, whether deists, radical republicans, or utopians. How acutely popular writers sensed the crosscurrents in American society remains unclear; there is no question, however, that they implicitly sustained the conservative position of the ruling order. Even the western humorists, including Mark

Twain, who rowdily satirized the affectations of the East, seldom disturbed the actual pillars of the American system. The nineteenth-century romances of the frontier, while not entirely free of subversive elements, mine western legendry within the context of progressivism; in nearly every instance, virtue is rewarded, honesty vindicated, and Manifest Destiny justified, whatever the cost to art and probability. Yet, these ostensibly innocent novels, concluding with pious progressive chords, subtly invoke notes of the primitive during the journey through the wilderness and obliquely betray cleavages in the American mind.

9 The Child of Nature

*"The artificial Noble shrinks into a dwarf before
the Noble of Nature."*—THE RIGHTS OF MAN

RATIONAL PROGRESSIVISM expresses the official rather
better than the private view of the expansion in the nineteenth
century; the main appeal of the frontier for much of the public
was its intimations of the primitive. While acknowledging the
doctrine of progress and upholding civilized values, frontier
chroniclers and romancers meant above all to satisfy the widespread interest in primitive modes of existence, an interest
intensified to the point of enthusiasm by European naturalism
in general and particularly by Rousseau's speculations about
man in the state of nature. If the untamed West of the Indian
and the heroic white hunter was by the commonsense view
only a barbarian wild standing in need of the civilizing process,
it also connoted for the urban imagination a desirable way of
life. The popularity of the Leatherstocking Tales suggests that
a considerable public held and enjoyed both conceptions without much conscious confusion. Yet the measure of approval bestowed on the ravages of progress was mixed with deep-felt
regret for the loss of the wilderness as a symbol of idyllic
felicity and unbounded freedom.

This ambivalence in regard to the West owed something to
the primitivistic element in romanticism and something also
to universal psychological factors. If not originally part and

parcel of progressivism, primitivism early crept into its fold and there with protective coloration subverted some of the main tendencies of the host. At the very height of the Enlightenment, when by the craft of the hand and the magic of the brain mankind had at last found substantial relief from physical discomforts and the burden of superstition, a new phase of primitivism was in an advanced stage of incubation. Numerous philosophers and poets affected a distaste for the consequences of progress and a preference for a primitive way of life, though in truth few seriously considered taking to the woods. It is perhaps the consummate irony that at each step up from savagery the human race has regarded the fruits of progress with a degree of misgiving and often longed against reason for a return to a simpler condition. Moreover, because social systems in conferring benefits necessarily enforce privations, there are always individuals who out of personal discontent project into past or future time or the remote present a situation superior to their own. Such inclinations toward the not-here and the not-now doubtless originate as wish-fulfillment phantasies floating up from the suffering unconscious mind, though none reaches the level of expression without a more or less rational garment. Men invariably invoke authority to cover their cultural retreats and seldom disclose as the true cause their own failure or disillusionment. Whereas the educated tend to seek justification in eccentric interpretations of history, others usually rationalize their impulses by appeal to tradition or Holy Writ. Whether sought out or not, the West was for many nineteenth-century Americans not only a wilderness to be civilized but also an exciting alternative to civilization, where man could escape the harassments of the social mechanism and complete his life in all desirable things. Much of this feeling centered on the frontiersman of the Boone type, who embodied all wished-for qualities and realized all wished-for experiences in the state of nature.

Officially, Daniel Boone made Kentucky and the West safe for the arts and industry and then out of distaste for crowded conditions retired beyond the Mississippi, but as a child of nature, leading the incomparably good life, he induced the civilized imagination to follow him deep into the forest. It is indicative of nineteenth-century thinking that Boone should have been installed in two different myths—progressivism and primitivism—which, though not in all respects antithetical, clash on several levels and ultimately point in opposite directions. An ideal frequently taken as a reality, the Boone type encouraged the belief that in primitiveness the hopeful assumptions of primitivism were actually verified. In other words, the idealized frontiersman, constructed out of the hypotheses of primitivism, was often regarded as living proof of the very theory from which he sprang. How the actual primitiveness of the West materialized in political, social, and religious attitudes inimical to rational progressivism is a subject for another chapter. At this point it is needful to consider the legendary Kentuckian, visualized most often as old Daniel, in the role of noble savage. The character conferred upon him by sentimental primitivists was to some extent transferred to the generality of backwoodsmen, who gladly accepted the prerogatives due nature's noblemen and often behaved as alligator-horses.

The child of nature varies according to time and circumstance, but, as H. N. Fairchild observes, he is normally a "free and wild being who draws directly from nature virtues which raise doubts as to the value of civilization."[1] Antiquity knew him as a Scythian or Arcadian; for the Enlightenment he was an Indian or Polynesian. The Indian on close examination proved less noble than supposed, and his place in the American imagination was largely usurped by the frontiersman. Filson's Boone, Cooper's Leatherstocking, and their congeners, though closely resembling the traditional antitype of civilized men, owed their special ideological content to the concept of the noble savage developed in the eighteenth century. This abstraction, in the opinion of C. B. Tinker, was invoked as an antidote for the debased image of man which religious orthodoxy fostered: "The 'noble savage' was the offspring of the rationalism of the Deist philosophers, who, in their attack upon the Christian doctrine of the fall of man, had idealised the child of Nature. Man in a state of nature, the Indian with untutored mind, was, they held, a noble creature—indeed, the noblest work of God. Take him untouched by the finger of civilisation, and you would find in him a potential perfection. Among his endowments there must be of course an artistic sense which would put to shame the artificialities of civilisation."[2]

As heirs of the Renaissance humanist tradition, the rationalists of the eighteenth century faced the old problem of freeing man and the world from the clutches of strict Protestantism, and in the tumultuous litigation of the period the child of nature figured as a prime exhibit. While agreeing in many things, Protestantism and the Enlightenment divided radically over a surviving particle of Augustinianism, namely, original sin. To the process by which man was at last acquitted metaphysically, if not theologically, of Adam's sin, Newton contributed importantly through placing beyond doubt the question of universal order in the physical world and intimating the autonomy of nature and intellect. Denied by the deists the function of mediating between these two spheres, God shed His supernatural trappings and became a master mechanic, regulating man and the cosmos according to immutable laws. Over against the manifold dogmatic religions, the deists set by analogy with the Newtonian synthesis the concept of natural religion, a simple, aboriginal structure of belief containing the valid core common to all faiths and accessible to men of whatever condition without the mediation of priests. Deism was not intended to destroy religion but to ease the friction between supernaturalism and science.

Perhaps inadvertently John Locke lent epistemological support to the deistic position when in *An Essay Concerning Human Understanding* (1690) he banished "native ideas and original characters" from the mind and therewith the likelihood of original corruption. Through the operation of the "light of reason," the Enlightenment held, civilized and savage alike could discover natural law and by following nature realize in themselves a corresponding harmony and balance, benevolence and wisdom. While the theological and philosophical deists deriving from Shaftesbury and Voltaire were far from conceiving human nature and the world in identical ways, their speculations tended to endow man in the abstract with freedom of the will, the capacity for understanding the laws of the universe and thereby God, and the power to perfect himself without supernatural aid. The rationalists were perhaps not profound thinkers, and assuredly their assumptions about man and mind were highly vulnerable, as David Hume demonstrated; nevertheless, they succeeded to some extent in emancipating the human spirit from the Calvinist slough of degradation and providing a philosophical basis for the exaltation of man in the garden. The tension between nature and grace, intellect and faith remained, but whether rightly or wrongly the optimistic view of man largely prevailed.

The Enlightenment perceived that the philosophical exoneration of man left him hardly less depraved than Calvinists imagined; in the state of organized society he was all too plainly much as the King of Brobdingnag suggested to Gulliver —a creature of unreason, hopelessly enslaved by his ungovernable passions, and more disposed to mischief than to benevolence. The secular explanation of man's wickedness is implicit in Shaftesbury's *Characteristicks of Men, Manners, Opinions, Times* (1711): after emerging innocent from the womb, man becomes good or evil in accordance with the sensations presented to his mind. For the cultural primitivists the blame rested specifically on modern society as an obstruction to the pure light of reason. This conclusion, reinforced by Locke's treatment of innate ideas, led in one direction to the associationism of David Hartley and inevitably to determinism, but perhaps more importantly it supported the concept of the blessed state of nature as the desirable alternative to civilization—not a new idea to be sure but one which the eighteenth century exploited as never before.

It remained for Jean Jacques Rousseau to write the classic exposition of the naturalistic myth, the epoch-making *Discours sur l'origine et les fondemens de l'inégalité parmi les hommes* (1754). The effect of this long essay was to reaffirm and activate both chronological and cultural primitivism with enormous political, social, and religious consequences for Europe and America. In the opinion of A. O. Lovejoy, Rousseau was not a primitivist but a progressivist who in no way endorsed the conduct of the savage.[3] While the *Contrat social* (1762) sustains Lovejoy's proposition very well, the *Discours* lavishes uncommon praise on some aspects of savage life. The condition which Rousseau appears to favor, although not the raw state of nature, is yet not fully evolved society either. The *Discours* speaks approvingly of a hypothetical intermediate stage combining the physical well-being and natural pity of the savage with the plainer virtues and acquired sociability of civilized man. His theory of social history may be accounted progressive inasmuch as it points forward to improvement of man's lot within a coherent social order, but his arguments appear also to confer respectability on libertinism, to legalize the cult of wildness, and even to sanction blind atavistic impulses. Jean Jacques visualized a utopia in which men voluntarily enter into the social compact for the common good and yet preserve their liberty and integrity by virtue of their inalienable rights under natural law. The rational element of Rousseau's philosophy may be said to have materialized in the ideal program of the French Revolution, but the Terror which followed all too plainly revealed its primitive, anarchic substratum. To blame him for the excesses of the three-quarters of a century following the *Discours* is however totally unfair, for he merely gave perceptible form and dramatic expression to tendencies implicit in the speculations of the rationalists, the colored reports of voyages into remote areas, and traditions stemming from classical antiquity. The thought that uncivilized peoples in a presumably natural state preserved something of the felicity of the Golden Age had occupied the mind of Europe for a good two centuries previously, and such works as Mrs. Aphra Behn's *Oroonoko* (1688), with its uncritical commentary on native life in the West Indies, in many ways anticipated Rousseau's views and generally prepared the public to receive them.

Philosophers of the eighteenth and nineteenth centuries ordinarily conceived nature as a contrary of civilization rather than as an absolute state. "State of nature" and "child of nature" were terms of social criticism meant not to define a particular condition so much as to condemn and eventually to reform an existing one. Nevertheless, romanticism spawned a set of enthusiasts for whom the noble savage, as sketched by the philosophers, was not only a device of social criticism but also an ideal to be emulated. Genteel savages all, they immersed themselves in the state of nature with the fond expectation of benefiting both morally and physically. Appreciation of country life was of course as old as Virgil's *Georgics,* but in no century before the eighteenth had nature been steadily and warmly admired for its therapeutic virtue. This aspect of primitivism culminated in Wordsworth, who regarded nature as the instrumentality of divinity and therefore a source of comfort and inspiration and a repository of eternal truths. While a laboratory for transcendentalists seeking impulses from vernal woods, nature was also a sphere for complete self-realization and wild adventure. With the assumed approval of Rousseau, poets tended to exalt atavism and license and to allow the individual uncommon freedom to realize himself in an excess of emotion. That rational primitivism should have ultimately furnished an excuse for the satisfaction of rather elemental longings can only be regarded as ironical, for philosophers originally conceived the state of nature as relatively free of irresponsible conduct. In the Romantic period individuals sought in the forest the freedom of action which the society pronounced corrupt by Rousseau attempted to control, and America became the scene of numerous individual and collective experiments in evading the compulsions perhaps necessarily imposed on human beings by old cultures.

The American frontier, while creating nothing, functioned as a catalyst to precipitate such barbaric modes of behavior as highly developed societies suppress. European travelers filled with fanciful notions about the state of nature were appalled by the appearance and manner of the real natural man in the backwoods. Yet numbers of American writers displayed in the face of frontier reality an extraordinary partiality for the sentimental view of nature and the noble savage—the white one in particular. There are several explanations for this apparent blindness to the facts: the romantic construction pleased the public and, moreover, served the needs of social criticism; and for most writers during their periods of authorship the frontier had grown a distant and increasingly idyllic memory.

When the legendary Kentuckian took his place in the long line of noble savages, he inherited all their implications. So much may not be immediately evident from Daniel Bryan's *Mountain Muse* or even from Filson's account of Boone, but the old hunter's ideological descent is plain in Byron's *Don Juan* (VIII.lxi-lxvii), composed between 1818 and 1823. A prominent heir of the Enlightenment, Byron recognized Boone as a child of nature and invested him with the nobility appropriate to his kind. The English poet had no particular interest in Kentucky story but, like Caesar and Tacitus, meant through idealizing the primitive people of a remote land to confront his own society with its conspicuous defects. Accordingly, the Boone kind in *Don Juan* are substantially Rousseau's generalized savages, conscious neither of their special virtue nor of their meaning for civilization:

> And tall, and strong, and swift of foot were they,
>   Beyond the dwarfing city's pale abortions,
> Because their thoughts had never been the prey
>   Of care or gain: the green woods were their portions;
> No sinking spirits told them they grew grey,

No fashion made them apes of her distortions;
Simple they were, not savage—and their rifles,
Though very true, were not yet used for trifles. (VIII.lxvi)

In American romances, however, the frontiersmen not only
know themselves to be children of beneficent nature but also
recognize the advantages of their condition over the civilized
mode. As nature's noblemen, they often feel competent to
pronounce cosmic judgments, and indeed the sum total of
their utterances may be taken as a rough statement of European naturalism. Filson bears some responsibility for their
arrogance and self-righteousness, as he first shaped Boone
in accordance with the eighteenth-century conception of the
noble savage and then endowed him with uncommon philosophical depth and the eloquence to express it. With Filson's
Boone and Cooper's garrulous Leatherstocking as models,
novelists at work on Kentucky frontier materials quite understandably tended to allow the natural man to preach what he
practiced.

The *Adventures of Col. Daniel Boon* contains the outline of
a portrait conceived in the libraries of Europe and not in the
Kentucky wilderness, Filson's statement about the origin of
this so-called autobiography notwithstanding. In accordance
with his philosophical background Boone asserts the superiority of the forest: "No populous city, with all the varieties of
commerce and stately structures, could afford so much pleasure
to my mind, as the beauties of nature I found here."[4] The
aesthetic sense herein displayed may trace to Shaftesbury, who
made moral excellence somewhat contingent upon refinement
of taste. At the same time, Boone as a man of sentiment in
Filson's portrait assumes a pose ordinarily reserved in romance
for the genteel hero; the Kentuckian of fiction tends to stoicism,
an attitude cultivated by the Renaissance but not by the
eighteenth century or the even more lachrymose nineteenth.
Perhaps to avoid the slings and arrows of sectarians, Filson set
forth Daniel's religious views rather cautiously. Averring that
"it requires but a little philosophy to make a man happy in

whatsoever state he is," the hunter defines that minimum rather vaguely: "This consists in a full resignation to the will of Providence; and a resigned soul finds pleasure in a path strewed with briars and thorns." While ostensibly sound Christian resignation, his statement agrees closely with Seneca's *De providentia* and in no way conflicts with deism. In this connection it ought to be recalled that in the *Last of the Mohicans* Hawkeye (Leatherstocking) is described as one "who imbibed his faith from the lights of nature, eschewing all subtleties of doctrine" (ch. 12). This is of course natural religion.

James Hall in *Legends of the West* discussed the sources of knowledge available to a backwoodsman on the order of Boone and frankly affirmed a tenet of deism, that all men are endowed with the capacity for discovering the laws of nature: "he forsook them [his friends] in the same spirit in which the philosopher retires to the seclusion of his closet—to enjoy unmolested the train of his own reflections, and to follow without interruption a pursuit congenial with his nature. Though unacquainted with books, he had perused certain parts of the great volume of nature with diligent attention. The changes of the seasons, the atmospherical phenomena, the growth of plants, the habits of animals, had for years engaged his observing powers; and without having any knowledge of the philosophy of schools, he had formed for himself a system which had the merit of being often true, and always original" (pp. 253-54). Whether Hall was wholly sensible of the deistical implications of his statement does not appear; in any event, natural religion as opposed to revealed was anathema to the evangelical sects of the frontier and less and less appealing to Americans in general.

Between the *Pioneers* and the *Deerslayer* Cooper completed the portrait sketched by Filson; Leatherstocking is substantially what the earliest Kentucky historian had in mind—a noble savage embodying the ideals of rational primitivism and to a large extent conscious of his exceptional endowment. For being uncommonly articulate, he is particularly useful for revealing the ideological content of the Boone type. Natty is the instrument by which Cooper opposes the forest to the city in the *Pioneers,* and in the *Prairie* the old hunter speaks for all noble savages in condemning civilization: "It is long sin' I took my leave of the waste and wickedness of the settlements and villages. If I live in a clearing, here, it is one of the Lord's making, and I have no hard thoughts on the matter; but never again shall I be seen running wilfully into the danger of immoralities" (ch. 33). Precisely what immoralities he stood in danger of at the ripe age of ninety are not disclosed, but the firmness of his conviction underscores the incompatibility of the two worlds; he dies, as he has lived, in the forest, the sphere, according to his statement in the *Deerslayer,* "ordered and ruled by a hand that never wavers" (ch. 1). Upon resuming the Leatherstocking Tales in 1840 with the *Pathfinder,* Cooper displayed an improved understanding of his famous character and confidently established him in the frame of eighteenth-century primitivism. Natty is likened to Adam before the fall and described as the product of nature undefiled: "In short, it was said of the Pathfinder . . . that he was a fair example of what a just-minded and pure man might be, while untempted by unruly or ambitious desires, and let to follow the bias of his feelings, amid the solitary grandeur and ennobling influences of a sublime nature; neither led aside by the inducements which influence all to do evil amid the incentives of civilization, nor forgetful of the Almighty Being, whose spirit pervades the wilderness as well as the towns" (ch. 9). Finally, in the *Deerslayer* Cooper finished the portrait of the natural man in action by conferring on Natty, with suggestions from Wordsworth, an aesthetic sense equal to his high moral excellence.

The creator of Leatherstocking may never have grasped the total meaning of his man, but it is safe to assert that he at no time intended him as a realistic portrayal of the frontiersman.

Admittedly, Cooper had little firsthand knowledge of life in the backwoods, but he could not have used real frontier characters in romance had he known them well. It is extremely doubtful, moreover, that the ante bellum public would have tolerated the grim and brutal West in fiction of any sort. The dime novels, dating from 1860, are not evidence to the contrary, for they are as innocent of reality as *Treasure Island*. Cooper managed very well—in some ways better than Chateaubriand—with his red noble savages, Chingachgook and Uncas, holding them at the margin of the plot and exploiting their symbolic value; they are not complete characters, nor were meant to be. He erected Leatherstocking on the theoretical foundation sustaining all noble savages but then proceeded to suspend him between the city and the forest, between Oliver Effingham and Chingachgook, with the consequence that he developed unexpected connotations. Under the circumstances, Cooper could not establish control over this his most interesting character, who was at once progressive and regressive, superior to civilized man and yet inferior, anarchic but uncommonly orderly in behavior. Such a character reveals his lack of substantiality when placed on intimate terms with personages of specific quality.

Through the ambiguous Leatherstocking, Cooper unwittingly exposed the logical defects of eighteenth-century primitivism, which fundamentally is not a philosophical system but an ancient myth appareled in superficially rational weeds. The myth of man in the garden shatters under close examination but serves humanity none the less well on that account; in the child of nature, a complex structure of symbols, discrete kinds of desiring are objectified and in some part satisfied. However, Cooper could not permit Leatherstocking to realize all of his potentialities and at the same time use him as a somewhat puritanical critic of civilization. In Kentucky literature the frontiersman conventionally proclaims the superiority of the natural state in order to instruct the genteel, but by his exuberance, unrestraint, and even love of violence he confesses in himself inclinations which Cooper conceals in Natty. Thus, while revealing the philosophical foundations of his kind Leatherstocking yet does not exemplify naturalism full blown so well as some of the Kentuckians.

James Weir bodied forth in *Simon· Kenton* (1852) a Kentuckian of the "half-horse, half-alligator" strain—boastful, violent, impudent, mischievous, but none the less noble. The author claims for Simon, who in real life enjoyed a reputation for high spirits, the virtues attributed to the savage by the philosophers without in any way divesting him of the qualities associated with the warrior of the heroic age: "His was a soul of bravery, and honesty, untutored, unrestrained, and unpolished, it is true; scorning the law and its formalities, but not lawless; despising the refinements and luxuries of civilization, but nevertheless kind, and gentle, and noble; ignorant of hypocrisy and treachery, and drawing all of his wild notions and emotions from the grand works of Nature alone!" (ch. 16). Weir's description of Kenton represents an effort to reconcile naturalistic theory with frontier reality, the notion that nature induces virtue and harmony with the fact of spectacular violence in the wilderness. He actually blended Filson's Boone with Mike Fink, two very differently evolved products of the same myth, the one exemplifying innate benevolence and love of nature, the other, utter freedom of action and expression. Weir had yet another purpose in lauding Kenton and that to establish a contrast in his novel between the naturally good savage—he calls Simon a "semi-savage"—and the urban villain, one Jean Montlack, "the child of fortune and refinement—the offspring of education and civilization, corrupted and degraded by vice and selfishness" (ch. 16). While exemplifying natural goodness and maintaining the opposition between forest and city, Simon yet behaves more plausibly than Leatherstocking and spares the reader the latter's largely gratuitous moralizing. In general, the legendary Kentuckian indicts society as much by example as by statement, and he enacts a heroic role in the context of primitivism without calling undue attention to the ambiguousness of his situation.

Understandably, the Kentuckian was less interesting to romancers as a living proof of the blessedness of the state of nature than as an actor in a drama filled with thrilling pursuits of buffalo and bear, hairbreadth escapes from ferocious Indians, and virile rural pleasures. Through the Boone species they issued the call of the primeval wild and stirred in the eternally adolescent part of man a longing for high adventure. Dreamy European romantics vaguely conceived life in the state of nature as a mingling of contented savages who, if sometimes moved to violence, in the main comported themselves after a benevolent and humane fashion. While paying lipservice to this view, American authors sketched for the enjoyment of a none too peaceable public a life of activity consisting largely of elemental experience with big game and cunning redskins. Although cast as an agent of progress or a fugitive from civilization, the indomitable frontiersman had in addition a decidedly less innocent meaning: he embodied the ingrained masculine inclination to behave as a beast of prey, seizing a domain with fang and claw and holding lesser creatures in frightened subjection. Spengler declared "Every real 'man,' even in the cities of Late periods in the Cultures, feels in himself from time to time the sleeping fires of this primitive soul."[5]

Needless to say, Americans in the nineteenth century were not members of a decayed culture, and they exalted their own savage side in the buckskin warrior. So humane a philosopher as Henry David Thoreau acknowledged himself drawn between the spiritual life and the savage. Emerson Bennett, who hardened the features of Filson's portrait, permitted Boone in the *Renegade* to confess unabashedly the motive which moves the beast of prey and the epic hero alike: "Why I war born to it—nursed to it—had a rifle for a play-thing, and the first thing I can remember perticularly, war shooting a painter, and it's became as nateral and necessary as breathing; and when I get so I can't follow the one, I want to quit the other. Weary on't, indeed! Why, thar's more rale satisfaction in sarcumventing and scalping one o' them red heathen, than in all the amusement you could scare up in a thick peopled, peaceable settlement in a life time" (ch. 1). Beadle's creatures borrowed the frontiersman as a symbol of violence from Bennett and for half a century satisfied the lust of America's adolescents for slaughter. None however hymned the life of the killer more enthusiastically than Charles Wilkins Webber, who approved warfare as a manly exercise and a means to eliminate the weak and certify the strong.[6] It is doubtful that his eloquent plea for militarism occasioned any surprise or alarm; in the nineteenth century, Americans—and especially those of the South and West—were a martial folk and generally accepted the proposition that battlefield experience is the making of a man.

As the rapid depletion of game attests, hunting in some degree provided an outlet between wars for the strong desire in Americans for conflict and conquest. On the frontier, survival often depended on the ability to kill buffalo and deer, but the wanton destruction of the large herds evidences what is nowhere denied, that sheer delight in killing as much as actual need motivated the hunters. Although Boone is supposed to have introduced a bill at the Boonesboro convention of 1775 for preserving game in Kentucky, he can hardly have been a conservationist in the modern sense; and legend depicts him as an indefatigable hunter. Yet, it is not recorded that Daniel ever participated in one of the mass assaults on the creatures which marred the westward movement. The wastefulness displayed by the hunters in the Kentucky wilderness, which because heavily forested afforded animals some protection, was a forecast of the spectacular outrages to be committed regularly against the magnificent herds of buffalo on the plains beyond the Mississippi.

There is no question that the frontiersmen sinned grievously against nature and moreover deprived their descendants of the incomparable excitement of big-game hunting. Nevertheless, they were not considered ignoble in the nineteenth century for accelerating the inevitable reduction of wildlife. In describing hunting as a "licentious idle life"[7] Crèvecoeur missed the point of the matter as surely as Sir Thomas More, who regarded the exercise as barbarous and assigned it to the inferior residents of Utopia. Early in the fifteenth century the second Duke of York set forth in the *Master of Game* the happy idea that hunting had cathartic virtue, relieving the mind of unwholesome passions and inducing a balanced physical state, and in this view American men generally concurred. Many of those reared on the frontier would not have quarreled with the duke's further observation "that hunters go into Paradise when they die, and live in this world more joyfully than any other men."[8] Thoreau readily understood the passion for hunting, having himself taken the road back to the forest; but he regarded it as a mark of adolescence, to be abandoned finally for loftier pursuits, though not to be condemned. No less humane than Henry David, the preacher James B. Finley had yet a finer appreciation of hunting, for having grown up on the Kentucky frontier and engaged in the pursuit of big game. His estimate of the life of the hunter is as perceptive as the Duke of York's: "A hunter's life is one of constant excitement. He is always on the look-out, and filled with constant expectation. His narratives always possess a thrilling interest, and are listened to with the greatest attention. His wants are but few, and he is not disturbed with cankering care about the future. His employment does not lead him to covetousness, and he is always characterized by a generous hospitality. His hut or cabin is always a sure asylum for the hungry and destitute."[9]

Finley doubtless recognized that the pursuit of wild animals enables man not only to satisfy his predatory instinct but also to demonstrate his worth according to an ancient though by no means forgotten standard. The primitive tribe, faced constantly with the harsh possibility of starvation, has traditionally honored the ability to take game. Hunting is then a challenge which even civilized men accept in order to show themselves to be adequate providers and thus to answer the query of ancestral voices about their merit. Thoreau observed in *Walden* (ch. 11), "There is a period in the history of the individual, as of the race, when the hunters are the 'best men'," which is perhaps to admit that the compulsions of the tribal stage survive in the unconscious mind and drive into the woods those in whom the primitive spirit throbs most insistently. The unrestrained slaughter of the buffalo and deer in the West is not on this account to be summarily excused; at the same time, cognizance ought to be taken of the likelihood that the seemingly brutal hunters of big game were moved by commendable impulses. Stirred themselves by the silent voices from the none too distant forest, nineteenth-century Americans of some refinement understood the hunter's motivation rather better than European philosophers or Romantic poets, who usually ignored the hard truth that real nature is red in tooth and claw.

Romantics were varyingly sensible, however, of a mystical element in the inclination toward the forest and endeavored to reflect it in literature. Their freely expressed contempt for the amenities of the metropolis, love of spartan simplicity, and interest in the life of the imagination confess a deep-seated malaise and perhaps a more or less conscious assumption that the pristine self—free, pure, and virile—may be rediscovered somewhere along the trace leading back from civilization to the primeval garden. By reestablishing contact with the spirit of the race in the forest where it was broken long before, the urban primitivist perhaps expected to cure his physical and spiritual ills and thus restore himself to the state of original perfection. In other words, it was for the fountain of primal virtue that he sought, and through its transforming magic, rebirth at the very beginning of the world. William Blake

expressed a longing for spiritual regeneration with specific
reference to the American West:

> Tho' born on the cheating banks of Thames,
> Tho' his waters bathed my infant limbs,
> The Ohio shall wash his stains from me:
> I was born a slave, but I go to be free.

The cult of nature in the eighteenth and nineteenth centuries, while no doubt dedicated to the magnification of God
through His splendid works, also represented an evocation of
the regenerative power vested in the earth spirit, the eternal
mother of creation. Much nature poetry of the period suggests
incantation without specific Christian reference. The type of
the wandering hero—a large class including the Boone species—
is among other things an objectification of man's unceasing
search for the lost self in the womb of the race. Charles Wilkins Webber divined this meaning in the legendary Boone
and, while ostensibly describing the hunter's individual tendency, in truth expressed the universal longing for rebirth and
the recovery of primal strength: "he had no educated purpose
but what he had learned from the deep breathings of nature.
What this purpose was, he never stopped to think—he only
felt yearnings—ungovernably strong—the meaning of which he
could not know—but which led him, deeper and deeper, with
yet more resistless strength, into the cool profounds of the
all-nourishing bosom of his primeval mother."[10]

The tendency toward asceticism in the buckskin hero of
frontier romance is explicable by reference to the psychology
of his engendering: as an objectification of the desire for rebirth in a bright new life, he is to some degree the fallen
Adam regenerated through returning to the ultimate source
of being. It is unlikely that Cooper would have conceded so
much, yet in the *Pathfinder* he described Leatherstocking as
"sort of type of what Adam might have been supposed to be
before the fall, though certainly not without sin" (ch. 9). The

obvious uncertainty and Calvinist afterthought notwithstanding, Cooper meant to conserve Natty as a symbol of purification through regression. Having reestablished the broken connection with nature, this noble savage realizes in himself moral and spiritual qualities desired by, though inaccessible to, men in a civilized state. But like Antaeus he must maintain contact with the earth in order to preserve his strength; in the settlements, removed from his natural element, he could only deteriorate and become like Childe Harold "Droop'd as a wild-born falcon with clipt wing." Leatherstocking is an anarch only in terms of the law made to govern corrupt man. In no sense a libertine, though jealous of his freedom, he orders his life with very nearly monastic severity. Cooper may have denied him a wife largely for lacking his female counterpart, the ladies being too high and the country wenches too low; even so, for entailing a loss of masculine vigor, marriage is as incompatible as luxury with the character of the wandering hero. In the dime novel *Walking-Bear* (1870) by Arthur L. Meserve, Simon Kenton appropriately vows to "keep his rifle, and give the women the go-by" (ch. 1); and the no less virile frontiersman of Colonel Prentiss Ingraham's *Lantern-Jawed Bob* (1908), a Beadle thriller, finds the prospect of matrimony actually revolting: "Darn the gals! . . . they're pooty enough to look at, as picters! but to marry one on 'em, an' have her around all the time, huggin' an' sich like, would be too much for human nater—turn me into a skeleton if it wouldn't!" (ch. 11). These uncouth sons of Leatherstocking, speaking for the benefit of adolescents, nevertheless deliver the only judgment possible to their kind, for as Adams cloistered in the bosom of nature they stand in mortal danger from the debilitating embrace of Eve. This is the central significance of their preference for the single condition, although considerations of social degree admittedly enter in. As a wish figure and as such exemplifying an ideal state of being, the legendary hero in buckskin can no more than the medieval anchorite enter into the Bower of Bliss without suffering a ruinous transformation.

That the nomadic hunters of Kentucky were not in reality ascetic or antifeminist is generally assumed, although early chroniclers provide less evidence than desirable. There is no reason for thinking that they indulged themselves less fully than their descendants, the western mountain men, whose excesses, to judge from Bernard DeVoto's colossal montage *Across the Wide Missouri* (1947), were during the 1830's spectacular, if not Gargantuan. The trappers essayed the seven deadly sins and the numerous subdivisions thereof with unexampled enthusiasm. Far from disliking women, these burly noblemen of the great outdoors groped and rifled every tolerably comely squaw who came within their purview between the Mississippi and the Pacific but left the victims reasonably satisfied with their handling. Leatherstocking's expression in the *Deerslayer* of a disinclination to "mix colors" probably represented the attitude of an insignificant minority in the West. It is likely that the American imagination seized as avidly upon the fleshly side of frontier life as upon the other, for libertinism is no less a part of the content of the garden myth than asceticism.

Kentucky as the mythical garden offering a happy alternative to the exactions of civilization existed for a while chiefly in the dimension of place. Although not wholly ignoring the time factor, romancers somehow created the impression of frontier Kentucky as an unchanging situation. Their practice was psychologically sound, for the Earthly Paradise—the heaven of uninhibited expression—by definition continues in existence, always in the distance yet in present time. It was understandably a matter of relative indifference to the urban imagination that Kentucky remained a wilderness and accordingly a favorable milieu for the buckskin hero, however conceived, less than half a century after the explorations of Gist and Walker. In contrast, men with some experience of the West could not very well regard Kentucky as a primeval garden in the face of rapid and sweeping change, but they could and did imagine that it had once been everything that early travelers reported. By simply adding the dimension of definite time to place, they preserved the garden for themselves and for posterity. Thus, a decade or two after the death of Boone, the period of the settlement had become in the western imagination something of a Golden Age, that is, the Earthly Paradise translated to the past. In T. B. Thorpe's sketch *The Flatboatman of the West* Mike Fink expressed somewhat crudely the view of life on the frontier which the collective imagination standardized in the nineteenth century: "I knew these parts afore a squatter's axe had blazed a tree; 'twasn't then pulling a —— sweep to get a living; but pulling the trigger business. Those were times to see; a man might call himself lucky. What's the use of improvements? When did cutting down trees make deer more plenty? Who ever found wild buffalo or a brave Indian in a city? Where's the fun, the frolicking, the fighting? Gone! Gone! The rifle won't make a man a living now—he must turn nigger and work. If forests continue to be used up, I may yet be smothered in the settlement. Boys, this 'ere life won't do."[11] Ulysses uttered the same anguished cry on the Ionian shore long before and sailed out of peace-ridden Ithaca with his old comrades of Troy, bound for the unknown world beyond the Pillars of Hercules and high adventure. And it was not Mike's fate to die at the sweeps on a Mississippi boat or to be smothered in the settlements; if legend is to be credited, death awaited him, as other fugitives from the crowded paradise of Kentucky, far out on the western plains.

Mike's lament, though expressing only the longing of the pioneer class for the good old days, recalls chronological primitivism. The idea of cultural degeneration, implicit in the Scriptures and conspicuously reflected in premillennialism, was a minor but a persistent theme in America throughout the nineteenth century. Fundamentalist pulpits condemned the consequences of progress and even in the face of national well-being forecast a steady worsening of conditions. It should be remarked, however, that by the 1830's the middle-class congregations of the cities tended to favor the kind of preacher who appreciated the spirit of Christian materialism and recognized that God wanted man to make money and enjoy it. Criticism of civilization has very frequently resolved into an attack upon luxury as a principal source of corruption. In *De providentia* Seneca exhorted man to flee luxury and enfeebling good fortune, and Boethius, under the influence of the Stoics, allowed few actual comforts to the golden race. The apostles made a virtue of poverty, and their example induced periodic reflexes in the body of the church, like the Franciscan rejection of property ownership and numerous severe monastic reforms. The ghost of Dives has always haunted the Christian mind, questioning the power of riches to provide true felicity. Lois Whitney observed that the theory of degeneration was chiefly used in the eighteenth century as an argument against economic theories which tended to sanction luxury.[12] It may be recalled that Bernard Mandeville in the *Fable of the Bees* (1714) readily granted the affinity of luxury and corruption but to the consternation of moralists denied that the social system suffered greatly on that account. In *Le Mondain* (1736) Voltaire facetiously defended luxury and ridiculed the glum primitivists who constantly despaired of the present and yearned for the simple, ascetic version of the Golden Age.

The chronological primitivism of the frontier preacher James B. Finley now seems magnificently absurd; it is nevertheless interesting evidence of a countercurrent to progressivism in the American West and as an argument recalling the ideas of the Stoics, the Reformation sectaries, and the eighteenth-century naturalists. Finley's father, a Princeton-educated Presbyterian minister, had schooled him thoroughly in Greek and Latin and at the same time permitted him to hunt through the forests of the Bluegrass and later to perfect himself as a woodsman in the company of Indians near Chillicothe, while Ohio was yet a wilderness. In old age, surrounded by the brazen effects of progress, he pronounced a Juvenalian verdict on society and in a Boethian strain sang the glory of the men and women of the golden frontier:

I imagine I hear the reader saying this was hard living and hard times. So they would have been to the present race of men, but those who lived at that time enjoyed life with a greater zest, and were more healthy and happy than the present race. We had not then sickly, hysterical wives, with poor, puny, sickly dying children, and no dyspeptic men constantly swallowing the nostrums of quacks. When we became sick unto death, we died at once, and did not keep the neighborhood in a constant state of alarm for several weeks, by daily bulletins of our dying. Our young women were beautiful without *rouge, color de rose, meen fun,* or any other cosmetic, and blithesome without wine and fruit-cake. There was then no curvature of the spine, but the lasses were straight and fine-looking, without corsets or whalebone. They were neat in their appearance, and fresh as the morning, in their homespun, without the paraphernalia of a la Parisian wardrobe and toilet.

Young ladies did not then weep over the sickly sentimentalism of a Bulwer, or Dickens, or Eugene Sue, or become corrupted by the yellow-covered literature which is now, like the frogs of Egypt, infesting our land. They were not annoyed with any Don-Juan-puff-cigaros, with his long hair and face resembling a worn-out hearth-brush, and whose long ears indicated to what species of the *genus homo* he belonged. The hard-fisted, honest yeomanry of the country, instead of being the mere product of the tailor or hair-dresser, were nature's noblemen, and their associates.[13]

Finley of course knew the reality of the frontier, but a preacher with a point to make can seldom control his rhetoric. There can be no doubt, however, of his attachment to the carefree hunting life, which might have claimed him permanently except for the ritual magic of Cane Ridge.

The bloom of the wilderness was shattered more than a quarter of a century before Timothy Flint arrived, but no writer ever affected a stronger interest in the Kentucky of myth. Whether he believed literally in the late perfection of the man and the garden or merely intended like Tacitus to shame his contemporaries, his accounts are shot through with chronological primitivism. Flint accepted the word of "venerable patriarchs" that most of the early Kentuckians were "perfect Apollos and Venuses," and his representation of the men is unmistakably classic: "These progenitors of the west were generally men of noble, square, erect forms, broad chests, clear, bright, truth-telling eyes, and of vigorous intellects." Their consummate excellence was owing not only to the "noble stock" from which they grew but also, according to Flint, to the original condition of the garden: "The air, before the forests were levelled, was generally remarkable for its salubrity. The chase yielded the most salutary viands, and immeasurable appetite and digestion corresponding. To these denizens of the flowering wilderness life was invigorating to hear the exhalatory interjection, the safety-valve respiration, as they struck their well tempered axe into the enormous trunk of the tree, they were about to fell."[14]

Finley and Flint, educated and perceptive men both, unconsciously revealed the force of primitivism and the garden myth; knowing full well the grim reality of the expansion and under none of the novelist's obligations to satisfy romantic expectations, they yet chose to describe the frontier according to the paradisiacal archetype. While both praised the olden times out of a desire to condemn contemporary society, neither seems to have idealized frontier life with intent to deceive. Finley and Flint fairly reflected the disposition of the nineteenth century not only to magnify the virtues of the pioneers but also to idealize men of whatever sort living a simple, rural existence. In consequence of the naturalistic tradition, which numerous travelers and romancers supported, the public tended to ascribe extraordinary virtue to primitiveness as such and to endow the illiterate backwoods class with morality and wisdom which collectively it was never shown to possess. Not all Americans were so uncritical as to accept the hypotheses of primitivism, but few clearly perceived that the child of nature was by definition a subversive element in the frame of progressivism and that permitted to realize himself he would in many things repudiate the Enlightenment.

10 The Rejection of Athens

*"This book [of nature] I can read,
and I find it full of wisdom and
knowledge."*—THE DEERSLAYER

THE PORTRAIT of Daniel Boone sketched by Filson had
no more objective reality than the Kentucky garden conceived
by enthusiasts. Filson's motive cannot now be divined, but
it is apparent that he clothed in buckskin an ideal form, namely,
the child of nature postulated by the Enlightenment for the
purpose of assailing the defenders of corrupt institutions, which
shackled man on the pretext that he was incapable of gov-
erning himself. Since only an exhibit in litigation over human
perfectibility, the "natural" man escaped close examination
from a multiplicity of angles; he was not expected—certainly
not by right-thinking philosophers—to materialize as a social
being markedly ignorant of his obligations in a civilized state.
For lacking accurate information about the intricate structure
of primitive societies, the eighteenth century conceded the
likelihood that savages of remote lands enjoyed something like
Arcadian simplicity and felicity. Clearheaded apostles of progress, however, had no thought of returning humanity to
Arcadia; the secular millennium was to be achieved by process
of evolution from one complex stage to another. In the minds
of progressivists like the *philosophes* the chief hope lay in the
perfection of the individual within the context of existing
institutions and in the application of reason and experience

to the collective errors of civilization. At the outset, the idea of progress had a rationalistic bias. Assuming a fundamentally moral and rational human nature, philosophers undertook as a preliminary step to emancipate man from superstition and absolutism. Their ultimate objective was to reintegrate society according to the immutable laws of nature, not to precipitate a wanton destruction of institutions or a retreat from civilization.

However useful as an instrument for the Enlightenment, the child of nature cannot be considered an altogether happy conception. Though meant only as a pawn in a metaphysical game, he symbolized a condition none the less desirable for being impossible and accordingly evoked considerable impatience with the coherent plan for social betterment devised by the rational mind of the period. His supposedly ideal state intimated an immediate solution of the ills of society, to wit, withdrawal from civilization and re-creation of a Golden Age existence. Suffering humanity understandably preferred this apparently easy course to slow, evolutionary process. Moreover, since the sixteenth century, Europe had been mildly intoxicated with the idea of the Earthly Paradise, where men lived without laws, without dogmatic religion, even without social organization in the restrictive sense. The later eighteenth century, increasingly antirational, dreamed of recovering not the sophisticated Augustan Age, after which Neoclassical poets yearned, but the mythic Golden Age. Partly in consequence of the paradisiacal archetype, the rational vision faded somewhat and with it respect for orderly process. The longing for Eden, intensified perhaps unintentionally by Rousseau, materialized in the French Revolution, in various utopian experiments, and in pure anarchism. More importantly for present purposes, the child of nature, who had been conceived somewhat abstractly at first, came in the romantic imagination to have a living and breathing actuality. Wordsworth plainly reflects the disposition of the times to endow men living in a rural condition with uncommon virtue and judgment.

Filson's Boone, the prototype of western heroes, sprang into being protected by a tissue of optimistic hypotheses, which had been advanced and elaborated between the Renaissance and the end of the eighteenth century. In him were realized the implications of natural goodness, natural law, and natural religion. From conning the great book of nature alone, Boone and his kind claimed essential knowledge (the law of nature and of God) and with it independence of magistrate, priest, and seer, each symbolic of human frailty though of cultural achievement too. It was apparently of no great concern to Filson, or indeed to the generality of sentimental primitivists, that the child of nature implicitly rejects the intellectual treasures of civilization along with the luxury and corruption. Cooper, an apostle of conservative progressivism, saw the problem fairly clearly and in the *Prairie* carefully placed a limit on the perfectibility of the Leatherstocking class in order to preserve the urban ideal, that is, the product of the cultural process. It is hardly likely that the master of Otsego Hall, though unfamiliar with the actual frontier, made the mistake of confusing Natty Bumppo with reality. So much discrimination cannot be allowed all social idealists, some of whom treated as fact what was only an assumed value—moral, rational, uniform—in a social equation. Earlier Tom Paine had declared in the *Rights of Man* (1791-1792) with magnificent confidence, "The artificial Noble shrinks into a dwarf before the Noble of Nature." With the aid of demagoguery and the speculations of visionaries enmeshed in apriority, the noble savage escaped his original context and suggested his capacity for reproduction in an actual social setting. But viewed as a member of society proposing to make moral judgments on the basis of the book of nature alone, he understandably loses much of his protective coloration and reveals lineaments of the alligator-horse, another name for unshirted barbarism.

Romancers rightly ignored the social and political significations of the noble frontiersman, inasmuch as romance, a genre conventionally associated with stable, aristocratic orders, is intended to entertain rather than to instruct. Moreover, the fictional wilderness presented an unlikely scene in which to bring the general problem into sharp focus. Cooper, however, contrived a situation which proves that he was perfectly aware of the fundamental anarchism and potential menace of Leatherstocking, though probably not eager to discuss it in basic terms. In the *Pioneers* Natty kills a deer out of season and further offends against the law by resisting search and assaulting an officer. He acts upon his natural right, at least in the matter of securing food, in opposition to the law of society upheld by Judge Marmaduke Temple, and like most anarchs in similar circumstances he goes to jail. Cooper shortly effects his release without, however, resolving the basic conflict between natural rights and arbitrary laws. Yet there can be no doubt that the sentence had Cooper's no less than Temple's approval, as both men conceived progress within a rational framework. The case is interesting for exposing the child of nature from a legalistic angle of vision. Although scarcely crossing the perimeter of civilization, Natty all too clearly reveals the menace of his kind when translated from the Edenic scene. The anarchism of the natural man is presented even more strikingly by the Kentucky backwoodsman of James Kirke Paulding's *Westward Ho!* In a speech to his employer Colonel Dangerfield, Bushfield unequivocally sets aside the law of society and affirms the efficacy of the inner light as a guide to conduct: "Laws! none of your laws for me, colonel. I can't live where there's laws or lawyers, and a feller don't know whether he's right or wrong without looking into a law-book. They don't seem to know any more about conscience than I do about law. Now, for my part, I do just what I think right, and that's what I call going according to my conscience" (vol. II, ch. 16).

Ominous indeed, Bushfield's statement of principle nonetheless echoes Old World commonplaces. The Enlightenment invested the generality of mankind with a moral sense (conscience, no less), despite Locke's sensationalist theory, and conjectured that this faculty operated most perfectly in the state of nature. Well before Shaftesbury, the efficacy of conscience had been affirmed in *De jure belli ac pacis* (1625) of Hugo Grotius, the supreme legal theorist of the Renaissance: "For God has given conscience a judicial power to be the sovereign guide of human actions, by despising whose admonitions the mind is stupified into brutal hardness" (II.xxiii.2).[1] Whether the idea of conscience necessarily assumes a rational human nature is debatable. Hume and Francis Hutcheson thought that it did not. Yet the eighteenth century tended to associate reason with the moral sense, and Grotius also, as his discussion of natural rights makes plain. The Enlightenment postulated the light of reason as an available and generally reliable guide to natural man, enabling him to intuit the great truths and to manage his life in complete harmony with cosmic law. He was thought unlikely to err for having only good and perfect impulses. There was of course small warrant for Bushfield's presumptuousness in Grotius, a humanist and respecter of tradition, nor did the sentimental primitivists mean so much. But in claiming what social philosophers for purposes of argument had freely granted the child of nature, the Kentucky frontiersman heavily underscored the fundamental tension between the state of nature and civilization, the noble savage and institutional man, inalienable rights and the social contract.

Grotius had postulated an absolute law of nature beyond the right of church or state to abrogate, and out of his theory of natural law and the humanist ideal of personal liberty evolved the doctrine of inalienable rights elaborated by Locke in his treatise *Of Civil Government* and incorporated in the revolutionary documents of Europe and America. Although natural rights presumably sufficed in the original state of nature, it was apparent even to extremists that man in society had to accept obligations and limitations. At one extreme, Godwin advocated the weakest conceivable central authority, and, at the other, Thomas Hobbes, viewing man as a creature of passion no less than of reason, argued for effective restraint.

Although favoring monarchy, Hobbes recognized the defects of all forms of government; but he believed that by his very nature man required an irrevocable power above him. In the *Contrat social,* Rousseau with Hobbes' *Leviathan* in mind rejected as unsatisfactory any system based on submission and compulsion, proposing instead a compact freely entered into and retaining force and validity only so long as expressive of the general will. For Hobbes the social compact represented an actual and permanent transfer of authority from the many to the one, for Rousseau only a blending of common sympathies and a bending of individual wills to the interest of the whole. It does not appear that Rousseau advocated a government without necessary sovereignty, but he skirted the command-and-obey relationship by identifying the particular with the general will. Locke and afterward Paine conceived the social compact more practically than Rousseau; for them it resembled a protective association in which the many delegated authority provisionally to the few for the common welfare. Whatever the differences, the political theorists deriving from Locke and Rousseau wrought with the hypothetical natural man in plain view and unquestionably granted to the individual the maximum freedom consistent with coherent government, though by no means enough to accommodate the vagaries of a robust conscience like Bushfield's. While protecting man in his natural rights, political reformers were nevertheless prepared to impose more or less effective checks upon caprice. Hence, even radical republicanism, because implying some restraint, could not give satisfaction to those who like the frontiersmen of romance insisted on preserving themselves in the condition of absolute liberty postulated of the Golden Age.

It must be admitted, however, that even anarchism was an easy, if not a legitimate, inference from moral-sense philosophy and the theory of associationism: man, innately good, could be otherwise only in consequence of important features of his environment, notably institutions. By this reasoning William Godwin in *An Enquiry Concerning Political Justice* (1793)

issued a radical indictment of political structures as such—
"since government even in its best state is an evil, the object
principally to be aimed at is that we have as little of it as the
general peace of human society will permit" (III.vii). Godwin
no more than Jefferson, who is supposed to have uttered a
comparable sentiment, advocated the abolishment of all government but proposed a gradual simplification directed by
liberals. With substantial equality achieved in consequence
of the reduction or elimination of property rights, vested interests, and aristocracy, he believed "Private interest would
visibly accord with public good, and civil society become all
that poetry has feigned of the golden age" (I.v). The political
ideal stated by Godwin cannot be distinguished from anarchy,
for he reserves to the individual so many prerogatives as to
forestall even minimal civil control. Yet Godwin, while proclaiming the integrity of the individual and the primacy of
reason, fell into materialistic determinism.

Although not unaware of social reality, the visionaries of
the Enlightenment unquestionably leaned much too heavily on
the naturalistic hypotheses. It is not surprising, therefore, that
they should have caused thoughtful men considerable apprehension and attracted to themselves harsh and often perceptive
criticism. Without much bothering to separate primitivists
from progressivists (and admittedly the distinctions blur at
the end of the eighteenth century), the English novelist
George Walker used the Kentucky scene in the *Vagabond*
(1799) to reduce the schemes of Rousseau and Godwin, among
others, to absurdity. A company of three philosophers pro-
fessing a hodgepodge of utilitarianism, materialistic determinism, cultural primitivism, and pure anarchism become disillusioned with England and thus determine to go in company
with two females to America in search of a utopian situation.
Philadelphia they find corrupted by commerce and are advised
by their landlord to seek Kentucky: "Then Kentucky is your
object; it is the most delectable spot on the face of the earth;
it is a second Arcadia—a continued scene of romantic delight,

and picturesque prospects. An author [Imlay] of *undoubted* veracity has given an history of that heavenly region. Sympathy, says he, is regarded as the essence of the human soul, participating of celestial matter, and as a spark engendered to warm our benevolence, and lead to the raptures of love and rational felicity" (ch. 14). The adventurers find no "blooming orchards and sugar-groves, with fine lawns beneath them," but they do find Indians in the state of nature who murder, lie, and steal. Further disillusionment awaits the men when they wander into a Godwinian utopia inhabited by one of the Lost Ten Tribes. There all are equal and all equally devoted to the public good; but without pressing incentive no one feels disposed to labor, and this communal state is fast going to wrack and ruin. The *Vagabond* is symptomatic of conservative reaction against the wild-eyed utopianism of the times. While somewhat unfair, it humorously and impressively underscores the discrepancy between the ideal and the real and unmasks the natural man of the eighteenth-century primitivists.

In Kentucky, Walker selected a likely scene for scrutinizing the garden myth. It was there that the frontiersman acquired ideal form and there that the Enlightenment as such made its farthest advance westward. What happened in Kentucky during the first quarter of the nineteenth century roughly prefigured the cultural pattern of the West; primitivism in a variety of forms interacted with and ultimately adulterated rational progressivism. Even before the cessation of Indian hostilities, apostles of the Enlightenment, largely from Virginia, planted central Kentucky to the finest flowers of Old World culture—humanism, rational theology, political liberalism—and for a season amazed the world with their promising displays. The brilliant springtime bloom was illusory, however; the plants sent down only shallow roots and had small defense against adverse conditions. While none perished from the land, all languished after the passing of the original gardeners —men like John Bradford, John Breckinridge, and Harry Toulmin. This result was perhaps inevitable, as the frontier was a sufficient catalyst to precipitate the antithesis contained in the thesis of progressivism. There was of course nowhere a total recoil from the structure of rational ideas furthered by the Enlightenment, but the reflex was sufficient in Kentucky—still new ground in the early nineteenth century—to prevent the establishment of a sound cultural tradition on a broad popular base. It is true that Kentucky fared culturally no worse than some other tramontane states of similar origin, but then Kentucky had superior opportunities to illuminate the "dark Barbarian World."

That Kentucky and the West went wrong in many things was not altogether the fault of the nobleman of nature turned social man. Nevertheless, in the development of western culture he expressed a set of attitudes inimical to the very kind of progress for which Filson and others had imagined him an advance agent. Accordingly, both as a noble savage and as a barbarous alligator-horse, the legendary Kentuckian is an appropriate symbol for the several forms of primitivism which defeated the Enlightenment. This is not to say, however, that he betrayed his sponsors; social optimists simply mistook him for the natural man of the eighteenth-century philosophers.

By definition the child of nature grows wise through discovering the great truths in nature. His apparent wisdom challenges the usefulness of scholarship and provides a basis for anti-intellectualism. In the *Prairie*, Dr. Battius,[2] an absurd naturalist intended as a comic character, contrasts unpleasantly with Natty, a being good and wise from consulting the book of nature alone; he rides an ass and behaves after an asinine, unmanly, and ineffectual manner. While expulsion from Yale can hardly have turned Cooper against the ideal of scientific investigation, in mounting scholarship on an ass he created a melancholy and portentous symbol, significant of a deep bias in the American mind.

It is of course possible to take Battius as an eccentric result of the cultural process and therefore deserving of ridicule, but the portrait accords altogether too well with a view

stridently and venomously proclaimed in Cooper's time and
after. The lower classes especially, but the upper somewhat
too, appear for one or more reasons to have regarded learning
with varying degrees of suspicion, mixed in some cases with
obvious hostility. One of Cooper's early imitators, Emerson
Bennett, who exploited the legendary Kentuckian in several
romances, pompously allowed that the "learning gained from
letters is a species of mental luxury."[3] Moreover, he embodied
the spirit of positive anti-intellectualism in Tom Sturgess, the
Kentucky frontiersman of the *Phantom of the Forest,* and set
this noble illiterate over against Harry Colburn, the romantic
and necessarily cultured hero. Although this novel is generally
conventional, Bennett almost certainly intended to satirize in
Colburn the effects of formal schooling and superior upbringing; otherwise, there would have been no purpose in representing him as a dainty man of sentiment, obviously over-
refined and incompetent to deal with hard reality. This
paragon of gentility professes the hunter's calling but uses his
time remarking the wonders of nature and sketching woodland
scenes. His companion Tom Sturgess understandably has
small sympathy for the cultivation of the fine arts and belles-
lettres and says as much: "I spect picturs and poetry is well
enough in thar places, in some old finiky settlement, whar
they sleep in feather-beds and git skeered at thar shadders;
but out yere they're no more use nor wings is to tadpoles"
(ch. 1). Harry's supercilious retort that there are "different
tastes and educations" doubtless causes nature's nobleman
some pain, for he asserts his own integrity with typical backwoods invidiousness: "Wall, I never had *any* edication . . .
'cept what I picked up in the woods; and whar's the use?
I had a tomahawk for a plaything when I war a baby, and a
rifle for a bed-feller; and when I growed up along, I larnt to
use 'em on beasts and Injuns. I kin hunt, fish, row, trail
Injuns and steal hosses; I can tell a skunk from a beaver, a
persimmon tree from a white-oak, a turkey-buzzard from a
chicken, and what more d'ye want? One man can't know

everything, I spect." The implication is that what Tom knows is much the best part and that the other ill becomes a man in any case. That Bennett to some extent shared this view can scarcely be doubted, but he was not on that account exceptional among Americans whether of high or low degree.

A Boone biographer, apparently distressed over his subject's illiteracy, stated what probably no one ever denied, that scholarly endeavor is incompatible with heroic conditions.[4] His explanation of the absence of intellectual interests among the pioneers, however, leaves out of consideration their manifest hostility toward learning and other conspicuous signs of culture long after the subjugation of the wilderness. Anti-intellectualism among the educated unquestionably owed something to the paroxysm of romanticism; but the distaste for intellectual achievement among the lower classes was probably significant less of actual contempt for knowledge gained from books than of social, political, and religious anxieties.

As a practical and theoretical beneficiary of the uncritical social optimism of the Enlightenment, the child of the backwoods at the polls understandably made his mark when opportunity permitted under the emblem of radical republicanism, and for reasons not difficult to fathom often voted for men of his own ignorant kind. While admiring Jefferson as an advocate of equal rights and maximum liberty, he doted on Andrew Jackson, with whom he had undeniable affinities. In the campaign of 1828 the backwoodsmen became politically articulate and instinctively supported the hero of New Orleans and Horseshoe Bend, who was something of a roarer and an alligator-horse too, a brawler and a gambler, but especially a champion of the uncouth West against the polished East. It was apparently a matter of indifference that Jackson was a capitalist rather than a hornyhanded yeoman farmer, that he fell far short of Jefferson's liberal ideal and on occasion behaved as autocratically as a crowned head; in western eyes he looked like a frontiersman and evidently possessed the "true grit." The frontier was unlikely to find serious fault with its own ignorant, highhanded, and even illiberal image. This is not altogether to deny merit to a man like "Old Hickory," who had the strength of his convictions, or to ignore the fact that he brought great energy and native intelligence to the Presidency. Nevertheless, his election reflected a notion widespread in the West that an uneducated son of the soil could fiddle about as well by ear as the aristocrat trained to read the score. It is ironical that the frontier while having benefited enormously in consequence of the labors of Jefferson should have displayed a marked hostility toward men of his station and background.

Wearers of broadcloth admittedly won offices, but by political acumen rather than by inherent fitness to serve. Whisky and oratory worked far more powerfully than reason on the "half horse, half alligator," who, confronted with political ideas beyond his power to analyze, behaved in the only possible way, that is, as mass man. Even political leaders of high purpose in the West had ordinarily to equivocate to gain election and afterward to take refuge in expediency to quieten their obstreperous constituencies. Alligator-horses, it goes without saying, adopted the tactics of their betters and took office in droves. A comical stump speech reported by the Port Gibson, Mississippi, *Reveille,* January 18, 1854, is certainly suggestive if not actually representative: "If I am elected to this office, I will represent my constituents as the sea represents the earth, or the night contrasts with the day. I will unrivet human society, clean all its parts and screw it together again. I will correct all abuses, purge out all corruption, and go through the enemies of our party like a rat through a new cheese. My chief recommendations are, that at a public dinner given to ——, I ate more than any two men at the table—at the last election I put in three votes for the party—I've just bought a new suit of clothes that will do to wear to Congress, and I've got the handsomest sister in old Kentuck."

Considered as a political force, the raw libertarian element of the West cannot in justice be fathered on Jefferson or even on Paine, as neither intended that the noble of nature cross over into civilization and undertake to perform the necessary functions of republican citizenship without training. They were at one with the generality of eighteenth-century progressivists in recognizing the basic need of the masses for education and in premising cultural progress on the growth and extension of knowledge. Jefferson and Paine were true sons of the Enlightenment inasmuch as they acknowledged modern man's 'great debt to the humanist tradition flowing down through the Renaissance from classical antiquity and as they hoped to recover something of the glory of the Athenian state through the liberation and instruction of the masses. Intelligent reformers everywhere understood that the people could not well protect themselves against exploitation without knowing the principles upon which their liberties rested. Hence, the emphasis upon Greek and Latin and natural science in the first half of the nineteenth century was owing to no pedagogical whim but to a firm conviction among thinking men that these studies together with Holy Writ and moral philosophy formed the only conceivable basis for a democratic Christian society. To know the substance of Homer, Plato, Euripides, Horace, Virgil, Seneca, and Cicero; Grotius, Copernicus, Galileo, and Newton; Shaftesbury, Kames, Rousseau, Hume, Diderot and the Encyclopedists, and the Gospels was to have the means to self-knowledge and knowledge of the world about in space and time. The eighteenth century may have lacked an acute sense of history (the point is debatable), but there was never any question in the minds of the educated about the dependence of the present on the past. That the American West entered political life with little learning and less historical perspective may be ascribed to a multiplicity of causes but not to the failure of the greatest minds among the Founding Fathers to perceive the necessary relation between a republican form of government and an educated electorate. While quarreling over particulars and indeed over first principles, they wrought in the full context of Western civilization, meaning to perpetuate in America something of the spirit of Athens.

There is no disputing the fact that the first generation of Kentuckians, ignorant though a majority of them were, included a considerable number who clearly recognized the value of the European cultural heritage and the necessity for implanting its substance in the commonalty. The achievement of Lexington—the "Athens of the West"—during the half century after the settlement, though including no monuments of permanent greatness, evidenced a strong intellectual impulse and a commendable striving for cultural distinction. From the pioneer period, men of vision labored mightily, if in the main ineffectually, to create a sound public school system. In his message of December 3, 1816, to the General Assembly, Governor Gabriel Slaughter pleaded for funds for education on the basis of principles which the Enlightenment had widely approved and to which the West as a whole subscribed with varying degrees of enthusiasm:

Knowledge and virtue are every where the surest basis of public happiness; the strongest barriers against oppression; a powerful check to mal-administration, by rendering it necessary for those in power to secure not the blind, but the enlightened confidence of the people. Every child born in the state should be considered a child of the republic, and educated at the public expence, where the parents are unable to do it. Such a system will not only improve the minds and morals of our youth, and thereby render our free institutions more durable, but by thus diffusing the benefits of government throughout the body politic, it will be strengthened in the affections of the people.[5]

Slaughter issued much the same earnest appeal a year later with much the same result.[6] While apparently not denying the governor's premises, the legislature was far from ready to implement his conclusion by levying sufficient taxes.

Even as Slaughter wrote, the condition of education worsened. The numerous academies reared during the past two decades on liberal grants of land from the state, their substance expended, were collapsing one after another; and adequate provision had been made meanwhile neither for common nor for any other kinds of schools. It was not until the appointment of Robert J. Breckinridge as state superintendent in 1847 that public education improved significantly. When he resigned in 1853, Kentucky had approximately the system requested by Governor Slaughter back in 1816. What Breckinridge had wrought, the Civil War largely dissipated, and at war's end—ninety years after the founding of Boonesboro and Harrodsburg—Kentucky was in some ways the same "dark Barbarian World" which the apostles of progress had thought to illuminate. In truth, the Enlightenment foundered in the first tramontane settlement despite the labors of men who well understood its importance for the American experiment, and the wilderness inhabited by the alligator-horse swallowed Athens. This development, if not foreseeable, was yet well-nigh inevitable, for really formidable countercurrents obstructed the course of rational progressivism in the West. What these were, the sad history of Transylvania University plainly reveals.

Thomas Jefferson died in 1826, Horace Holley resigned the presidency of Transylvania in 1827, and Andrew Jackson won the campaign of 1828—three unrelated events but all symbolic of intellectual reflex and recrudescence of primitive ideas. Like Jonathan Edwards, Jefferson was the consummate genius of a rich but declining tradition; unlike Edwards he looked forward as well as backward and touched his period at all points. He charted the nation's course according to the ideals of the Enlightenment, looking to the West and Kentucky in particular for a demonstration of the efficacy of his program of agrarianism, liberal republicanism, and public education; but natural enemies lurked in the wilderness, including the Reformation spirit so well exemplified in Edwards. With the support of a landed aristocracy chiefly derived from the same milieu as Jefferson, Holley brought Transylvania into national prom-

inence as an intellectual center between 1817 and 1827. His
first board included Henry Clay, Edmund Bullock, Robert
Trimble, John T. Mason, Jr., Robert Wickliffe, James Prentiss,
Hubbard Taylor, John Pope, Lewis Sanders, Samuel H. Wood-
son, John Brown, Charles Humphries, and Thomas Bodley—
men of superior intelligence, high position, and incontestable
culture, though in the opinion of religious conservatives plain
corrupters of the youth. Holley shaped Transylvania after a
fashion agreeable to the intellectuals of the "Athens of the
West," employing a faculty according to ability rather than
piety and inculcating the spirit of free inquiry and sound
scholarship. A Unitarian minister by profession, Yale-educated,
and urbane, he exemplified liberalism without radicalism but
nevertheless became a monstrous symbol for backwoods Protestantism, in process during the first half of the nineteenth
century of evangelizing the state. There can be no doubt after
the investigations of N. H. Sonne that the Presbyterians more
than any other sectaries were responsible for forcing Holley's
resignation and pulling down the citadel of humane learning.[7]
They were not as a group conspicuously anti-intellectual, but
their activity against Transylvania coincided with the rise of
men who were—the noble savages of the frontier actualized
politically as Jacksonian Democrats.

The proprietary interest taken in Transylvania by the Presbyterians is understandable; for between about 1785 and 1799
they labored diligently to bring about the establishment of
an institution of higher learning adequately supported with
state funds. Their motive was ultimately sectarian, but then
religious bodies as a rule have not lent their support to liberal
education as such, the Congregationalists of New England
having been exceptional in this respect. The intellectual
climate of Transylvania was a matter of practical concern to
them inasmuch as they required a well-educated ministry, in
contrast to the Baptists and Methodists. Obviously, a Unitarian president had other concerns than the inculcation of
Calvinism in Presbyterian youth, and the possibility that he

might relax the doctrinal rigor of his charges was doubtless very real. Yet it is exceedingly unfortunate that the Presbyterians sought to make a state facility an instrument of church policy. As a nonsectarian public school, it might have preserved, despite the vicissitudes attending the Civil War, the rich intellectual heritage borne into Kentucky by the Virginia gentry and in due course supplied educational leadership; but as a sectarian public school, it could under no circumstances have withstood the opposition of the rising Baptists, who were rather indifferent to learning but as adamant about the separation of church and state as about immersion.

The opposition of the Presbyterians to the liberal program instituted by Holley was historically consistent, as Protestantism, excluding the Anglican Establishment, had never concurred wholeheartedly in the humanist view of the world and the intellect. It is doubtless true, as R. W. Battenhouse has recently argued, that Calvin was influenced by the Neoplatonism and humanist thought issuing from the Florentine Academy and that he was accordingly sensible of the claims of humanism as opposed to theology and of reason as opposed to revelation,[8] but the Reformation and the Renaissance are little nearer accord on that account. Calvin understood the issue and kept the spirit of Augustine to haunt the bright new world vacated by the papacy in the sixteenth century. While less awesome in the regard of the learned than of the ignorant, the thought of total depravity and the fate appointed for the souls of the unregenerate abided in the Christian imagination. By the terms of the Protestant charter every sinner became his own exegete and confessor and faced a more or less angry God in his own naked individuality. Whereas before the Reformation a sympathetic, if sometimes venal, priesthood gave absolution and mediated between the faithful and the Lord, the Protestant assumed responsibility for probing his own conscience and readying himself for divine grace. John Calvin created an additional source of anxiety by incubating the predestinarian germ enclosed in medieval theology, thus evoking in his followers a grim, otherworldly demeanor, doubtless meant to signify membership in the elect of God. For the evangelical sects, lately sprung as a consequence of Luther's revolt from the solid Thomist edifice and beset by arbitrary authority in various forms, life in this world was an altogether serious matter, perilous to the soul and painful to the flesh.

Yet humanism, because generally congenial to the temper of the times, survived the doubts of the old Established Church and of Protestantism, with considerable unofficial support from both. In this connection, it ought to be recalled that the medieval church, despite obvious theological queasiness, conserved in the Roman classics the foundations of humanism. Augustine, the greatest theologian among the fathers, loved Virgil; and Dante, the greatest religious poet, loved Augustine and Virgil both. Although opposed to this brighter view of man and the world, the Reformation found the integrity and independence of the individual postulated by humanism congenial to its soul, and this area of agreement, it is important to note, expanded into a political philosophy ultimately fatal to despotism of many sorts. Through the seventeenth century, humanism as such was accorded more or less toleration, or perhaps neglect, by the several orthodoxies, though separated from them by the width of the abyss between nature and grace, human exaltation and human degradation; but the fundamental tension endured and produced corrosive effects on the Enlightenment both in Europe and America.

The Protestant reaction to deism is a measure of the basic conflict. Deism originated from the impact of the speculations and discoveries of the scientists—among others Copernicus, Galileo, Francis Bacon, the members of the Royal Society—upon supernaturalism; it was a compromise adopted by rationalists in the humanist tradition, including of course Anglican divines and adherents, to relieve a serious cause of anxiety and friction. Calvinists had no difficulty in perceiving the implications for dogmatic theology of a set of postulates which placed a serious limitation on divine power and intimated the ade-

quacy of moral conduct and right reason; the acceptance of
deism was very nearly tantamount to the substitution of ethics
for religion. In assimilating God to a mechanistic theory of
the universe, the deists deprived Him of the power to awe, to
bestow favor, and thus the means to exact reverence. The
Puritans at least among the Calvinists' were not contemptuous
of intellect, but they reasoned from theological, not scientific,
premises and accordingly preserved the Lord's absolute authority. Moreover, the deistic solution was no solution for the
commonalty, as witness the rise of a religion of the heart,
Wesleyanism, burning from the center of the Establishment.
The Methodists thirsted after the juice of religion, fear and
trembling, divine favor, and above all, salvation for all seekers.
"Enthusiasm" (the word has lost the old sense of excessive
zeal) repelled Anglican divines, but it is the true means to
religious satisfaction for the poor and the afflicted, as both
heathen and Christian priests have always known. Evangelism
flared south from New England along the frontier, more heat
than light, but ultimately effective to prostrate the robust
sinners of the wilderness before the Lord. Rational theology
held no appeal for an uneducated folk who sinned in a hot
passion and preferred to repent in the same manner.

No professor of religious history has as yet fully chronicled
the progress of enthusiasm in America from the Great Awakening to the period of the Civil War, nor is one likely single-
handed to accomplish the task in face of the amazing com-
plexities. All Protestant bodies seem to have suffered from
schism; most threw off several splinters, which in some cases
divided further. There was concurrently a regular shifting of
individuals from one church to another, often for other than
doctrinal causes. Moreover, denominations underwent subtle
transformations from the influence of social and economic
forces. The spiritual upsurge began as early as the revival
conducted by the imposing Edwards at Northampton in 1734-
1735, although the height of the Great Awakening was hardly
reached before the sensational tour in 1739-1741 of George

Whitefield, the English Methodist with Calvinist reservations. W. W. Sweet, however, argues persuasively for a beginning a decade or two earlier in the pietistic revival in the Dutch Reformed church of New Jersey and in the awakening of the Presbyterian Irish throughout the Middle Colonies.[9] This whole series of convulsions was perhaps less important for increasing church membership than for activating radical bodies which favored emotionalism and democratic process in religion. For after all the stirring preaching, the church member was yet exceptional among the colonists in 1760;[10] but the Baptists and Methodists had established themselves and given fair indication of their ability to win converts, especially among the poor and poorly educated. Congregationalism and Presbyterianism experienced flurries of emotionalism during the eighteenth century and tended to personalize Calvinism and liberalize church polity, though without significant doctrinal concessions. Neither developed a lasting evangelical impulse, perhaps for having in the main educated and relatively prosperous adherents, and both in the next century after a period of schism settled back into well-regulated, middle-class religious activity alongside the less staid Episcopalians. There can be no doubt that the Great Awakening arrested the general drift of the eighteenth century toward secularism and softened the somewhat forbidding intellectualism of orthodox Calvinism and Anglicanism. In consequence of religious enthusiasm, the evangelical bodies in time were augmented enormously. The Baptists and Methodists most fully embodied the new spirit of free religious expression and accordingly reaped the harvest, especially in the West, where men and women during the pioneer period cared less about ecclesiastical polity and fine doctrinal discriminations than about the deep emotional experience of religion.

The evangelical impulse lasted long enough in the Presbyterians to precipitate the Great Revival in the West, beginning about 1797 in Logan County, Kentucky, and culminating in the frenzy of Cane Ridge, Bourbon County, in August, 1801.

Chief responsibility for this series of frenetic revivals rests with a Scotch-Irish Calvinist from Pennsylvania, James Mc-Gready, who, after incurring ill will in North and South Carolina by his inflammatory preaching, moved into southern Kentucky. Of his spectacular success came the camp meeting, which R. H. Gabriel describes as a "unique American contribution to Christianity," whether ironically is not clear.[11] The host to the crowd of from ten thousand to twenty thousand at the Cane Ridge meeting was the Presbyterian minister Barton W. Stone, afterward a schismatic. He seems to have been assisted not only by preachers of his own sect but also by Methodists, who later employed the camp meeting with considerable profit. Though ardent revivalists, the Baptists appear to have had no official part at Cane Ridge, doubtless from a traditional disinclination to interdenominational traffic. All shades of Protestantism on the frontier were probably represented in the multitude, as well as all degrees of depravity and roguery. At the center of the vortex day after day stood the preachers declaiming of sin and salvation, hellfire and damnation, arousing sympathetic resonances in the simple backwoods folk and evoking violent expressions of religious ecstasy: "falling, jerking, rolling, running, dancing and barking exercises and visions and trances."[12]

The preachers hymned the glory of the Christian faith, but in a way to summon up primitive responses, and the mass of pulsating, ecstatic humanity reacted according to archetypal patterns rather than conventional form. The passion sublimated at the center apparently precipitated on the perimeter into frank eroticism, to judge from the aftereffects; and the plentiful supply of corn liquor doubtless sustained the state described by observers as general disorder. True, there were American and European precedents for violent manifestations at Christian assemblages, but the fact remains that the means to conversion at Cane Ridge was orgy unpleasantly reminiscent of ancient rites like the Dionysiac. This the most sensational display of religious enthusiasm among Christians on the North

American continent and also the most primitive filled staid Presbyterians and others with disgust, and reaction accordingly set in. Camp meetings with the characteristic seizures in "coming through" continued, though with increasing disapproval; the subdued, fairly rational revival, however, was the chief means by which the evangelization of the West was accomplished by the Baptists and Methodists. The spectacle of Cane Ridge remains important as a mass demonstration of instinctive action in a period filled with fanciful ideas about natural man; the noble of nature, when incited by his priests, unerringly chose the one true way into the darkest corner of the forest.

Religious enthusiasm, emphasizing the heart rather than the head, necessarily begets anti-intellectualism in some degree. It is in the very nature of things that learning should suffer as a consequence of the revival spirit, which, compounded of faith and feeling, omits rational process from the steps to salvation. The western preachers were as a class poorly educated men who, having heard the "call," mounted the rostrum with scant preparation, relying upon God and conscience to reveal the Scriptures and guide their utterances. Moved and sustained by faith, these backwoods zealots naturally granted it primacy over reason. During the period of intensive evangelization, the Baptists and Methodists seem not to have desired a learned clergy, and admittedly the unchurched West needed plain, honest preaching rather than profound exegesis. There seems small justification, however, for the proposition advanced by these ministers that education actually hinders preaching and even less excuse for their reproaching Presbyterians for having formal training in theology. The anti-intellectualism of the intensely democratic Baptists was owing in some measure to their long, hard struggle against the Virginia Establishment to gain religious liberty and equality; the association of education with privilege and class became fixed in their minds together with distrust of learned preachers.

For the anti-intellectualism of western evangelists there was precedent of a kind and something of a tradition too. The question of the efficacy of learning as a moral guide had been raised from time to time in the medieval church and variously answered, though usually not to the positive detriment of the seven liberal arts, the traditional foundation for theology. Varying degrees of anti-intellectualism appear in the writings of Tertullian, Pope Gregory the Great, Bernard of Clairvaux, Pope Innocent III, and Peter Damiani, among others less well known. Nor are these scattered reflexes surprising in view of the popular doctrine of the fall of man in consequence of his desire for forbidden knowledge. While granting the usefulness of the liberal studies, Bernard in *De gradibus humilitatis et superbiae* advanced the self-evident truth, that many a man has found salvation though in ignorance of them. In this view frontier preachers enthusiastically concurred and further pronounced education to be an actual obstacle to the service of the Lord.

In the *Discours sur les sciences et les arts* Rousseau considered the question, whether the arts and sciences had contributed to the purification of morals. Reasoning *post hoc ergo propter hoc,* he maintained that the liberal studies, together with luxury, had figured importantly in the decay of old civilizations. The hard consistency of Rousseau's answer cannot be denied, as the arts and sciences were integrally related to the social structure which he found unsatisfactory on all counts. What effect the *Discours* had is uncertain, but Gilbert Imlay, embowered in the Kentucky paradise a few years after the settlement, reflected on man and the world and pronounced a Rousseauistic judgment, with specific reference to the evil effects of education: "Far from being disgusted with man for his turpitude or depravity, we feel that dignity nature bestowed upon us at the creation; but which has been contaminated by the base alloy of meanness, the concomitant of European education; and what is more lamentable, is, that it is the consequence of your very laws and governments."[13] Nothing exceptional toward the end of the eighteenth century, Imlay's view is significant of a growing suspicion of learning.

Distrust of rationalism and even of intellectual process is evident in romanticism as well as in religious enthusiasm, which may be considered in certain respects the formal Christian counterpart of the other. The glorification of the noble savage, the child, and the peasant implies a rejection of intellect, for these simple beings, in contrast to men in a complex social situation, act not from reason but from impulse, and, in the opinion of sentimental primitivists, act rightly. While Wordsworth and Keats intimated the superiority of feeling over reason as a moral guide, Blake in *Jerusalem* and *Milton* unequivocally rejected rational demonstration and upheld faith and inspiration. It ought to be remarked that a basis for antirationalism appeared in a quarter of eighteenth-century thought besides primitivism: Francis Hutcheson and later Hume called in question the effectiveness of the reason for moral discrimination and on empirical grounds asserted the necessary primacy of feeling. Distrust of reason as a basis for a system of ethics need not lead to rabid anti-intellectualism; at the same time, there is small warrant for liberal education and the cultivation of the mental faculty if man has the capacity, from an innate sense of right and wrong, to arrange his life satisfactorily. While anti-intellectualism in the American West appears to have been intensified by local causes, it was obviously a part of the cultural heritage of the settlers.

As a Unitarian, President Holley symbolized heresy for Kentucky Presbyterians; but their attack upon him probably sprang from pure anti-intellectualism as well as from theological antirationalism. While their distrust of learning came partly of the effect of religious enthusiasm, other factors were unquestionably involved. The Presbyterians, like the much less numerous Episcopalians, drew their membership to a considerable extent from the well-to-do, landholding class, in whom by 1827, the year of Holley's resignation, reaction against some aspects of Jeffersonianism had already started. Merle Curti has described this evolving attitude with admirable insight: "it put less emphasis on natural rights, on public education for a republican society, on intellectualism, and on humanitarianism than had the philosophy of Jefferson. It tended to attach importance to historic institutions rather than to natural law; it questioned and finally denounced humanitarianism; . . . it substituted for the older rationalism of the plantation aristocracy the middle-class doctrine of morality, piety, and orthodox religious faith."[14] This reflex may be regarded with some justice as the revival of the Puritan state of mind, a practical, common-sense way of looking at matters, generally opposed to speculation and deviation. Moreover, it agrees in some things with the evangelical mind, particularly in discounting the nonutilitarian pursuit of knowledge and generally deprecating the life of the intellect. As long recognized, the respect for authority and the personal discipline inculcated by Puritanism were conducive to material success; and of course its adherents in the nineteenth century had no great difficulty in harmonizing their commercial interests with divine intention. The Puritan mind ordinarily discovers in speculation a threat on the one hand to social stability, and thereby to profits, and on the other to orthodox belief. There is obviously a basic incompatibility between this intellectual conservatism and the spirit of free inquiry.

Attacked for his religious liberalism, Holley had yet to endure criticism for his political conservatism, for he was a confessed Federalist during the season of agitation over relief. As a recipient of state aid, Transylvania came under the scrutiny of the Relief party, composed in the main of the lower and debt-ridden classes, understandably of strong republican sympathies. That Holley inculcated federalism seems improbable, but rumor was basis enough for the enemies of his school. As a Bluegrass institution, supported by aristocracy and inevitably drawing students to a considerable extent from the upper class, it was a symbol of social and economic superiority in a state filled with raw equalitarians, who loudly claimed all of the faculties and privileges conferred on the natural man by Rousseau and concurred in by Godwin and Paine. In his messages of 1825 and 1826 to the General Assembly, Governor Joseph Desha repeated the by then familiar charge of aristocratic exclusiveness against Transylvania, with the approbation of the same levels of society which had abandoned reason for instinct in the camp meetings.[15] In many ways this was a more damaging charge than heterodoxy, for backwoods republicans had come to regard learning as a badge of aristocracy, perhaps no less offensive than powdered wigs and lace cuffs three or four decades earlier. That they should have resented marks of distinction of whatever kind without reference to individual deserving was perhaps inevitable; for, as Franz Alexander observes, the emphasis in a democratic society on individual achievement produces inequities which mediocre men, rationalizing their own envy, tend to regard as contrary to the principle of equality.[16]

In Transylvania under President Holley, Kentucky had an exceptionally fine instrumentality for realizing the cultural ambitions of the transplanted Virginia gentry and for ultimately providing the masses with light and with enlightened leadership. His faculty was nothing short of distinguished even by eastern standards.[17] It is fair to assert, moreover, that no other state in Transappalachia possessed during its pioneer period a comparable institution. Transylvania as a liberal college was nonetheless doomed. Antithetical forces gathering in western civilization for the century past were focused on the school, and its defenders, including John Bradford and Robert Wickliffe, were powerless to avert the catastrophe. It is of course not literally true that the Enlightenment in the West depended solely on Transylvania, but the departure of Holley and the withdrawal of state support from this the most conspicuous guardian of the arts and sciences in the tramontane region signaled the rejection of Athens.

The failure of Kentucky and the West to provide adequately for education may be ascribed to a number of local and general causes. Public education unquestionably suffered from the lack of taxable resources and the thinness of population, as well as on account of conservative reaction, religious fundamentalism, and republican invidiousness. Coulter leaves the impression that Kentucky erred in beginning at the top instead of the bottom—that is, with the academies and Transylvania rather than common schools[18]—but he neglected to explain how otherwise teachers could have been trained. In truth, learning has always radiated from intellectual centers, and the state of education in a region at a given time has seldom been better than the scholarship of its universities. The fact is that a state of mind, evoked largely by primitivism and the paradisiacal archetype, defeated education and the Enlightenment. Behind Holley's departure there was active opposition to the humane tradition and a corresponding indifference to the life of the mind and the spirit of free inquiry. It is accordingly not surprising that throughout the century educational programs in the West should have received at best unenthusiastic support. An anecdote printed in 1832 by Lunenburg C. Abernathy is now less striking as humor than as prophecy: "Two members of Congress, one from Connecticut, the other from Kentucky, were travelling in company, when they chanced to spy a drove of mules going to market. Says the Yankee to the Kentuckian, do you know what animals those are? 'Indeed I do,' replied the latter; 'they surely must be your constituents.' 'No doubt,' rejoined the Yankee, 'and I suppose they are travelling to Kentucky to be employed as schoolmasters.' "[19] Mounted on an ass like Cooper's Dr. Battius, scholarship in the Garden of the West came inevitably to be served by men who suited the part. This situation probably could not have been foreseen by Jefferson and Paine, who imagined that the people longed for the knowledge that would set them free and give them power. Nonetheless, the rejection of the authorship of seers, as of magistrates and priests, followed logically from the psychology of the westward movement.

Anti-intellectualism clearly issues from every part of the

structure of primitivism. Withdrawal from civilized process, while in some things probably beneficial, entails sacrifice of the fruits of the creative imagination and the analytical faculty, besides a loss of historical perspective. While not unaware of the cost, sentimental primitivists and optimistic social reformers judged the compensations adequate in the state of nature, where the noble savage, innately virtuous and uncorrupted by society, manages his life by reference to the infallible book of nature—instinct, no less. Leatherstocking in the *Deerslayer* solemnly declares, "This book I can read, and I find it full of wisdom and knowledge" (ch. 24). But what wisdom and knowledge? Not, surely, such as would perfect man and usher in the secular millennium of the eighteenth-century philosophers. Liberated body and mind by Renaissance humanism, the rationalism of the Enlightenment, and the republicanism of the romantics, and left to follow instinct for the one true way, men often displayed a preference for the path back into the primeval forest. And in this tendency they were encouraged somewhat by visionaries, who desired to translate the eternally fascinating myth of man in the garden into a way of life—clearly an impossible dream for reasons familiar to Calvin and indeed well understood by philosophers from Plato to Hobbes.

11 The Frontier Mind

"We rarely looked back but rather pressed forward eagerly to what was before us."— THE GREAT FRONTIER

THE DEVELOPMENT of society in the West may be regarded as a grotesque jest at the expense of the Enlightenment, for the actual pioneers displayed few of the qualities predicated of men living close to nature, and the defective culture which they erected in the fabled garden land disappointed even modest expectations. Unquestionably primitive, nature's noblemen yet outraged romantics by their violence and animality. While readily approving that part of the progressivist program leading to luxury, they debased the concept of progress by rejecting the arts and sciences. Supremely confident of their capacity for making value judgments, they wrought as if unaware of the pure light of reason allegedly shining in the state of nature, and the record of their social, political, and religious activities abounds in startling eccentricities. This is not altogether to withhold credit from the picturesque barbarians who harassed the Indians from Kentucky to the Pacific. Neither their compelling attractiveness nor the national debt to them can be denied; they won an empire through their devastating haste and leaped—an imperishable image—into the collective imagination. Their virtues, however, were appropriate to a heroic age. While eagerly accepting the benefits bestowed upon the individual by the Enlightenment, nature's noblemen largely refused the implicit responsibilities, meaning to preserve their unprecedented liberties and at the same time their social and intellectual innocence. What came of this refractoriness was nothing of cultural value but a curious orientation, which may with propriety be called the frontier mind.

The frontier mind resulted from hardship, cultural deprivation, and superficially satisfied desiring. It was then not so much a consciously fostered condition as a psychic growth evoked by the peculiar circumstances of the emigration. Kentucky and Tennessee were settled principally from the eastern slopes of the Appalachians by backwoods families who, standing one to three generations from a unified cultural frame, had regressed perceptibly under the impact of the frontier. True, the culture which their fathers and grandfathers left was on many counts unsatisfactory; Europe had become increasingly since the Middle Ages a divided mind and a disordered house. Even so, the Old World preserved traditional social and religious forms, which, if irksome to some, gave the individual a sense of identity and imposed upon him obligations appropriate to his station. Except to his family, the frontiersman ordinarily acknowledged no very strong allegiances—social, political, or religious; and he characteristically frowned on all symbols of authority. He was his own man, a free agent in the state of nature, but necessarily a man, culturally speaking, without a home. His progress westward from Kentucky was accompanied by a further loss of traditional references and by an increased distortion of vision.

It cannot be said, however, that the West altogether escaped Europe, for the concepts with which the pioneers wrought were chiefly of European provenience. The West suffered at the outset not from the lack of fruitful ideas but from the lack of an efficient myth in which to frame them, and perhaps in consequence there was no general agreement in those matters most significant for cultural unity and health. Unhappily for American civilization, the West united mainly in opposing programs implying discipline and discrimination. The expectations of the emigrants considered, their reluctance to sort men according to ability and virtue and to legislate correctives for license is in no way surprising; assuredly, all are equal in Eden and all equally unrestrained. Whether for good or for ill, though perhaps inevitably, the West made out with the doubtful myth which had sustained the emigration, that is, the garden myth, with its overtones of libertinism, materialism, and isolationism.

The emigration was enacted to a large extent in the context of primitivism. While receptive to the idea of infinite material progress into the future, the illiterate generality tended to regard Kentucky and to some extent the whole West not as a cultural extension of the Old World but as the lost garden. They had the sense of going back in the history of civilization to a hypothetical point of general equality, felicity, and abundance, with the expectation of building anew without the former errors. Sanction for this curious movement backward into the future may be found in Rousseau, his progressivism notwithstanding, and in later reformers like Paine. It is a question, moreover, whether Jefferson himself was not influenced by the paradisiacal archetype, for his intense agrarianism, his faith in the common man of the backwoods, and his fear of strong government bespeak a degree of recoil from the metropolis and the institutions thereof. As a practical politician Jefferson was far from acting on the basis of vague misgivings or utopian visions, and as much may be said of most other American leaders. Yet it cannot be doubted that all classes of society experienced some effects from the primitivistic inflections of contemporary social theory. The majority of Americans appear, moreover, to have had some sense of divorcing the European culture area and of creating a rich new life without necessary reference to the old. The East nevertheless maintained contact with Europe, but the West stridently proclaimed its cultural autonomy and defended its accomplishment with more fervor than reason.

The criticism of traditional institutions, which in Paine, Godwin, and other zealots became highly destructive, and the pictures of the Earthly Paradise sketched by visionaries induced in Western civilization a pronounced orientation toward the future, though nowhere more than in the American West a corresponding disdain for the common cultural heritage. The Graeco-Roman world had been oriented toward the past and the Middle Ages toward the afterlife; the Renaissance, Janus-like, looked backward and forward. Out of the study of classical antiquity Renaissance thinkers restored the long-neglected humanism and from examining the world about them devised the new science. Upon this foundation the Enlightenment speculated and brought forth the liberal concepts from which democratic societies evolved. The ideological capital borne into the West by the pioneers was obviously nothing of their own creating but a European legacy. Ungrateful indeed, they increasingly ignored the debt and came in time to imagine their preconceptions to be original. Walter Prescott Webb, who studies the course of history from deep in the heart of Texas, stated of the expansion a sadder truth than he appears to have realized: "In making this conquest, we rarely looked back but rather pressed forward eagerly to what was before us."[1]

The failure of the emigrants to take bearings produced no ill effects at once; spared the dead weight of outmoded institutions and filled with liberal ideals, they wrought impressively in many things. The foundations of western society, though lacking a unifying principle, unquestionably embody much of the best European thought. Moreover, the energy generated in the settlers from the prospect of an existence lacking in no good thing transformed the wilderness from the Valley of Virginia to the Great Plains within the space of Boone's life. The incredible fertility of the garden land unfortunately encouraged a philosophy of abundance and a reckless extractive economy, while the sense of fulfillment born of liberty and plenty contributed to a general neglect of spiritual and intellectual values. In consequence, the West tended to look no farther back than the first settlements; for viewed from new-found Eden the past has no significance, neither the hard lessons of history nor the painful lucubrations of philosophers wracked by experience. Thus, in transcending the cramped European way of life, the settlers broke firm contact with the culture from which their ideals sprang. While the enlightened among the first generation thought on Athens and proposed the arts and sciences for all men capable of learning, their descendants, denied the broadening effect of a liberal education, became so engrossed with exploiting the garden as to lose historical perspective. Somewhat from their own perversity and somewhat from evil circumstance, the backwoodsmen assumed the responsibilities of citizenship with almost nothing of that basic education which Jefferson thought indispensable in a republican state. It is not strange therefore that at the end of the expansion the intellectual horizons of the American West should have corresponded roughly to its geographical limits.

A multitude of exceptions may properly be lodged against the foregoing generalizations. The Enlightenment never quite died in the West, and the West never ceased to pay respect of a kind to liberal education. Admittedly, the well-to-do desired the appearance if not the substance of learning for their children. French and Spanish centers preserved something of Old World culture despite the barbarian invasion, and German and Scandinavian emigrants entering the Old Northwest after 1830 clung tenaciously to their European heritage. Moreover, self-improvement societies of one kind or another sprang up in Anglo-Saxon communities, evidencing at least a mild interest in the humane tradition among the educated minority. Nonetheless, the frontier mind prevailed. Even after the wild, anarchic West became the conservative agricultural West, the garden as such remained the chief interest and the preservation of it the chief concern. What seriously occupied the mind of the West during the nineteenth century was not then intellectual or even spiritual values but the tariff, public lands, internal improvements, Indian affairs, and markets. Rugged and self-reliant individualists by reputation, Westerners from Kentucky to the Pacific yet assumed that the national government had a special obligation to help them with the garden, and at the polls they regularly underscored their assumption. Since the garden yielded magnificently, life was abundant in material things; and the conclusion could hardly be resisted that prosperity was the truest measure of well-being. With riches came a sense of power and importance and a desire to win the world's approval. Radically affected by the garden psychology, the West could not fully realize that wealth was only one of several criteria by which the rest of the world judged cultures.

The somewhat battered frontier theory of Frederick Jackson Turner, whatever may have been his conscious motive, came of an unconscious desire to defend the frontier mind, to justify the culture of the West, and to enhance its importance in the eyes of America and the world. That it should have been enthusiastically and uncritically received confessed a deep-felt yearning in historians, professional and amateur, for an angle of vision which would magnify the achievement of America as an independent culture. By Turner's view, the distinctive quality of American character and institutions came of the frontier experience: "This perennial rebirth [through a return to primitive conditions at every stage of the emigration], this fluidity of American life, this expansion westward with its new opportunities, its continuous touch with the simplicity of primitive society, furnish the forces dominating American character."[2] From this astigmatic and primitivistic view, Turner could to a considerable extent explain the political, social, and economic development of the nation by reference to western influences; and he of course leaped to the happy conclusion that European culture was a less important factor than the West in the growth of all America.[3] Indeed, Turner seems to have been half persuaded that there was no important European influence in what counted most: "Western democracy was no theorist's dream. It came, stark and strong and full of life, from the American forest."[4] This mystical statement tends to invest the forest with creative force and to repudiate tradition. Jefferson and Paine knew very well that democracy arose elsewhere and came from afar. What came out of the forest was the alligator-horse invested with all the rights and privileges of republican citizenship and ill prepared to exercise them; and even he was a consequence, though quite unexpected, of the speculations of the Enlightenment.

As Henry Nash Smith has shown, Turner was confused by the garden myth: while lauding the simple, agricultural society, he yet approved the evolutionary process leading necessarily to the city; and from thinking largely in an agrarian context, he tended to slight factors associated with industrialization.[5] Turner later attached more importance to the European background, but meanwhile his original hypothesis, stated in 1893, had profoundly altered the interpretation of American history. Founded in the garden myth and motivated by nationalism, Turnerism provided a superficially rational basis for shifting the world's center westward and for conceiving the distinctive American culture as western, indigenous, and above all valid. In all fairness to Turner, it must be said that he hardly meant so much, and perceptive historians nowadays are inclined to qualify his conclusions. Even so, Walter Prescott Webb has recently applied the frontier hypothesis to the course of European history from the Middle Ages to the present, in the process slighting the impact of classical antiquity on the Renaissance mind and violently wrenching the world's cultural axis as well. The importance of the frontier granted, strange biases come of contemplating Western civilization exclusively from that angle.

Sometime before 1925 J. B. Hubbell was struck with the implications of the frontier theory for literature: if American character and institutions had been considerably shaped by the western experience, it followed logically that literature had been similarly affected. Adapting a passage from Turner,

Hubbell asked, "May not one at this late day dare to assert that in American literature likewise the true point of view is not New York or New England but the Great West?"[6] Hubbell elicited from Turner what he regarded as support for his proposition, but the passage quoted from the historian's letter seems evasive: "I agree thoroughly that what is distinctive in American, in contrast to general English literature, comes out of our experience with the frontier, broadly considered." Hubbell maintained that the frontier gave writers materials and a new point of view, but the literature which he cited suggests neither a widespread nor a particularly beneficial influence. A further statement, "The frontier has been a great stimulus to the imagination of American authors—even of those who never saw it," is as unlikely as it is unprovable. In effect denying Hubbell's thesis, Gregory Paine observed a few years later, "If it is not too heretical to suggest it, perhaps the frontier as a factor in American literature will prove less important than, in our first enthusiasm, we have thought"—a tactful statement indeed by a scholar who had investigated the matter thoroughly.[7] Perhaps taking his cue from Hubbell, Webb confidently extended Turnerism even to European art, accounting for much of the glory of Renaissance literature by reference to the stimulus of the frontier.[8] It goes virtually without saying that his evidence is unimpressive. What Webb apparently reckoned without was the likelihood that the frontier activity of European nations and their cultural achievement stood not in a cause-and-effect relationship but came simultaneously of humanism, the new science, and renewed interest in the world as such.

The frontier theory in whatever form cannot conceal the fact that the literary achievement of Transappalachia in the nineteenth century was negligible. No better result should have been expected, the circumstances of the settlement considered; but many American scholars have been reluctant to admit the truth and even when admitting it have taken refuge in critical relativism. Although Paulding and Emerson confidently awaited the appearance of native talent capable of hymning the glory of the westward movement,[9] such writers as appeared showed themselves inept or slavishly imitative. The respect accorded them by chroniclers of American literature is significant not of their intrinsic merit but of the pervasive influence of Turnerism. In this century poets and novelists of transcendent genius have risen in, though not in consequence of, the West. Hubbell and Webb can take little comfort in them, for they have with few exceptions damned or ignored the region of their birth. Far from acknowledging the blessed influence of the frontier, the greatest of these have in varying degrees sought out the fountainheads of Western civilization and have perfected their art to a large extent by conning the masters of the Old World. By the nature of their achievement they suggest the continuing virtue of the humanist tradition flowing down from Athens.

Considered as a stronghold of democracy and rugged individualism and accordingly a principal formative influence on American society, the West appears in a favorable light; but regarded as virgin land planted to the finest concepts of European liberal thought, it is decidedly less attractive. For while making respectable use of their enlightened preconceptions in drafting constitutions, the pioneers neglected the very foundations of their system and allowed the old culture to languish without evolving a valid substitute. Obsessed with the garden myth and admittedly oppressed at times by the hard circumstances of existence, the West actually receded culturally and substantially abandoned the rational social, political, and theological bequest of the Enlightenment. Generation after generation of roistering alligator-horses came to maturity without light save that of nature, which even Rousseau thought insufficient in the state of civilization. Yet such of these as were cunning and adaptable underwent subtle changes, acquiring the manners, attitudes, and formulas necessary to material success, though nothing resembling a liberal education. Rising in the social scale, they tended to lose their saving graces—elan and individualism. Without standards adequate for fine discrimination, they lacked moral and intellectual means to behave independently and yet rationally in a civilized state. At the same time, their reluctance to recognize superior education and intellect inevitably produced a vertical drag on quality, with the consequence that leadership became increasingly mediocre. The veneered alligator-horses moved in the direction of unreflecting Christian materialism—unthinkable position!—and ultimately engendered images of Sinclair Lewis' George Babbitt. It cannot be said that perceptive Americans have failed to lash the West for its cultural defects or for its political isolationism, but the frontier mind is not easily disabused of the myth of the Earthly Paradise, which has been the cause both of its achievement and of its affliction.

Kentucky saw it all—the hungering pilgrims descending like locusts upon the fabled garden, there to rend and devour nature's bounty; the hopeful planning of apostles of the Enlightenment and the blighting of their fair program; the legendary frontiersman, embodiment of several kinds of romantic desiring, turning an alligator-horse and confronting the metropolis with the image of its own dark unconscious mind. Out of the garden came abundance without fulfillment, religious fanaticism without religious unity, the profession of equalitarianism and lusting after class distinctions, envy of superior merit and rank anti-intellectualism. Men sought to live, as they had journeyed, by the garden myth, and accomplished works consistent with their materialism and secularism. Indifferent to the warning writ large in Kentucky, the West reached the fateful conclusion that the experience of settling a garden provides better answers to the great questions about life and death and eternity than the collective wisdom of the founders of Western civilization.

Notes

1. A Long View of the Frontier

[1] *A Trip to the Prairies and in the Interior of North America*, trans. Andrew Evans (New York, 1934), 44.

[2] *The Frontier in American History* (New York, 1920), 253.

2. Eden Recovered

[1] *American Museum*, XI (1792), 12.

[2] *Travels to the West of the Alleghany Mountains*, in R. G. Thwaites (ed.), *Early Western Travels* (Cleveland, 1904-1907), III, 229-230.

[3] *The Western Country in 1793*, ed. Marion Tinling and Godfrey Davies (San Marino, Calif., 1948), 72.

[4] *American Museum*, XI (1792), 12. Cf. Charles Lyell, *Travels in North America, in the Years 1841-2* (New York, 1845), II, 53.

[5] Toulmin, 72-73.

[6] *A Topographical Description of the Western Territory of North America* (2d ed., London, 1793), 222-23.

[7] Michaux, 231. James Hall, *Letters from the West* (London, 1828), 188, gave the range as from twelve to twenty feet.

[8] C. B. Firestone, *Bubbling Waters* (New York, 1938), 79. The etymology of *Kentucky* has been much disputed: according to W. E. Connelley in the *History of Kentucky*, ed. Charles Kerr (Chicago and New York, 1922), I, 1-2, it is derived from Wyandot *Kah-ten-tah-teh* "the land of tomorrow"; but Lucien Beckner, "Eskippakithiki: the Last Indian Town in Kentucky," *Filson Club History Quarterly*, VI (1932), 373-74, takes *Kentucky* to be an Iroquoian form (*kenta*—"level") referring specifically to Indian Old Fields.

[9] *American Museum*, XI (1792), 13.

[10] *The History of Kentucky* (2d ed., Frankfort, 1824), I, 20.

[11] C. W. Alvord, "The Daniel Boone Myth," *Journal of the Illinois State Historical Society*, XIX (1926-1927), 21.

[12] For accounts of the Long Hunters—not always in agreement—see Brent Altsheler, "The Long Hunters and James Knox Their Leader," *Filson Club History Quarterly*, V (1931), 169-85; R. G. Thwaites, *Daniel Boone* (New York, 1919), 91-93; T. D. Clark, *A History of Kentucky* (New York, 1937), 46-48.

[13] *The Discovery, Settlement and Present State of Kentucke* (Wilmington, 1784), 27; Edna Kenton, *Simon Kenton: His Life and Period, 1755-1836* (Garden City, N. Y., 1930), 63.

[14] Lewis Collins, *History of Kentucky*, rev. R. H. Collins (Covington, Ky., 1874), II, 723.

[15] Daniel Drake, *Pioneer Life in Kentucky, 1785-1800*, ed. E. F. Horine (New York, 1948), 25.

[16] R. C. Buley, *The Old Northwest* (Bloomington, Ind., 1951), I, 31.

[17] p. 26.

[18] W. D. Funkhouser and W. S. Webb, *Ancient Life in Kentucky* (Frankfort, 1928), 40-46.

[19] Thomas Ashe, *Memoirs of Mammoth, and Various Other Extraordinary and Stupendous Bones* (Liverpool, 1806), 40-49.

[20] Kenton, 148; William Fleming, *Journal of Travels in Kentucky 1779-1780*, in N. D. Mereness (ed.), *Travels in the American Colonies* (New York, 1916), 636.

[21] *Recollections of the Last Ten Years* (Boston, 1826), 63.

[22] *A Winter in the West* (New York, 1835), II, 141.

[23] *Relation de ce qui s'est passé de plus remarquable aux missions des peres de la campagnie de Iesus, en la Nouvelle France, és années 1661. & 1662* (Paris, 1663).

[24] R. G. Thwaites (ed.), *The Jesuit Relations and Allied Documents* (Cleveland, 1896-1901), XLVII, 145, 147. Thwaites, 316, identified the Ontôagannha as Shawnee, who, when first known, dwelt in western Kentucky.

[25] *Voyage au Kentoukey et sur les bords du Genesée* (Paris, 1821), 156-57.

[26] It is well to remark that the referent of the garden images in this study is most often the primeval forest, for, in contrast, H. N. Smith, *Virgin Land: The American West as Symbol and Myth* (Cambridge, Mass., 1950), 123, uses "Garden of the World" with reference to the West conceived according to the agrarian ideal.

[27] p. 138.

[28] Alvord, 19, observed that Jean Couture, the French-Canadian explorer who possibly visited the Bluegrass between 1690 and 1693, reported rich mines and abundant furs.

[29] Cf. *Autobiography of Rev. James B. Finley or, Pioneer Life in the West*, ed. W. P. Strickland (Cincinnati, 1853), 22; Timothy Flint, *The First White Man of the West, or the Life and Exploits of Col. Dan'l. Boone* (Cincinnati, 1849), 52.

[30] R. E. Banta, *The Ohio* (New York, 1949), 266-67; W. R. Jillson, *The Boone Narrative* (Louisville, 1932), 62, which locates the second poem in Flint's *The First White Man of the West*—it is not in the printing of 1849.

[31] *The Christian Traveller* (New York, 1828), 47-48.

3. The Garden Archetype

[1] Alvord, "The Daniel Boone Myth," 24. Murray Kane, "Some Considerations on the Safety Valve Doctrine," *Mississippi Valley Historical Review*, XXIII (1936-1937), 187, argues persuasively that contrary to received opinion the westward movement was accelerated by prosperity rather than by depression. See further in connection with the profit thesis C. W. Alvord and Lee Bidgood, *The First Explorations of the Trans-Allegheny Region by the Vir-*

ginians, 1650-1674 (Cleveland, 1912), 22-23; Alexis de Tocqueville, *Quinze jours au désert* [and] *Voyage en Sicile*, ed. J. E. Mansion (Oxford, 1904), 14-15.

[2] *The Lure of the Frontier: A Story of Race Conflict* (New Haven, 1929), 5. Cf. *North American Review*, LXII (1846), 87.

[3] "A Memorandum of M. Austin's Journey from the Lead Mines in the County of Wythe in the State of Virginia to the Lead Mines in the Province of Louisiana West of the Mississippi, 1796-1797," *American Historical Review*, V (1899-1900), 525-26.

[4] M. R. Audubon (ed.), *Audubon and His Journals* (New York, 1897), II, 455.

[5] *Recollections of the Last Ten Years*, 241-42.

[6] Socialist colonies, notably those of the Shakers, Owenites, and Rappites, have been studied recently by A. E. Bestor, Jr., *Backwoods Utopias* (Philadelphia, 1950).

[7] *Travels to the West*, 192.

[8] See Banta, *The Ohio*, 107.

[9] *Travels in America, Performed in 1806* (London, 1808), 171.

[10] *Millennium and Utopia: A Study in the Background of the Idea of Progress* (Berkeley, 1949), x.

[11] Gilbert Chinard, *L'Exotisme américain dans la littérature française au XVIᵉ siècle* (Paris, 1911), 4.

[12] *L'Amérique et le rêve exotique dans la littérature française au XVIIᵉ et au XVIIIᵉ siècle* (Paris, 1913), 219. For some indication of the sanguine regard of Renaissance writers for America, see R. B. Heilman, *America in English Fiction 1760-1800* (Baton Rouge, La., 1937), 16-26.

[13] Merle Curti, *The Growth of American Thought* (2d ed., New York, 1943), 261-62.

[14] *The Literature of the Middle Western Frontier* (New York, 1925), I, 42-43.

[15] *Revivalism in America* (New York, 1945), 2-4. Cf. A. S. Withers, *Chronicles of Border Warfare*, ed. R. G. Thwaites (new ed., Cincinnati, 1895), 129.

[16] Isgrig's manuscript has been made available to me through the courtesy of the owner, Mrs. Mary Frances Isgrigg Hamilton of Greensburg, Indiana.

[17] Everett Dick, *The Dixie Frontier: A Social History of the Southern Frontier from the First Transmontane Beginnings to the Civil War* (New York, 1948), 225, calls attention to the revealing statistics buried in early court records.

[18] *Personal Narrative of Travels in Virginia, Maryland, Pennsylvania, Ohio, Indiana, Kentucky; and of a Residence in the Illinois Territory: 1817-1818,* ed. F. A. Ogg (Cleveland, 1906), 182.

[19] *Famous Frontiersmen, Pioneers and Scouts* (Chicago, 1886), 202.

[20] *A Study of History* (London, 1934-1954), V, 478-80.

[21] *Memorable Days in America*, in Thwaites (ed.), *Early Western Travels*, XII, 13.

[22] *Recollections of the Last Ten Years*, 66-67.

4. The Tenant of the Garden

[1] *Man and Technics*, trans. C. F. Atkinson (New York, 1932), 69-70.

[2] T. P. Abernethy, *Three Virginia Frontiers* (University, La., 1940), 41-42.

[3] *Westward: The Romance of the American Frontier* (New York, 1938), 49.

[4] F. L. Paxson, *History of the American Frontier, 1763-1893* (Boston, 1924), 116; Theodore Roosevelt, *The Winning of the West* (New York, 1905), I, 134. J. C. Campbell, *The Southern Highlander and His Homeland* (New York, 1921), 65, dissented mildly from the usual view, claiming a slight numerical superiority for the English.

[5] The borderers, whether nominally English or Scottish, were racially much the same stock.

[6] *Races and Immigrants in America* (new ed., New York, 1920), 38.

[7] *The First Explorations of the Trans-Allegheny Region,* 27.

[8] Fortescue Cuming, *Sketches of a Tour to the Western Country,* in Thwaites (ed.), *Early Western Travels,* IV, 137.

[9] For an authoritative discussion, see J. G. W. Dillin, *The Kentucky Rifle* (Washington, D. C., 1924), i-ii, 1-69.

[10] Buley, *The Old Northwest,* I, 160-61; Clement Eaton, *A History of the Old South* (New York, 1949), 129.

[11] W. A. Pusey, *The Wilderness Road to Kentucky* (New York, 1921), 55.

[12] See George Robertson, *Scrap Book on Law and Politics, Men and Times* (Lexington, 1855), 272-73, for a concise summary of the Virginia land law as relating to Kentucky.

[13] Attempts by the Virginia legislature to improve the situation seem merely to have increased the confusion, largely because orderly surveys, though fundamental to a workable land program, were not provided for. See Clark, *A History of Kentucky,* 86-90.

[14] *Two Years' Residence in the Settlement on the English Prairie, in the Illinois Country,* in Thwaites (ed.), *Early Western Travels,* X, 274-78.

[15] *Pioneer Life in Kentucky,* 107-108.

[16] "Attack of Bryant's Station," *Western Monthly Review,* III (Sept., 1829), 116. Though unnamed, the author was surely Flint, who edited this periodical.

[17] *Travels in America,* 241.

[18] *A Topographical Description,* 160.

[19] Drake, 101.

[20] Dick, *The Dixie Frontier,* 293-94. André Michaux, *Journal of Travels into Kentucky,* in Thwaites (ed.), *Early Western Travels,* III, 70, reported that the French at Kaskaskia in 1795 commonly affected this apparel.

[21] *Personal Narrative of Travels,* 181.

[22] Mann Butler, *A History of the Commonwealth of Kentucky* (2d ed., Cincinnati, 1836), xiii. Cf. Clark, *A History of Kentucky,* 31.

[23] S. C. Williams, *Tennessee During the Revolutionary War* (Nashville, 1944), 191.

[24] *Adair's History of the American Indians,* ed. S. C. Williams (Johnson City, Tenn., 1930), 377-79.

[25] p. 216.

[26] Marshall, *The History of Kentucky,* I, 44-45, readily conceded that the early settlements could not have withstood a determined attack.

[27] "Attack of Bryant's Station," 115. Cf. Clark, 97-98.

[28] Butler, 195.

[29] Cincinnati *Western Spy, and Hamilton Gazette,* March 11, 1801.

[30] *Letters from an American Farmer* (New York, 1904), 67. Crèvecoeur was not basically hostile toward the frontiersmen but considered them invaluable agents of progress as H. C. Rice points out in *Le Cultivateur américain: étude sur l'oeuvre de Saint John de Crèvecoeur* (Paris, 1933), 185.

Notes for Pages 67-90 253

[31] *The Frontier in American History*, 6.

[32] I, 360.

[33] *Letters from the West*, 5.

[34] *A Winter in the West*, II, 139.

[35] *The First White Man of the West*, 107.

[36] "The Kentuckian in New York," *Western Monthly Review*, I (1827), 88.

[37] *Letters from Illinois* (Philadelphia, 1818), 134.

[38] *The Americans as They Are* (London, 1828), 50.

[39] *Travels in America*, 191-241.

[40] *A Pedestrious Tour . . . Through the Western States and Territories*, in Thwaites (ed.), *Early Western Travels*, VIII, 344.

[41] T. P. Abernethy, "Democracy and the Southern Frontier," *Journal of Southern History*, IV (1938), 6; Abernethy, *Three Virginia Frontiers*, 58-60.

[42] While veterans of the French and Indian War benefited from the Preston survey, Patrick Henry, William Byrd III, John May, William Fleming, Andrew Lewis, Arthur Campbell, and William Christian, among other speculators, also procured sizeable tracts, according to T. P. Abernethy, *Western Lands and the American Revolution* (New York, 1937), 103.

[43] "The Daniel Boone Myth," 24, 30.

[44] p. 273.

[45] Eager for revenue, Virginia apparently sold warrants in excess of the available land. Speculators also bought up in large quantities warrants issued to veterans of the Indian wars and the Revolution. However, many Revolutionary War veterans took up land in Kentucky, as Collins, *History of Kentucky*, I, 5-9, demonstrated with obvious pride. According to the list of Virginia grants (1782-1792) prepared by W. R. Jillson, *The Kentucky Land Grants* (Louisville, 1925), 15-139, more than fifty individuals claimed tracts aggregating 50,000 acres or more.

[46] G. W. Featherstonhaugh, *Excursion Through the Slave States* (New York, 1844), 82.

5. The Buckskin Hero

[1] *The Frontier in American History*, 1.

[2] *Six Months in America* (London, 1832), II, 63.

[3] *Travels on an Inland Voyage* (New York, 1810), II, 21; *Echoes from the Backwoods; or Sketches of Transatlantic Life* (London, 1846), II, 15.

[4] *The Hunter-Naturalist: Romance of Sporting or Wild Scenes and Wild Hunters* (Philadelphia, 1852), 177.

[5] Audubon (ed.), *Audubon and His Journals*, II, 241, 459-60.

[6] *Autobiography*, 83-84.

[7] *The Drama in Pokerville* (Philadelphia, 1846), 108-11. According to J. A. McClung, *Sketches of Western Adventure* (Covington, Ky., 1872), 26-27, Tontileaugo, the Indian companion of the renowned captive Colonel James Smith, consistently ran down bear, deer, elk, and buffalo, though he failed to catch three horses even after an all-day pursuit.

[8] *The Way to the West* (Indianapolis, 1903), 73.

[9] II, 11-12.

[10] R. M. Dorson, *Davy Crockett: American Comic Legend* (New York, 1939), 84-85.

[11] *Dramatic Life as I Found It* (St. Louis, 1880), 237-38.

12 Clark, *A History of Kentucky*, 191-93.

13 M. W. Fishwick, "Daniel Boone and the Pattern of the Western Hero," *Filson Club History Quarterly*, XXVII (1953), 119, maintains correctly that the portraits of Crockett, Kit Carson, and the wild West cowboy owe something to Boone.

14 *Memorable Days in America*, 178.

15 New Orleans *Weekly Picayune*, July 5, 1841, p. 153. Lewis Cass, *France, Its King, Court, and Government* (2d ed., New York, 1841), 48-49, remarked the readiness of British travelers to credit preposterous stories told them in America.

16 Frank Triplett, *Conquering the Wilderness* (New York, 1883), 283-88.

17 *Ibid.*, 329.

18 Dick, *The Dixie Frontier*, 257. The Indian hater as a type often figures in frontier romance. For a full-length portrait, see James Hall's *The Western Souvenir. A Christmas and New Year's Gift for 1829* (Cincinnati), 256-72.

19 John Bradford began printing the *Notes* in the *Kentucky Gazette* on August 25, 1826. The next year G. W. Stipp printed twenty-three of the installments in the *Western Miscellany* (Xenia, Ohio, 1827).

20 J. W. Coleman, Jr., *A Bibliography of Kentucky History* (Lexington, 1949), 293. The edition of 1872 contains a biography of the author by Henry Waller.

21 p. 45.

22 *Daniel Boone, and the Hunters of Kentucky* (Boston, 1870), 224-25.

23 *Daniel Boone*, 59.

24 *Master of the Wilderness: Daniel Boone* (New York, 1939), 162.

25 pp. 161-64.

26 McClung, 197-98.

27 *Ibid.*, 86; *Simon Kenton*, 86-88.

28 See Kenton, 102-44, for a detailed account of Simon's capture and escape.

29 Kenton was not without justification, as the Indians continually stole horses from the whites. Butler, *A History of the Commonwealth*, 195, quoted contemporary authority to the effect that between 1783 and 1790 upwards of 20,000 horses were taken by the Indians.

30 Kenton, 197-200.

31 p. 216.

32 *The Hero in America: A Chronicle of Hero-Worship* (New York, 1941), 182-83.

33 *Recollections of the Last Ten Years*, 67. Cf. Finley, 43; *Heroes and Hunters of the West* (Philadelphia, 1858), vii.

6. The Playful Savage

1 The barbarous Kentuckian figures prominently in sketches, anecdotes, and tall tales widely scattered through the New York *Spirit of the Times*, the St. Louis *Reveille*, the New Orleans *Picayune*, and a large number of unfamiliar provincial newspapers.

2 *Recollections of the Last Ten Years*, 78.

3 *Echoes from the Backwoods*, II, 4.

4 *Memorable Days in America*, 198-99.

5 II, 30-31.

[6] *A Visit to North America and the English Settlements in Illinois,* in Thwaites, (ed.), *Early Western Travels,* XII, 220. Cf. Cuming, *Sketches of a Tour,* 137-38.

[7] *The Americans as They Are,* 112.

[8] *Porter's Spirit of the Times,* I (Jan. 17, 1857), 316.

[9] New Orleans *Weekly Picayune,* May 16, 1842, p. 97.

[10] *Ring-Tailed Roarers: Tall Tales of the American Frontier 1830-60* (Caldwell, Idaho, 1943), 16-17.

[11] *Travels on an Inland Voyage,* II, 21.

[12] pp. 142-43.

[13] *Letters from America,* in Thwaites (ed.), *Early Western Travels,* IX, 113.

[14] II, 145-46.

[15] *A Narrative of a Journey of Five Thousand Miles Through the Eastern and Western States of America* (3d ed., London, 1819), 274.

[16] Huntsville, Ala., *Southern Advocate,* Feb. 2, 1833.

[17] Frederick Marryat, *A Diary in America* (London, 1839), pt. 2, I, 254.

[18] *The Keelboat Age on Western Waters* (Pittsburgh, 1941), 87.

[19] "National Character of the Western People," *Western Monthly Review,* I (July, 1827), 138.

[20] I, 253. For a day-by-day relation of the hardships of river travel, see Samuel Postlethwaite's "Journal of a Voyage from Louisville to Natchez—1800," *Bulletin of the Missouri Historical Society,* VII (1951), 312-29.

[21] "National Character of the Western People," 137. For an excellent description of the many sorts of boats using the western waterways, see Flint's *Recollections of the Last Ten Years,* 13-14.

[22] Kenton, *Simon Kenton,* 318.

[23] *The Harp of a Thousand Strings* (New York, 1858), 292-93.

[24] Quoted from T. D. Clark, *Rampaging Frontier* (Indianapolis, 1939), 73-74.

[25] *Letters from an American Farmer,* 82.

[26] "The Kentuckian in New York," 85.

[27] *Personal Narrative of Travels,* 223.

[28] T. Flint, *Recollections of the Last Ten Years,* 32-33.

[29] p. 15.

[30] pp. 222-23.

[31] *American Humor: A Study of the National Character* (New York, 1931), 38, 70-76.

[32] The play was located and edited by J. N. Tidwell, *The Lion of the West* (Stanford, Calif., 1954). The original title was subsequently changed to *The Kentuckian, or a Trip to New York,* a circumstance which has caused some confusion.

[33] *Spirit of the Times,* XIII (Nov. 18, 1843), 456

[34] St. Louis *Weekly Reveille,* Jan. 20, 1845, p. 219.

[35] II, 28-29.

[36] Little Rock *Arkansas Gazette,* Feb. 13, 1827.

[37] *Spirit of the Times,* XIX (Mar. 3, 1849), 20.

[38] *Ibid.,* VII (Aug. 12, 1837), 202-203.

[39] *Carrollton* (La.) *Star,* Dec. 29, 1855.

[40] Huntsville, Ala., *Southern Advocate,* Dec. 8, 1832 (attributed to the New York *Constellation*).

[41] *Spirit of the Times,* X (Apr. 25, 1840), 85.

[42] New Orleans *Louisiana Spectator,* Aug. 31, 1853.

[43] *The Indian in American Literature* (New York, 1933), 145; Introduction to *Nick of the Woods or the Jibbenainosay* (New York, 1939), xxxiv.

[44] Cf. *Spirit of the Times*, XIII (Nov. 18, 1843), 456. In J. B. Jones, *War-Path* (1860), Simon Kenton performs this silly exercise.

[45] R. M. Dorson, *Jonathan Draws the Long Bow* (Cambridge, Mass., 1946), 13-15.

7. The Agent of Progress

[1] S. J. Case, *The Millennial Hope* (Chicago, 1918), 187-202.

[2] Tuveson, *Millennium and Utopia*, 59.

[3] R. S. Crane, "Anglican Apologetics and the Idea of Progress, 1699-1745," *Modern Philology*, XXXI (1933-1934), 273-306, 349-82.

[4] J. B. Bury, *The Idea of Progress: An Inquiry into Its Origin and Growth* (London, 1921), 128.

[5] *The Course of American Democratic Thought* (New York, 1940), 4.

[6] According to J. D. Hart, *The Popular Book: A History of America's Literary Taste* (New York, 1950), 27, forty-five editions of *An Essay on Man* were issued in America between 1747 and 1799—explanation enough of the large number of allusions to this highly quotable poem in the articles and editorials of early American newspapers.

[7] *A Collection of Some of the Most Interesting Narratives of Indian Warfare in the West* (Lexington, 1821), reprinted in the *Magazine of History*, extra no. 26, (1913), 7.

[8] *A History of the Commonwealth*, 19.

[9] *The Adventures of Col. Daniel Boon*, appended to *The Discovery, Settlement and Present State of Kentucke*, 81.

[10] *Life and Times of Colonel Daniel Boone* (Philadelphia, 1860), 72-74.

[11] *Conquering the Wilderness*, 32.

[12] *Daniel Boone*, 84.

[13] *Pioneers of the Old Southwest: A Chronicle of the Dark and Bloody Ground* (New Haven, 1921), 105-106.

[14] *Daniel Boone*, vii.

[15] "The Daniel Boone Myth," 16.

[16] *The Hunter-Naturalist*, 171.

[17] *Personal Narrative of Travels*, 180.

[18] The *Kentucky Gazette*, February 13, 1790, announced a meeting of the organization at Danville in December, 1789.

[19] *A Narrative of a Journey*, 204-205.

[20] *History of the American Indians*, 16-230.

[21] *The Savages of America: A Study of the Indian and the Idea of Civilization* (Baltimore, 1953), 61-62.

[22] *The Winning of the West*, I, 109.

[23] Quoted by Collins, *History of Kentucky*, I, 579. Cf. Triplett, 21; J. K. Paulding, *The Backwoodsman* (Philadelphia, 1818), 90.

[24] *Utopia*, trans. Ralph Robynson, 1551, Bk. II, ch. 5.

[25] "Civilization and Savagism: The World of The Leatherstocking Tales," *English Institute Essays—1949* (New York, 1950), 104-105; *The Savages of America*, 76-77.

[26] pp. l-li.

Notes for Pages 161-203

8. The Romance of the Frontier

[1] *Recollections of the Last Ten Years*, 67.

[2] For an unblushing defense of Kentucky as a region "calculated to give poetical inspiration," see the *Lexington Intelligencer*, Aug. 21, 1838.

[3] Simms set forth his theory of romance in a letter to Samuel Henry Dickson, printed as a preface to the *Yemassee* (1835). He modified his position considerably in the revision of 1853. See the edition of Alexander Cowie, *The Yemassee* (New York, 1937), 2-7.

[4] *The Literature of the Middle Western Frontier* (New York, 1925), 1, 328.

[5] *Conquering the Wilderness*, 21-23, 26.

[6] Smith, *Virgin Land*, 100, notes the rise of the self-made western hero to the status of lover in Deadwood Dick, a dime-novel hero introduced in the 1870's by Edward L. Wheeler.

[7] *The American Novel* (New York), 46.

[8] *The Rise of the American Novel* (New York, 1948), 115.

[9] Chinard, *L'Amérique et le rêve exotique*, 60-63.

[10] Other Indian novels besides Cooper's appeared in the 1820's—John Neal's *Logan* (1822), Paulding's *Koningsmarke* (1823), Lydia Maria Child's *Hobomok* (1824), and Catharine Sedgwick's *Hope Leslie* (1827).

[11] James Hall in 1832 published *Legends of the West*, a collection of tales and sketches, and in 1833 the *Harpe's Head*, a long tale.

[12] As a rule, the title of the nineteenth-century romance of the frontier—but not that of the twentieth century—contains the name or sobriquet of the chief Indian fighter.

[13] Pearce, *The Savages of America*, 203-204, takes Natty as "a type which is created as an intermediate result of the civilizing process."

[14] R. H. Pearce, "The Leatherstocking Tales Re-examined," *South Atlantic Quarterly*, XLVI (1947), 525.

[15] While nineteenth-century romancers ordinarily present their aristocrats with excessive solemnity, James Hall in *Legends of the West* (rev. ed., 1853), 245, mildly satirized the preference of his contemporaries for handsome heroes and peerless heroines and then proceeded to announce facetiously that his own were nothing inferior to others in beauty and merit.

9. The Child of Nature

[1] *The Noble Savage: A Study in Romantic Naturalism* (New York, 1928), 2.

[2] *Nature's Simple Plan* (Princeton, 1922), 88-89.

[3] "The Supposed Primitivism of Rousseau's *Discourse on Inequality*," *Modern Philology*, XXI (1923-1924), 165-86.

[4] See *The Discovery, Settlement and Present State of Kentucke*, 53-58.

[5] *Man and Technics*, 43.

[6] *The Hunter-Naturalist*, 17-33.

[7] *Letters from an American Farmer*, 69.

[8] Edith Rickert (comp.), *Chaucer's World*, ed. C. C. Olson and M. M. Crow (New York, 1948), 220.

[9] *Autobiography*, 96.

[10] p. 162.

258 Notes for Pages 206-243

[11] Charles Cist (comp.), *Cincinnati Miscellany* (Cincinnati, 1845-1846), II, 333.

[12] *Primitivism and the Idea of Progress in English Popular Literature of the Eighteenth Century* (Baltimore, 1934), 44.

[13] *Autobiography*, 152-53.

[14] "Attack of Bryant's Station," 114; *The First White Man of the West*, 107.

10. The Rejection of Athens

[1] *The Rights of War and Peace*, trans. A. C. Campbell (Washington, 1901).

[2] The name *Battius* was assuredly meant to be derisive; the elegant Latin suffix clashes with the root, which recalls "batty," "blind as a bat," "bats in the belfry."

[3] *Wild Scenes on the Frontiers* (Philadelphia, 1859), 69.

[4] Bogart, *Daniel Boone*, 23.

[5] *Niles' Weekly Register*, XI (Feb. 8, 1817), 392.

[6] *Ibid.*, XIII (Feb. 7, 1818), 386-87.

[7] *Liberal Kentucky 1780-1828* (New York, 1939).

[8] "The Doctrine of Man in Calvin and in Renaissance Platonism," *Journal of the History of Ideas*, IX (1948), 447-71.

[9] *Revivalism in America*, 26-28.

[10] Sweet, 18, estimates that one out of eight was a member in New England, one of fifteen to eighteen in the Middle Colonies, and about one in twenty in the South.

[11] *The Course of American Democratic Thought*, 32.

[12] W. W. Sweet, *Religion on the American Frontier: The Presbyterians* (New York, 1936), 88.

[13] *A Topographical Description*, 43.

[14] *The Growth of American Thought*, 440.

[15] Sonne, 248-54, discusses the political and class implications of the conflict over Transylvania. For clear indications of the sorry state of education at all levels, see Kerr (ed.), *History of Kentucky*, II, 753-68.

[16] *Our Age of Unreason* (Philadelphia, 1942), 281.

[17] According to W. H. Townsend, in Kerr, II, 1056, the faculty assembled by Holley for the academic year of 1821-1822 included in the college—R. H. Bishop (philology, belles-lettres, and mental philosophy), J. F. Jenkins (natural philosophy and history), John Roache (mathematics), Constantine S. Rafinesque (natural history, botany, and modern languages), J. W. Tibbatts (tutor), and B. O. Peers (tutor); in medicine—Charles Caldwell, Benjamin W. Dudley, Samuel Brown, W. H. Richardson, James Blythe, and Daniel Drake; in law—William T. Barry and Jesse Bledsoe.

[18] Kerr, II, 753.

[19] L. C. Abernathy, *Laughable Anecdotes* (Frankfort, 1832), 272-73.

11. The Frontier Mind

[1] *The Great Frontier* (Boston, 1951), 418.

[2] *The Frontier in American History*, 2-3.

[3] pp. 22-23.

[4] *Rise of the New West 1819-1829* (New York, 1906), 69.

[5] *Virgin Land,* 250-60.

[6] "The Frontier in American Literature," *Southwest Review,* X (Jan., 1925), 84-92.

[7] "The Frontier in American Literature," *Sewanee Review,* XXXVI (1928), 236.

[8] pp. 352-55.

[9] See Paulding's *Backwoodsman* (1818) and Emerson's Phi Beta Kappa oration at Cambridge in 1837.

Index

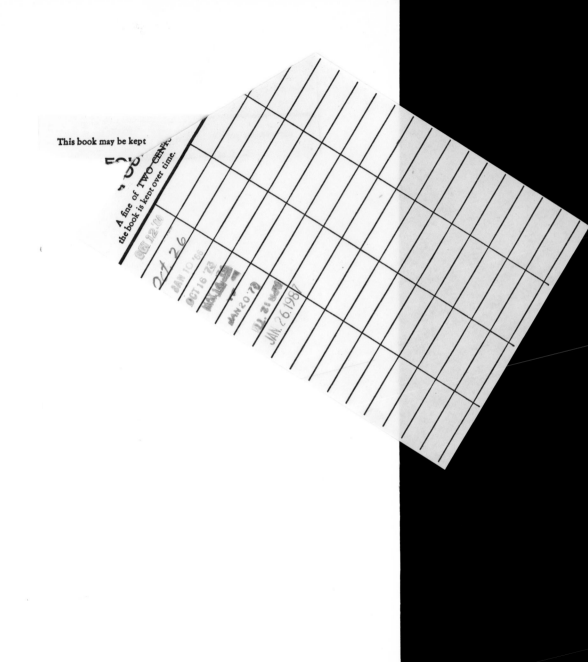